Maiden Voyages

Rochelle Girson

MAIDEN VOYAGES

A Lively Guide
for the Woman Traveler

Harcourt, Brace & World, Inc., New York

Parts of this book appeared in slightly different form in
Saturday Review and *The Atlantic*.

This book is for the girls who got me started: Minnie, Virginia, and Helene.

Contents

1 One with the World 3

2 Charting a Milestone 12

3 In the Black with the Green 36

4 Red Tape from Scratch 61

5 Ready-to-Wear on the Wing 83

6 Victuals and Vins 97

7 Carriers Away 113

8 At Sea with the Language 137

9 P's and Q's in Aix 149

10 Keepsakes in the Bargain 165

11 Snapping Memories 182

12 Covered with Old Glory 199

13 Globes of New Friends 218

APPENDIX: Sources of Information 247

INDEX 259

Maiden Voyages

1

One with the World

All my life I've wanted to meet somebody in the casbah. Do you think I could have achieved this with a girl friend in tow? Do you think I swung it even without one? I said to Hank, who coincidentally was going abroad the same evening as I, "Meet me in the casbah." He said, "I can't. I promised my father I'd go to Israel." Okay. I did the casbahs with hired guides. One can't have everything. I have, however, stacked up other lovely memories I never would have if I had been traveling all these years yoked to a pal.

To be sure, I've observed couples touring in sin who really seemed to be having a lark. And I've encountered wedlocks that were not corroded by a long humid journey—even though the parties thereto didn't appear to have any more to say to each other over rice in Hong Kong than over mashed potatoes in Kansas City. I've even known women whose friendships have survived the magpied togetherness of going abroad as a duo, trio, even quartet. Nevertheless, faced with the alternatives of traveling alone or joining a group tour, any woman without husband or available companion need not hesitate to go solo. Traveling alone can be the greatest adventure of her life—as I discovered through trial and error.

For years Lu and I had been buddies. I tagged along with her opinions and, until that sorry jaunt to Mexico, we guffawed at each other's wheezes and sneered at the same drips. We had spent moderately pleasant vacations together at a couple of resorts and planned to join forces the following summer for our first trip to Europe. The previous year she had made personal history aboard a

3

luxurious Norwegian freighter loading bananas from the Caribbean to Guayaquil—which, I suppose, technically justified her going on so about "when I was in South America . . ." Not only had she presciently become fair-haired for the occasion, but, by the grace of Neptune, found herself to be the youngest woman aboard, with the entire vessel's jovial Scandinavian personnel to entertain her.

Counting heavily on a repeat performance, she was gloomily disappointed that on our spartan Ward Line ship the captain was preoccupied and the other officers merely clean- and crew-cut American lads. Nor did she rejoice, as did I, that of the eight passengers the two we were seated with at meals were affable Mexican gentlemen. True, one was nineteen, the other about seventy, whereas we were—well—more or less mature. Although I soaked up their intelligence about the Mayans, Toltecs, Aztecs, and Acapulcans (I am very earnest about Other Cultures), I must concede they were miscast for moonlight.

Whether it was their lack of romantic potential that made Lu peevish or the heat, which she abominated, she sulked for the whole voyage. By the time we landed at Veracruz I was clenching my molars, determined to enjoy my first foreign land. It wasn't easy, because, even when it came to deciding if we should go to Cholula, to Taxco, to Querétaro, have a look at the Pyramids of the Moon and the Sun, or just loaf about the Zócalo, there was friction. I wanted to cram twelve days' sightseeing into five and a half; Lu, who was still tired after an arduous year, preferred to relax on the patio. Our compromises left us disgruntled, and by the time we picked up the return ship at Tampico we were exchanging unpleasantries. Someday I must give that country another chance.

I don't mean to imply that I was completely without blame. Most likely I was at fault at least twenty-five per cent of the time. It was evident that Lu, who made a virtue of her total lack of palate, found my strictures about the ship's soggy blueberry muffins a bit gross. And I am aware that my bouncing energy can render others absolutely flaccid. If I retched at her use of the fruit bowl as a wastebasket and ashtray, doubtless my festoons of dripping-dry panties were to her equally painful. I don't remember which of us monopolized the bathroom, but certainly she scored my having brought a cocktail skirt on a tramp trip as pure treachery.

To her credit, it was Lu's idea that we bribe the room steward on the return sailing to let me move into the empty cabin; she had already begun to unpack, so said she would stay where she was. I was glad that it was her idea, because she had miscalculated the position of the afternoon sun and wound up hopping mad that I had the cool, shady quarters.

Since by this time we had pretty much abandoned amenities, Lu ceased being a good sport about joining me in a preprandial cocktail (she is really as insensible to spirits as to food).

The only other passengers on board were an elderly Marxist, his pert old Russian pixie of a wife, who skipped about the deck in scuffed ballet slippers, and—an extraordinary woman—a catalyst in my life. (Last time I saw Virginia she'd just returned from a spin about the South Pacific and was wearing an understated little pink silk sheath she'd had run up in Fiji.) Virginia and I shared apéritifs for the balance of the voyage while, torn with envy, I followed her tales of adventures she had had traveling the ends of the earth unaccompanied. It was Virginia who convinced me that it is neither dangerous nor lonely, but infinitely more exciting, to trip about solo.

To begin with, you can be totally selfish, which is soothing. Save for the tyranny of timetables and back-to-work deadlines, you can go where you wish and when, stay as long as you like without deferring to a companion. At the same time, strangers, both American and foreign, more readily strike up conversations with—and extend invitations to—a woman alone than one flanked by sopranos. Life is rarely so bountiful that the man who has asked you to dinner has a crony to accompany yours. Even if one is with the ideal friend, usually nothing very adventurous happens to pairs. Let's say you're a good deal the prettier, or perhaps she is. Why, in the first instance, inhibit your potential—or, in the second, be overshadowed?

Particularly in transit it is practically inevitable that one's seatmate will before long, out of an apparently insatiable curiosity about the United States, begin to ask personal or political questions. They may not be in English, but no mind: you're getting to know the people of the country, however unintelligible. Assistance, too, is more quickly volunteered to a solitary woman clumsily coping with her luggage or puzzling out a map than to a team of flustered females. When Ruth returned from her first trip abroad, she reported that she had felt as if the whole country—and this was the reputedly cold and aloof England—were looking out for her, and she had never previously ventured alone farther than from Boston to New York. People universally like to help and advise; it gives them a sense of contentment.

Without the distraction of a best friend suffering from adhesive office problems, a break with her beau, or a compulsion to relate her menstrual history, impressions are as sharpened as if you'd chewed cactus. I shall never forget how sappily I fell in love with the first kiosk I encountered after we docked at Marseilles during my Maiden Voyage. Or what a marvelous sense of invisibility I had snooping alone behind the cadaverous, hood-eyed gamblers at Monte Carlo, the only sound at the roulette table the raking of the chips by the croupier. Those pasty senior citizens with purple bags under their eyes were like a macabre sketch by George Grosz. And afterwards, how right that across the room from me in the cocktail lounge of the Casino—looking as withered as the dolls the Flathead Indians used to fashion from dried apples—Somerset Maugham should be reflectively sipping a cognac.

How bewitching to stumble over the pebbles of a dead civilization like that of the kingdom of the Khmers, to pad silently through the jungles of Angkor, which ring with the whistles of millions of miniature birds while wild monkeys sneak between the thicket of branches overhead. A comment—even an intelligent one —from a companion would surely have broken the spell. As it did the second time that I saw the Taj Mahal. (May I say, in passing, that there's going to be quite a lot of place-name dropping in this book.)

The flight from New Delhi is so scheduled that one lands at the Agra airport late in the afternoon. Absolutely frantic to see the Taj before nightfall, I engaged a taxi to drive me directly there, extravagantly bypassing the free hotel limousine, which was tardy in arriving. After inching along at the pace of a No play, I arrived in an apoplectic state at Shah Jehan's overwhelming mausoleum for his number-two wife, the much-loved Arjmand, who died giving birth to their fourteenth child. It was dusk, and the hordes of Moslem pilgrims who were swarming the area for the feast after Ramadan had gone to their inns. I was the only person before the pool and, reflected there, unearthly in the twilight, was the most poetically proportioned structure I had ever seen. The experience was absolutely sublime, and I don't blame Philip Wylie for having burst into tears when he first saw it. I almost did so myself.

That evening's dinner was abbreviated by the rush of tourists to see the Taj by moonlight, and when I was invited by a young Indian to join him, I readily accepted. Although you will usually meet a nice sort of chap in my memoirs, this one wasn't the sort to make you fall down kissing. Whatever the gain socially, spiritually the evening was a loss, because he chattered away all the magic.

Surely I would have delighted more in the canal trip about Amsterdam without the exhaustive history of the steamboat which the shipyards inspired a flat-toned Midwestern schoolteacher in the next seat to recite. And I doubt that, first time I saw its original in Florence, the "Madonna of the Chair" would have raised quite the goose pimples if I had had to listen to an explication of the picture studiously recalled from a chum's semester in art appreciation. I remember all that jazz myself about how Raphael had to curve his design to conform with the barreltop on which it was painted— and, well, you can see what an irritable type I am.

Free of an anchor from home, you can immerse yourself in foreign surroundings, feel completely *away*, forget yourself. Nevertheless, the first time I went abroad alone I was frightened. Like any other tenderfoot, I subconsciously felt there was something unwholesome about foreigners and had alarms about going amongst them unprotected. How would I find my way around in strange cities? Having absolutely no sense of direction, I am frequently confused even on Fifth Avenue, and readily get lost in labyrinths more exotic. I am, moreover, a moron in mathematics; I was sure I'd never learn to decimate into tips lire, piasters, drachmas, and francs. Unlike Montezuma, who changed his clothes four times a day and never wore a garment twice, I was troubled about my wardrobe: how could I possibly be adequately dressed for fall, winter, and a heat wave within a plane's forty-four-pound baggage allowance?

I worried whether it would be possible to dine unescorted in even the local beaneries, let alone the great restaurants I needed to plump out my education. Happily, I have the digestive tract of an incinerator, so I wasn't as squeamish as others might be about eating foreign food; indeed, there is practically nothing short of human flesh that I won't hazard. And, having nourished myself with New York's international cuisine, I can sound out the victuals on menus written in French, German, Dutch, Spanish, Portuguese, and Italian. However, without pictographs, I'm a dead loss in Chinese, Arabic, Hebrew, and Greek.

As for speaking any of those tongues, I am the archetypal dunce. Even my four years' high-school and college Spanish are all but totally forgotten. However, innocent that I was, it never occurred to me before my first trip abroad that, although English is the lingua franca of the airports, it has a long way to go before acquiring currency throughout the world.

Finally, I was as fanciful as the next woman about the possibility of lecherous attacks upon my person. (I'm no Aphrodite, but who knows how ruttish those foreigners might be?) And what if I became manic-depressive through an acute sense of isolation? Oh well, I comforted myself, I have resources: I talk to myself.

Most women on their own sensibly wet their peripatetic toes in Western Europe, which is so well organized for tourism that it's a breeze to get about unaccompanied. However, I was confronted with the bargain of a lifetime, and it was that which galvanized me into venturing such a scary initiation.

The summer following the Mexican fiasco I couldn't make up my mind how to spend my vacation, and by mid-July still had no plans. I was toying with the idea of taking a Norwegian freighter when it occurred to me that maybe Helene, a co-worker in charge of travel advertising, could get me a discount on the Alcoa Line, whose cruises were highly praised at the time. "Not a chance," said Helene crisply. "Alcoa's booked solid. Why don't you go to Egypt? I can get you de luxe accommodations for the minimum rate on one of the Stockard Line ships. They have a fifty-one-day Mediterranean cruise to Alexandria for five hundred and eighty dollars."

"But, Helene," I said anxiously, "that's more than seven weeks. I couldn't possibly get that much time off." "Well, think it over," she said, and spun on a sassy spike heel to bring in more linage, little realizing she had at that moment altered the course of my life.

I brooded for about seven minutes. Why shouldn't I go to
Egypt, I asked myself, reaching for the atlas. I deserve to see something of the world. What am I living for? Just to be a grind? I've
never heard of a trip so cheap. Fifty-one days for $580. It's fantastic.
I won't—I can't—let it pass by! It's against nature.

I already had a couple of hundred dollars in the bank, and by a
bit of quick but faulty arithmetic figured I could save the necessary
balance before the last sailing of the year, leaving New York just
before Thanksgiving. Of course, I would need a little extra cash—
say, $250? Never were expenses so grossly underestimated.

The first problem solved, I tackled the stickier one of how to
persuade the management that it would be more economical for
them if I were to stay away seven weeks rather than the three to
which I was entitled. The scheme I came up with was ingenious; it
was also exhausting, the idea being that I borrow one week from
the following year's vacation and take three weeks without pay,
which moneys would be used to hire a substitute to handle the
work it would be impossible for me to do in advance. After securing the permission of everybody from the publisher to the scrub-
woman, I was set. By that time I was so eager to go floating down
the Nile with a bullrush between my teeth I would have sacrificed
a goat.

Exhausted, I boarded the S.S. *Khedive Ismail* which, after a
day's fretful delay in Hoboken's cheerless harbor, finally set sail.
She was a heavy-beamed, semicargo ship with the drab appointments of an old English chophouse and a passenger capacity of
seventy-five. There were only thirty-two of us aboard; and immediately I had to start making adjustments, because we were predominantly Egyptian, Armenian, Lebanese, and Syrian, whereas—my
being a brunette notwithstanding (I am a commonplace Mediterranean type)—I had been conditioned by a prevailing Anglo-Saxon
culture to be mistrustful of the swarthy.

We were a motley crew, representing as well ten other nations. There was a French medievalist voyaging from Brooklyn to
Marseilles for a family reunion; a spry, seventy-eight-year-old refugee from East Berlin who was headed for Alexandria to visit her
children; a broad-faced Swedish farmer, naturalized in Michigan,
who was off to Lebanon to inspect a couple of orphanages he had
founded. The West Indies *caballero* said he did a fair rumba, and

the hot-eyed young Iraqi, who wore a white woolly sweater imprinted "University of Illinois," raced all day about deck, shouting "Hi!" His father had prospered vending dates in Baghdad, and the youth himself gave every evidence of a quickening talent for trade.

Only three of us were native Americans. All female, one was prone with prolonged *mal de mer;* the other came of a milieu somewhat tonier than mine: it was her wont to spend Saturdays riding to hounds in New Jersey, whereas I generally vacuumed the flat. Nevertheless, we got on amiably, since I am ever ready to bridge this sort of social gap. Happily, the ratio of men to women was decidedly favorable, so it was easy for us to be belles aboard ship. The Moslems, to whom alcohol is forbidden, companionably sipped Coca-Colas while we Westerners were kept festive with brandy and Scotch, provided by renegade Egyptian officers at, respectively, thirty-two and twenty-six cents a shot.

Hour after hour our ears were stung by the amplified, quartertone strains of Arabic wails and at least four different recorded versions of "Hey, Joe!"—an air that none too quickly sank into oblivion. A young intellectual whistled Coptic liturgical chants, and for variety we picked up frequent broadcasts from Algiers, during which selections of popular native refrains were from time to time dedicated to "six of the gang": Mohammed Sherif, Mohammed Kamal, Mohammed Kaddah, Mohammed Sami, Mohammed Ali, and Mohammed Alexan.

We were told that in warm weather guests danced on the decks, but this was the economical off-season and, as the florid-faced British captain conservatively put it, "The sea is a bit boisterous, you know." During a particularly rambunctious night, due to what he described as "a lively gale," there were loud crashes in the bowels of the vessel, a deckhand broke his arm, the elderly German lady fractured her hip, and the stolid brown-leather sofas flew insanely across the saloon. To a somewhat lesser degree the ship rolled and pitched in the rain for twelve days.

Ignoring the tumult, the turbaned Sudanese stewards, sparkling in their white balloon trousers, red cummerbunds, and scroll-embroidered boleros, continued serenely to clang the *seneas,* the large brass trays with which they summoned us thrice daily to a high-caloric diet: for breakfast, horse beans; for luncheon and dinner, Italian pastas, meat, potatoes and Turkish, Dutch, and Egyptian cheeses—the last a derivative of water-buffalo milk. Sunday's *pièce de résistance* was roasted pigeon imported from Egypt (at least, they said the pigeons were from Egypt, and not simply shanghaied from the New York Public Library steps).

The majority of the passengers were sick in their cabins, but the girl from New Jersey didn't even need a Dramamine, and, after but one, I too kept my head high. For daytime entertainment we careened vigorously through the spray or conversed with the equally hardy Egyptians, most of whom were engineers or scientists who had been studying in the States. They taught us some Arabic, quickly forgotten, and, as it was shortly after the revolution that unseated Farouk, talked enthusiastically about the "new Egypt" they were then evolving. I tingled at the thought of being in this Mainstream of History, on this very Threshold of the Future.

As we approached Gibraltar, the high waves subsided. Stimulated by their steadied endolymph, some of the Asians swiped a *senea* and, slapping it like a bongo, one of them beat out a Lebanese polka while the rest clapped their hands and swayed to the rhythm. Snapping imaginary castanets and rippling her shoulders in an Oriental shimmy, a portly Theda Bara, who until then had been confined to her quarters looking green and so *tragique*, began trilling a coloratura tune, to which her fellows stomped a folk roundelay that looked half American Indian war dance, half mambo. "They're hep," remarked the boy from Baghdad.

Hungrily we devoured the impromptu buffet set up by three of the matriarchs, who had chased the cook out of the galley and prepared a big *mezza* of Arabic hors d'oeuvres. Included were *mihshee warak inab* (grape leaves filled with rice and ground lamb), *tabouli* (cracked wheat, chopped parsley, mint, onions, and tomatoes), and *kenafe bi jiben* (vermicelli pastry stuffed with soft cheese and served in a bath of syrup).

When the chubby first officer invited me to share a *mezza* like that with him in Beirut, I couldn't help thinking that travel might well prove to be too broadening.

2

Charting a Milestone

"You'll be seeing an awful lot of water during those fifty-one days
—but darned little else," remarked my colleague, travel-writer Hor-
ace Sutton, to whom I showed the *Khedive*'s itinerary. "Here," he
said, "take a look at it on the map. Why don't you leave the ship at
Marseilles? Pick up a bus there and drive along the Riviera. Stop
over in Nice and Rapallo, then go on to Florence and have a look
at the art. From there you can take the *rapido* train down to Naples
and rejoin the cruise. Tell you what: if I were you, on the way back
I'd fly from Cairo to Rome and Paris. You can go by train to Marseilles, and board your ship there." Although I tended in those days
to be mulish about unsolicited advice, I was so dazzled by these
unthought-of vistas that I obediently acted upon his suggestions.

From them I learned a number of lessons, foremost of which
was plan a trip carefully, four to six months in advance, checking
possible routes against a clearly detailed map. If you like to travel
by bus or private car, note especially the topography: the plains of
Spain, not to say the Ukraine, are scarcely more diverting than
those of the Dakotas. Telescope them in flight and save motoring
hours for the picturesque and the awesome. If not available locally,
order the maps that you need from the Hammond Map Company.
Two of my most dog-eared possessions are *Hammond's Ambassador World Atlas* and the *Hammond Map Library*, a boxed port-
folio containing huge maps of the world, the United States,
Canada, North America, South America, Europe, Asia, Africa,

Australia, and the South Pacific. Excellent, too, is the *New Cosmopolitan World Atlas* put out by Rand McNally.*

If you've never explored outside North America, your initial venture alone might be the British Isles, the countries of Western Europe, Mexico, Bermuda, the better-known islands in the Caribbean, the Holy Land, or Greece—all of which are so well organized for tourism they present no problem to the soloing tenderfoot. Unless one is accompanied by a guide or on a conducted group tour, many countries in Asia, Africa, and South America require more travel expertise, the sort of know-how almost anyone who has traveled in Europe would have. Hong Kong and the Union of South Africa would be exceptions. And, though tourism is not so highly developed in Australia and New Zealand, the fact that they are English-speaking nations offsets any difficulty in getting about. Only—who goes Down Under the first time?

It is normal at the outset to lack confidence in one's judgment about what to see and to rely on the word of a travel agent, since, to heed the propaganda, you'd think they had not only displaced the dog as man's best friend but were pervasively omniscient. Both debatable premises. Knowledgeable to a degree about the most-frequented sites, even the largest agencies have scant information concerning such offbeat targets as Ceylon, Indonesia, and the hinterlands of India and Japan. (I know at least one to whom it was news that New Delhi has excellent restaurants and that there, as elsewhere, the traveler need not—indeed, should not, if she wishes to get any real taste of the country's exciting cuisine—eat all her meals at her hotel.)

Because of the reduced group rates they receive from bus companies and railroads, travel agents can profit more and save themselves desk work by sending clients on packaged tours. Even when these seem good values with respect to mileage and monuments covered, they shortchange one in terms of adventure, tailored as they must be to shepherded activity. A journey of this type can be pleasurable and enlightening; it can also be a drag. Depends on your temperament and tolerance for the failings and foibles of other passengers.

Voicing a typical objection, Helen said of her first trip to Eu-

* All addresses appear in the Appendix, beginning on page 247.

rope, as a member of a group tour to the Scandinavian countries, "Not having to handle luggage and worry about reservations and getting to and from places was wonderful. But being on a set schedule was frustrating, because I saw things I didn't care about and missed out on others."

The same can be true of the so-called FIT, or Foreign Independent Trip, as planned by a travel agent for individual tourists. A West Coast travel agent, who boasts "scores of thousands" of satisfied clients, recommends to readers of his European guidebook that on their initial "Grand Tour" of the Continent they spend five days in the British Isles, three of which can be lavished on London. First time I visited there I took one ecstatic look at the city and promptly canceled plans to cram Scotland and Wales as well into a couple of weeks. The same authority suggests that during an Oriental fling, one day, less time out for a nice nap, is sufficient to inspect the acres of miraculous excavations in Cambodia; however, he insists that no less than eight be devoted to Hong Kong. For a hedonistic shopping spree the British Crown Colony is great—but eight days? The individual has to decide for herself. It's her trip. Not the travel agent's—or mine.

When planning your trip, be candid with yourself about what you really enjoy—and what leaves you cold. It's no smirch on one's sensibility to yawn over Florentine Renaissance art and prefer a brisk hike around Bergün, Andermatt, or Leukerbad.

For a condensed view of the possibilities, *Travellers Digest,* a 416-page guide to 101 countries, available for a pittance from British Overseas Airways Corporation, provides the most information compactly that I've seen. Another marvel of *multum in parvo* is *Other Lands, Other Peoples: A Country-by-Country Fact Book,* by Elizabeth M. Thompson, available for $1.50 from the Committee on International Relations, National Educational Association of the United States. Miss Thompson describes each nation in terms of its size and location, geographical features, capital city, economy, people, religion, and language, political background, government, education, food, and holidays. In some instances, cultural and historical notes are added. Not least of the book's value are the explanations of the major religions of Asia. For an enlarged, easily understood exposition, read *Three Ways of Asian Wisdom:*

Hinduism, Buddhism, and Zen and Their Significance for the West, by Nancy Wilson Ross (Simon and Schuster).

Some travelers like to read as much as possible about a country before they visit it; others find their appetite for additional information keener after the trip. In either case an excellent source for titles of works about various lands is the *Subject Guide to Books in Print* at your public library.

Besides BOAC, many international airlines offer booklets—generally free—describing the highlights of the countries they serve. Several have helpful brochures addressed to women that include currency converters and intelligence about tipping, restaurants, shopping, packing, and the maximum clothes (I always take much less) that one needs seasonally in various locales. Tops among them are Sabena, Pan American, BOAC, Qantas, Air France, and TWA. All have distaff travel consultants.

For practical hints about traveling on the Continent, read Fielding's *Travel Guide to Europe* (Sloane); for Asia, David Dodge's *Poor Man's Guide to the Orient* (Simon and Schuster). When you've thinned down the possibilities, look at one or two of the guidebooks to individual countries for details about the attractions and characteristics of those you are considering. None are infallible; however, a series that I have always found exceedingly useful —*Fodor's Modern Guides* (McKay)—was also recommended by more foreign government representatives whom I queried than any other. *Travellers Digest,* Fodor, and *New Horizons World Guide* (Simon and Schuster), edited by Gerald W. Whitted for Pan Am, are all good for checking the average temperature and inches of rainfall usual each month in various cities and countries—an important precaution if you must take a summer vacation or are weighing the advisability of off-season travel. Don't forget that in many areas there's a reason for the off-season: the weather's apt to be foul, which doesn't matter if you don't mind sloshing around in the rain or sneezing in drafty marble museums and hotels without central heating—commonplace outside the U.S. Conversely, though on-season, summer is an undesirable time to be in many countries where during July and August the temperature and humidity are hellish.

If you flip over folk and cultural fetes, write to the United States representatives of foreign government tourist offices or consulates for a current schedule of the year's events. You might also secure from SAS the publication *Festivals*, which lists the dates for major music, dance, and theatrical performances throughout Europe. These, plus film festivals and a global variety of meets, appear in *Saturday Review*'s annual "World Travel Calendar," published in the first issue of January.

A travel calendar could be crammed with exotica. One might begin it in Palermo January 6, when the Sicilians don spectacular costumes for the Epiphany celebrations, which, following the Byzantine rite, end with a volley of doves and the blessing and distribution of oranges. In February, escaping the slush, you might sun in Trinidad or Tobago and catch the calypso singers tuning up for Carnival, which, of course, would have to be spent in Rio gamboling with the Cariocas.

At Easter you might prefer to be across the world in Jordan, where you could climb to a roof contiguous to that of the Church of the Holy Sepulchre in Jerusalem to watch under a starlit sky the Abyssinian Holy Saturday rite. In a long, narrow tent draped with brocaded hangings and carpeted with Oriental rugs, the litany is chanted to the beat of giant tom-toms and to the tinkle of silver sistrums, rattles that date back to the devotions of Isis. Climaxing the service, a procession of clergy—walking beneath red, green, or blue velvet ceremonial umbrellas fringed with gold—circles the roof searching for the body of Christ.

If you were in the Holy Land at Passover, permission might be secured to observe on Mount Gerizim an ancient rite known as "the sacrifice," during which, in a night-long ceremony, the Samaritans re-enact the Exodus from Egypt exactly as described in the second book of the Old Testament. For the entire week following the paschal supper the Samaritans live in tents and booths on Mount Gerizim—held by them to be the sacred Mount Moriah, where Abraham set Isaac upon the sacrificial altar.

Thailand's Water Festival, Songkran, would be the target in mid-April. Although sprinkling Buddha images, monks, parents, and other senior citizens is a gesture of veneration, the solemnities in Paklat, a village near Bangkok, tend to turn into a good-natured splashing of all bystanders. A neater celebration occurs in the town of Chiangmai with its pageant of gilded floats, flags, and bands, followed by beautiful Thai maidens in brilliant *panungs* and unicorn caps, performing the traditional fingernail dance.

Flamenco dancing might lure you in May to Spain's sherry land, Jerez de la Frontera, gala with bullfights and Andalusian parades, during the Spring Fair. In June and July, how about Italy's Festival of the Two Worlds at Spoleto, some Greek tragedy at Epidaurus, or Dubrovnik's Summer Festival of theatre, music, and folklore? The latter days of July could, of course, find you in Salzburg for the Mozart, or perhaps in Hol, as member of a Norwegian peasant wedding, procession, and feast. Afterwards it would be easy to skate up to Mo i Rana for the presentation of the Arctic Circle princess—unless you opted for the Mackerel Fiesta in Kristiansand.

Naturally, on the first day of Bhadra (variously in August or September) you'd want to be in the Katmandu valley for Gaijatra. As described by the Nepalese Department of Tourism, "Those whose family members have died during the year send out persons disguised as cows to parade the main thoroughfares of the city. The procession of cows and other grotesque figures are very much fascinating. Dancing, singing, making hilarious humors are spectacular phenomenon." Open-air dramatic performances accompanied by music also take place during those eight bovine days.

Since it would have been too hot in Java in August for Karapan Sapi, why not cheer the finals of these bull races in October? On the day they occur, the Indonesians report, "the bulls, decorated with bells and gilded ornaments and protected by ceremonial umbrellas, are paraded through the streets accompanied by musicians carrying drums and flutes." The races "also feature a beauty contest of nicely decorated cows." Moreover, the competing bulls "are bathed, brushed, and massaged every day and entertained with medical herbs, raw eggs, and honey."

I don't know how they entertain the greyhounds that race through Eire from the first of February to the end of November, but I do know that Dublin's Oireachtas in October features literary, musical, drama, and chess competitions, as well as Gaelic games and an art exhibition—just like the Eisteddfod in Wales.

There are lots of Oktoberfests in addition to the beery bacchanals in Bavaria. For instance, on the ninth day of the Chinese

Festival of the Nine Emperor Gods in Penang, mediums seated on spiked chairs with skewers through their cheeks are carried in the procession that rejoices the return of the Gods of Heaven. Climax of these Malaysian mysteries is a fire-walking ceremony at Kew Ong Yeah Temple—atop Paya Terubon Hill, in case you're curious how to get there.

Or you might like to be in Mysore for Dashahara, which commemorates the triumph of Good ("the righteous and valiant Rama") over Evil (the demon Ravana) as depicted in the *Ramayana*. During the ten-day dramatization of the sacred Hindu epic the city is gay with bunting and arches and jubilant revelers led by a richly caparisoned elephant, on which the governor of the state rides. This performance, subject to the lunar calendar, occurs in September or October.

And where would one be on Christmas Eve but Bethlehem, where children wait for Santa Claus to lope across the eastern desert on a camel, and a radiant, black-haired baby doll representing the Infant Jesus is removed from its crib in the Church of the Nativity to be carried in joyous procession through the little town, in which women still wear the Crusaders' dress—on sale at the Bethlehem Stop 'n' Shop.

Unlike my friend Fannie, a veteran solo traveler, who successfully planned her last itinerary to include Kandy for the Ceylonese Festival of the Tooth—Buddha's, that is—somehow I always seem to skirt the really swell rites. There are *moussems*—holy pilgrimages followed by folk celebrations—throughout the year in Morocco, save for the twenty-eight-day Moslem fast, Ramadan, when thoughtlessly I chose to be there. You'd think I couldn't have missed in Mexico or Nepal, since sacred or pagan performances go on practically every week. Not only did I not get to that big cow bash, but I missed by twenty-four hours the last of Indra Jatra, when the Living Goddess, a vestal virgin, is paraded through Katmandu in a chariot, along with Bhairav, the God of Destruction; Ganesh, the lovable and auspicious elephant-headed first-born of the Lord Shiva; and Kumari, a god with whom I am not acquainted.

Although the efficiency of their personnel varies (my queries to the Australians, for instance, were ignored), the foreign government tourist offices in the U.S. (abroad usually referred to as "the States") are generally quick to provide descriptive brochures, as well as specific information. It is particularly wise to secure from them the government-fixed price range of approved hotels, inns, pensions (boarding houses), and motels. In some places erstwhile monasteries have been converted into hotels; there's a gem in Taormina where the public rooms are palatial, the gardens sublime, and the bedrooms monastic. Should you prefer to dream in a castle, you'll find scores of them in Germany, Austria, Belgium, France, Holland, Portugal, Spain, Switzerland, Britain, Scotland, and Ireland, where, moreover, they're haunted. The government bureaus can provide names and addresses.

Information is also available—though less copiously—from the foreign consulates in American cities.

In general, tourist offices are not permitted to recommend individual hotels or to make reservations, but they will advise approximately how much food and accommodations cost in the various tourist classifications, as well as sightseeing rates for groups or with private car and guide. The latter is pure extravagance in Europe, where there are countless motor-coach trips with multilingual guides. However, in a few farflung areas one has no other choice.

After reading the preliminary information, select the places that intrigue you, discard or postpone any that seem expendable on the Maiden Voyage. Have no fear: if you go abroad once, you will do so again and again. Nothing makes a woman stuff money into the mattress and wheedle extra time off like a series of geographical goals.

It is an enormous temptation to cram too many countries into a brief vacation. Even so, fleeting impressions are better than none, and during a concentrated trip one tends to concentrate one's attention. I don't hold with those who maintain that it isn't worth while going abroad unless one has sufficient time to "get to know the people of the country." That could easily take years. Opportunities to become friendly with the locals can occur during brief visits.

With their "optional stops" the airlines make it easy to pop into and out of numerous countries at no additonal fare if one does not backtrack in the process. As example, at this writing TWA offers these possibilities on a New York-Rome round-trip flight: eastbound—New York, Lisbon, Madrid, Barcelona, Genoa, Nice,

Rome; westbound—Rome, Florence, Milan, Geneva, Paris, London/Shannon, New York, or Rome, Zurich, Munich, Amsterdam, London/Shannon, New York. The trip of which I have the blurriest recollection was the one greedily choked with optional stops, during which too much time was squandered driving to and from airports, waiting for planes, and going through entry and exit formalities.

Since then I have found it the best system to list vertically on a lined scratch-pad the dates I will be gone and alongside them the days of the week on which they will fall. For short stays this is important since sightseeing may be circumscribed by legal or religious holidays. Guidebooks or foreign government tourist bureaus can tell you about local observances. For example, a pamphlet from the Finnish Tourist Association reports that "shops and offices are closed on the following days: January 1 (New Year's Day); January 6 (Epiphany); May 1 (Spring Feast and Labor Day—Student Festivals); the Saturday closest to June 24 (Midsummer's Day and Finnish Flag Day); the Saturday closest to the end of October or the beginning of November (All Saints' Day); December 6 (Independence Day); Ascension Day; and Whitsunday."

Then, in geographical sequence, I fill in on the scratch-pad the number of days I should like to spend in each of the "must" places, remembering that, with respect to sightseeing, arrival and departure days can be almost total losses. Evening flights are preferable but infrequently available except between major European capitals. And, while travel is tremendously exhilarating, it can also be tiring; so a day now and then has to be set aside for relaxation.

Invariably there is an overflow on the itinerary. Either the number of places or the length of the visit has to be curtailed—ever a painful and perplexing procedure, because before seeing them how can anybody be certain of making the right decision? Best thing to do is to quiz advance scouts among your friends; they will not be stingy with advice. If your interests coincide, follow their counsel; if they conflict, do exactly the opposite.

The preliminary itinerary may now be taken to a travel agent, who can route your transportation, alter your schedule as necessary to accommodate the carriers' timetables, and book hotel reservations in the price range you prefer. If there is no travel agency in your vicinity, write to the American Society of Travel Agents, Inc., to recommend one in the nearest town. Those displaying their insignia, ASTA, are supposed to be reliable. As in all enterprises, there are exceptions.

Among the "de luxe" or "luxury" category hotels are the very American Hilton and Intercontinental chains, along with the regal Old World establishments. Although one of the kicks of traveling is, at least occasionally, to patronize a patrician hotel, the hauteur of their help has, I confess, at times cowed me. In such palaces the guests are likely to be largely well-heeled Americans, from whom heavy tips are expected.

Because a hotel's rating is often determined by its size and number of elegant lounges rather than bedroom and plumbing appointments, a lot in "Class A" or "Class I," while more reasonably priced, are also luxurious. And multitudes in "Class B" or "Class II" are comfortable, even if they range from less attractive to downright gloomy. Save for students, few Americans knowingly choose hotels rated as low as "Class C" or "Class III." Adequate in Europe, Class B accommodations are not, by and large, recommended for South America, Africa, and Asia.

Some travel agents levy a service charge for securing hotel reservations if they do not contract for your steamship or air ticket, on which they get a commission. Others charge a percentage of the bill regardless of the circumstances. Most claim there is no charge to the traveler for their services. This is because, in general, agencies are supposed to get 10 per cent of the chit from hotels; however, I am told that many in Class B and below refuse to comply. Therefore, it is not unreasonable that one will be booked in Class A or de luxe accommodations, which, after all, most Americans want. Unfortunately, the hotels themselves often place tourists coming to them through travel agents in more expensive lodgings in order to have a larger pot left for themselves after paying the commission.

I have found this especially true in the Orient, where you're put in a Westernized, air-conditioned room even if the temperature is down to seventy degrees and your travel agent, following instructions, has specified one of those nice old Colonial rooms with a lazy, big-bladed fan on the ceiling. As but one example, in Bangkok at the Oriental Hotel I stood in the queue behind a young French

couple who had no reservations. "Sir," I heard the reception clerk
inquire, "would you mind a room in the old wing without air-
conditioning?" Tingling at the prospect of reclining under the
breezes of a large punkah (when it comes to historic color, I am
decidedly reactionary), I gave the woman my reservation receipt. "I
am sorry, madame," she said, "we do not have a small single room
left in the old wing. They are all accommodations for two people.
But we have a very nice room reserved for you in the new wing."
Nice it was, with about eighteen square feet of floor space, twin
beds, and a terrace, which, of course, commanded a heightened
tariff. The Waldorf has as much Siamese spice.

Again, perhaps because of the commission they receive, agents
habitually try to book travelers' local sightseeing in advance. This
in turn gives the nervous tourist a sense of security knowing that
she won't be floundering like a poor lost thing about a strange city.
What she doesn't realize is that these same excursions are listed on
billboards or in pamphlets at her hotel, where they may be reserved
through the concierge or hall porter (same thing), usually the
same day and sometimes for considerably less money than if
booked in the States. Obviously, this is preferable, since she can opt
for the sightseeing the prevailing solar or lunar situation suggests.
She might spend an unpredictably inclement day delightfully in
the Louvre and postpone those tours of Paris till tomorrow. Moreover, who can be sure that three months from the following
Wednesday a slight intestinal misery won't make an all-day motor
trip along the fabulous Amalfi Drive a worrisome discomfort?

To get a line on the sightseeing alternatives—available to any
individual—collect brochures of packaged travel plans from the
various airlines. Or, when writing to the government tourist offices,
ask what guided tours are conducted. Not all will have them listed,
but typical of the excursions in Western Europe and, to a lesser
degree, other major tourist centers are the following for Rome com-
piled by, and secured from, the Italian State Tourist Office in New
York. One dollar is currently worth 625 lire; thus a tour costing
2,000 lire comes to $3.20.

MORNING TOUR NO. 1

St. Peter's Basilica, Borghese Gallery (daily)   Lire 2,000

MORNING TOUR NO. 2
The Vatican City Museums and Galleries (daily)   Lire 2,000

AFTERNOON TOUR NO. 1
The Capitol, the Roman Forum, Colosseum (daily)   Lire 2,000

AFTERNOON TOUR NO. 2
The great Basilicas, the Catacombs (daily)   Lire 2,000

AFTERNOON TOUR NO. 3
Olympic and Modern Rome (E.U.R. District) (daily)   Lire 2,000

EVENING TOUR NO. 1
Rome by night (daily) (refreshments included)   Lire 4,500

EVENING TOUR NO. 2
Tivoli, Villa d'Este, illuminated fountains   Lire 3,000
(Tuesday, Thursday, Saturday and Sunday from April to October)

HALF-DAY EXCURSION NO. 1
Tivoli, Villa d'Este, Villa Adriana (daily)   Lire 2,800

HALF-DAY EXCURSION NO. 2
Castelli Romani, Castelgandolfo (twice weekly)   Lire 2,100

FULL-DAY EXCURSION
Etruscan Ribbon (Thursday and Sunday from 3/31 to
10/31) (includes lunch)   Lire 7,500

Letting a travel agent make your arrangements can save you time
if not cash, since, their protestations notwithstanding, it does cost
more to use one—though not too much if you allow them sufficient time to write rather than cable for accommodations and if
you are at least somewhat savvy as to overseas prices.

Certainly I could have been heartlessly swindled on my first trip
abroad. A couple of weeks before I was to depart I set about—be-
latedly even for the off-season—to secure hotel reservations. Having selected for my commerce one of New York's most prominent
travel agencies, I acquainted them with my plans and, being leery
about the refinements of Continental plumbing, specified several
luxury hotels that were recommended by guidebooks or friends—
an American conceit that still makes me wince. Could he, I asked
the travel agent, estimate what it would cost. No, not immediately,
but he would send me the itinerary and bill within a few days. The
legal-sized document I received was truly stunning: beautifully
typed in triplicate, its calculus made me see stars. Even with the

bank loan I had taken as a cushion, I couldn't possibly afford the trip.

In consternation I telephoned for an itemized breakdown in charges. That, I was told, would be impossible; it was an exceedingly complicated task. With a heavy heart I hung up. I had read the guidebooks. How, I beat my brow, could I have miscalculated so badly? Forced out of pure desperation to use my head, I called up representatives in New York of the French Government Tourist Office, the Italian State Tourist Office, and the Egyptian Consulate, asking in turn if they could kindly tell me the highest rate with all taxes and service charges for a single room with bath imposed by the hotels at which I was booked in their country. Then I telephoned the New York offices of Europabus, the French National Railroads, and the Italian State Railways and got the price of the first-class rail and bus tickets unnecessarily reserved for me between points. When I added it all up, the sum came to precisely half that on the travel agent's bill.

Choking with anger—as much at being taken for a sucker as for the afternoon's nuisance—I rang up the travel agency and informed them that I *had* found it possible to itemize their bill; would they, therefore, be so good as to cancel their arrangements? "But," the agent sputtered, "you are being met by our representatives at every port of entry, helped through customs, and taken by private taxi to your hotel." "That," I snapped, "doesn't come to two hundred and fifty dollars." And hung up.

A few minutes later the head of the firm telephoned back. "I am a-fraid," he said, "that we shall have to impose a service charge for the work we did on your itinerary." "*Service* charge!" I screamed, quite losing my gentility. "You just try sending me one, and I'll forward it directly to the Better Business Bureau with full particulars." That was the last I heard of a service charge.

Having been told by the government tourist offices that I could write to hotels myself requesting reservations, I did so, and all were honored upon my arrival. The incident had so shattered my trust that for the next seven trips I made all my own travel arrangements—which, when finally completed after weeks and weeks of loving revision, always gave me an intoxicating sense of achievement, not to say narcissism.

h the airline office to find out what their policy is with
a refund in case of cancellation. And be sure to recon-
r flight with the airline forty-eight hours before departure.
irst several itineraries I planned with manic zeal. Not con-
th noting the flight schedules of the various airlines I would
ng, I obtained from government tourist offices ferry, rail, and
r-coach timetables as well. Only too often I found upon ar-
at my destination that their routines had been changed. Now,
ond determining that there is transportation between points
ery day or several days of the week, I leave the minutiae to whim
n location.

Sometimes an airline overseas will say they have no flight on the
day that you wish. Persevere. Ask if any other carrier has such a
flight; between large cities chances are that they will. In general, I
have found TWA and Pan Am offices in foreign cities much better
informed about such possibilities than their counterparts from
other nations. Once, for reasons that still mystify me, it was so
sunny, I was grounded in Beirut for twenty-four hours en route to
Turkey. When I arrived in Istanbul I asked at the Air France office
if I could fly to Athens on Friday instead of Thursday, as shown on
their ticket. *Non*, they had no flights on that day; I would have to
lay over until Saturday. It wasn't until some brand-new friends remarked that they were flying to Athens on Friday that I realized
there were alternatives to Air France.

Whether you're making arrangements yourself or getting a FIT
from an agency, guard against the jam-packed schedule that zips
you in and out of cities before you have a chance to see them. I
once asked a travel agent to provide a stopover in Banaras between
Calcutta and Katmandu. His first itinerary had me arriving in Banaras at 9:45 A.M., "here connecting with Indian Airways 252 departing at 12:30 P.M." the same day. Even if I had in fifteen
minutes gotten my baggage checked through to the next flight and
rushed by taxi to the Ganges, that would have allowed me a scant
half hour to marvel at the hordes of holy men and pilgrims purify-
ing themselves in the sacred river.

Although extremely careful not to compete with travel agents,
many airlines, besides routing your flight, will without charge make

If you like to put together jigs~
plenty of time, it is enormous f
Moreover, the information th.
wish or have to change plans ov

Many authorities try to make t.
plex procedure. It isn't cabalistic. It
not going on a chartered flight, telep.
reservations office and ask them to book
farthest destination on your itinerary, lea
date, and inquire about the optional stops.
sional courtesy, they will probably suggest th
agent handle the trip for you. Reply that you p.
self. When the airline realizes that you are not jus.
questions, they will probably be happy to tell you t.
bilities on the days you wish to go from one city or co
next. In this respect I have always found TWA person.
tionally patient and responsive.

Although the routing may involve the use of various a.
your ticket will be issued by the parent company. South Ameri
the only continent where I have found any reluctance between ca
riers to transfer a portion of a ticket.

Let's assume that between Paris and Rome you have the choice
of Pan Am, TWA, Air France, BOAC, and SAS. One leaves at
6:30 A.M., another at noon, another in midafternoon, the fourth
early in the evening, and the last close to midnight. Will you feel
like getting up at 4:00 A.M. to get that 6:30 flight? Are you willing
to sacrifice another morning in Paris to have extra daylight hours in
Rome (remember, you'll have to be at the terminal at 10:00 A.M.
for that noon flight). And bear in mind those time changes: Rome
is an hour later than Paris. Finally, for long flights, don't forget to
inquire, "How much is that in hours?" On paper it may look like
absolutely nothing, but if you have to keep setting your watch
back, a flight can easily add up to an exhausting ordeal.

Ask the airline how much deposit they require, when they wish
it, and when the balance is due. They may have to call you back to
confirm the space you have reserved; sometimes they can okay it
immediately. Under any circumstances, confirmed space will be
held unless you neglect to pay the deposit on time, or the balance.

advance hotel reservations in the countries they serve, and some-times others, when you purchase your ticket from them, or upon arrival at your destination. They will also book a room for your next stop and cable cancellations. Among those that will do so are BOAC, Pan American–Grace Airways, Pakistan International Airlines, Sabena, Finnair, Aerolineas Argentinas, Swissair (when disembarking from their planes), Aer Lingus (which will also han-dle car-hire bookings), Northwest Orient Airlines, TWA, Iberia ("in certain areas"), and Japan Air Lines (in any city in which they have an office, even one that is off-line).

Pan American World Airways has a hotel reservation service that extends all over Europe. In a matter of minutes, through their electronic reservations system—Panamac—they can determine the availability of hotel accommodations, rates, etc., in any of the cities served by Pan American in Europe, while their rapid wire service to other cities brings replies within a few hours.

That foreign carriers can secure excellent modest quarters in their own countries I discovered when I asked Swissair to get me a room in Zurich. They put me into a small, newly-built neighbor-hood hotel that was a five-minute walk from the center of the city. It had no cocktail lounge, library, or lobby—just a cheerful little dining room—but my bedroom and bath were commodious and attractive, the fondue was as aromatic as any in town, and the rate was comfortably low. However, when I tried the same trick in Am-sterdam through KLM, I found that impromptu bookings made by airlines at the height of the season can prove as costly as those secured any other way.

This service is not to be confused with the packaged tours some airlines promote in co-operation with travel agents.

I didn't intend to use a travel agent before going to Japan, for I had boned up with *Japan: The Official Guide* and other manuals. I had also minded quantities of advice from everyone I knew who had traveled or lived there, and I had read a number of supplemen-tary works on Japanese culture as well. When I was quite clear about what I wanted to see, I went to the Japan National Tourist Office in New York and asked for a list of hotels and inns, together with their rates in yen. Here I ran into a snag. I was told I had to have a travel agent write for not only hotel and inn reservations, but intercity railroad accommodations too—this because little English is read, let alone spoken outside Tokyo, and I had chosen to go to Japan in the autumn, which, what with all those chrysanthemums, is the country's busiest holiday season. So, loath as I was to be held to an inflexible schedule, I secured from the tourist office a list of Japanese travel agencies in New York, on the theory that they would know more than others about their land. The first one I approached turned out to be a "wholesaler," who served as middle man for American travel agents, but the second took care of bookings for both agents and individuals.

The itinerary I had blocked out with the aid of a map seemed to him quite practicable, save for one idyllic inn that the guidebook did not indicate was inaccessible without a car. Within a short time I received a marvelously detailed, formal itinerary, accompanied by a letter itemizing in yen the room charges. Although, as customary, they asked that I pay in advance for hotel accommodations, for which I would be issued the usual vouchers, they did not press the request when I stated I preferred to pay each hotel or inn upon checking out, which is always advisable if a woman wishes freedom to exercise a time-honored prerogative. The agent's office in Tokyo was to collect for the train and steamer tickets when delivered to me there.

Shortly before leaving I was introduced to the New York representative of a large Japanese advertising agency, who hospitably cabled his home office in Tokyo to get out the red carpet. They would, he said, undoubtedly have someone at Haneda International Airport to meet me. So I was not surprised when I reached the waiting room there to be approached by a Japanese gentleman, who, after establishing my identity, said he would drive me to my hotel. It wasn't until I got into the taxi that I discovered that he was identified with the travel agency rather than Nippon's Madison Avenue. When I registered at the Asabu Prince Hotel, the hall porter handed me a letter from the hucksters, forwarded earlier that evening by the Akasaka Prince Hotel, also a former royal mansion, to which it was addressed.

The letter read: "We are very happy to extend to you our hearty welcome to Japan. We have dispatched to Haneda Airport

our car and driver, who will take you to the Akasaka Prince Hotel.
In order that you may know him he will display a large placard on
which is your name. May we take pleasure of inviting you to a
luncheon with us sometime during your stay here, about which we
shall contact you soon for further details. Please, be informed accordingly and we look forward to the pleasure of meeting you."

The first item of the transportation invoice, presented to me the
next morning was "Meeting Assist with Transfer, ¥3,600."
"What's that for?" I asked the chubby Japanese girl who was conscientiously going over the itinerary at my hotel.

"That, madam," she said, "is for the services of the man who
met you at the airport last night, and the taxi."

"It comes to about ten dollars in American money, doesn't it?" I
said grimly, thinking *how* you have to *watch* people. "I specifically
told your New York office that I did not wish to be met. You can
see from their itinerary that it says, 'Upon your arrival, you will
clear customs and immigration government formalities, then transfer to your hotel by airport limousine service. . . .' Furthermore,
they wanted only five dollars for being met. How come you are
charging me twice that?" Then I weakened because she seemed so
very vulnerable and was trying so earnestly to be helpful. "Tell you
what," I said with rather more grace than I'd previously exhibited,
"I'll give them eighteen hundred yen because of the extra effort
that *you* have gone to—but not one penny more."

When I returned to the States, I learned from my friend Carol,
who was traveling alone about Japan at the same time, that it was
unnecessary to make reservations in advance. When she arrived in
Tokyo she had merely strolled over to the Japan National Tourist
Office, which booked accommodations for her at the price she
requested.

To be fair, I found the itinerary drawn up for me enormously
helpful, containing as it did instructions like the following: "Date:
September 25, Tuesday. Place: Tokyo. Remarks: Early morning
transfer to Ueno station either by subway or taxi. 9:20 A.M. Lv.
Ueno. Japanese National Railways train No. 33. 'Aoba' express to
Sendai. Upon your arrival at Sendai station you are required to
change train in the same station via Sengoku Line to Matsushima
Kaigan. The train leave out of the same station but different track

every 20–30 minutes. Take approximately 45 minutes. Upon your arrival at Matsushima Kaigan station, transfer to your hotel at: MATSUSHIMA PARK HOTEL, 10, Namiuchihama, Matsushima-machi, Miyagi-ken; Tel.: Matsushima 103, 153." In the event all that wasn't perfectly clear, I could show any passer-by my destination written in Japanese on yellow lined paper.

The thoughtful travel agent also arranged that the American Plan, typical of Japanese inns, not apply to an American unused to getting a room and three meals at such a low price; so more than once I had to persuade the proprietor that I was not to pay extra for food. "Travel agent say . . . " they would protest.

"Never mind what the travel agent said," I'd interrupt. "Japanese pay one price for room and meals; Americans should not pay more." Sometimes I won out, or at least got a compromise. In Osaka I was told, with a deep bow, that honorable lady could seek other premises the next day.

Many guidebooks list and describe hotels. Most concentrate on the posh. At their true rates, the hotels used (with inflated prices) in the more expensive packaged tours are excellent values, both attractive and comfortable, so for ideas pick up a variety of brochures. En route, of course, travelers exchange guide and hotel tips the way clubwomen swap recipes. Usually tourists prefer to be centrally located and, if they plan to get about by railroad or bus, to be situated reasonably near their depots.

If you do not have reservations at your next destination, the hall porter at the hotel you are in will telephone or wire for a booking, a service for which you tip him fifty cents to a dollar, in addition to the cost of the calls or telegrams. One caution: in a city like Paris a Class B hotel may be perfectly charming; in a smaller town, decidedly dreary. Many women couldn't care less, and my hat is off to them.

Hotels in popular tourist centers usually have English-speaking personnel, who will understand a typewritten letter even if they can't cope with the average American hand. Before going to Yugoslavia, however, I was told by the head of its government tourist office in New York that because of language difficulties it was virtually impossible to secure accommodations by writing directly to the various hotels, although he gave me a list of them, along with their price range. Disgruntled, for I was still gun-shy with travel agents, I sent a letter to the Putnik (travel agency) in Zagreb, indicating the hotels I wished to stop at during the fortnight I had allotted to the Dalmatian Coast. And in due course I received an itinerary, together with the itemized charges that I had requested. These were appreciably higher than the rates quoted in New York.

Immediately canceling Putnik's reservations, I asked a German-speaking friend to draft a form letter that I could use to communicate with the hotels. The speedy replies that I received, all of which confirmed the government list prices, added to my disillusionment, not to say chagrin for not having thought of writing in German in the first place. I knew it was Yugoslavia's alternate tongue.

Should you write for accommodations, do so at least four but preferably six to eight weeks in advance of your arrival. Send an air-mail letter to the manager of the hotel requesting a quiet, well-ventilated, single room—with "attached bath and toilet" if you wish to indulge yourself in handy conveniences. Just specifying "private" or "adjoining" bath isn't sufficient; you may get your own tub and discover that the toilet is down the hall a ways, or vice versa. If you are your own hairdresser you may wish to reserve a room with a private bath or shower for shampoo days rather than be caught in the corridor with a wet head. In first-class and luxury hotels most tubs have marvelous metal hand sprays.

Rare is the bedroom in Europe without attached bath that does not have a sink with at least one spigot, as well as a bidet—a clumsily low plumbing device resembling an elongated, seatless toilet—by means of which civilized folk abroad of both sexes lave their lower torso.

Unusual also in the older hotels is a "single" room without at least two beds or what the Italians call a *matrimoniale*. The price won't be half that for double occupancy, but the rate will reflect a rather slighter "supplement" than that charged by all packaged tours for a private room.

The request for "quiet" is important. Once I found myself a few yards from Buckingham Palace in a hotel that was so genteel I didn't have the spunk to order anything in its Victorian parlor more intoxicating than sherry. Came night, though, and what a clangor of crashing china and boisterous shouts. Having had scarcely a wink of sleep, I testily approached the manager the next morning.

"I didn't," I said, "reserve a room here two months in advance just to be assured of a location above the kitchen."

"But, madam," he countered, "you asked for a minimum-rate room." I always ask for minimum-rate rooms; if dissatisfied, more costly surroundings can generally be procured, and usually inexpensive rooms are quite adequate; they simply lack a view.

Ask the hotel to state in their confirmation of the reservation the price for lodging and whatever table d'hôte meals you expect to take with them—Continental breakfast (rolls, jam, coffee *au lait* or tea), demi- or full pension (two meals or the works—either of which may be mandatory), plus service charges and all taxes. You can't lose by requesting that these be quoted in the currency of the country; if there are fluctuations in the exchange, you may save a bit by it. Inquire also how much deposit they wish in order to hold the reservation. Usually a personal check covering the first night's occupancy (or even as little as five dollars) will do it. To insure airmail replies, enclose return postage with your letters in the form of international mail coupons, available at post offices.

When you send your deposit, indicate in your letter to the hotel the approximate hour of your arrival, as well as your means of transportation into the city since, should there be a delay, you will not thereby forfeit the reservation. When you leave on your trip, take all letters confirming reservations for presentation to the reception clerks at the various hotels; occasionally there's a misunderstanding.

While I don't advocate the practice, it is sometimes safe to travel off-season without advance reservations (regardless of the local religion, the week between Christmas and New Year's is in-season). Just taxi to the hotel that you fancy. The driver will know the addresses of all but the most obscure, and he can frequently suggest a good one if you are unacquainted with the possibilities. In small places hotels with vacancies often have their cars at the station soliciting guests, in which event the transportation may be free. Moreover, many airports and railroad stations maintain tourist accommodations desks, which can immediately book a room for you (if there is no convention going on).

Not thinking to check in advance whether by chance there was a conclave in Paris, late one August I blithely ducked a tempest in Biarritz and entrained for the City of Light. The tourist-accommodations desk was shut down when I arrived about seven in the evening, but that did not unnerve me. I simply asked a cab driver to take me to a rather more elegant hotel than I had previously frequented, confident one can always secure opulent quarters. The annual automobile show was in progress, the reception clerk told me, and there wasn't a room anywhere to be had. That, I replied, is nonsense, and returned to my hack driver, whose snarls at other motorists were nostalgically reminiscent of Manhattan.

We tried the gamut of luxury hotels, the Class A, the Class B, the C's, the D's. My nettlesome driver became fatherly, even ingenious about hideaway hostels, but, although he was now serving as entrepreneur, I was beginning to blanch. Would we be driving through eternity and, ultimately, would I be able to pay for the haul? With arched eyebrows we exchanged Gallic shrugs. Eventually, on a side street near the Etoile, he found a room for me in a fleabag of exquisite dilapidation. The claustrophobic cage that served as lift creaked up four flights to a rundown eyrie, where a single gray sheet on the lumpy, unblanketed bed tattled of previous occupants, and the pillows lacked cases. A tempestuous wind lashed at the room, in which the only concessions to the fastidious were a tiny screened-off wash basin and, unsteadily perched on a stand, a tin makeshift bidet.

I asked the taxi driver what I owed him, uneasily calculating my resources. Would he want ten bucks, twenty, fifty? We had been riding for hours and hours. He asked the equivalent of three. And when I gave that thorny apache as much again in a tip, his eyes filled with *merci*-ful tears.

When, on a whim, Jane, too, innocently arrived in Paris during an automobile show, she had to spend two nights in a bathroom—albeit one big enough to house a narrow cot. "It was nice being so close to the facilities," she said, "and I got all caught up on my laundry."

The opposite can as easily happen; indeed it did the summer I traveled through the Tyrol without reserved accommodations. After two nights in Innsbruck at different hotels, I was in no mood to vacate a third—once again to make room for a foresighted guest.

Besides, it was teeming in the Alps. More debonair than the height of the season warranted, I took a train to sunny Velden, a chic resort in southern Austria. Not a room was free—not a single or double one, at any rate. I was finally put up in a dormitory sleeping six—and had to pay for each of the beds. Without even *Wiener brot* and *Kaffee* on the house.

On the other hand, through the *Reisebüro* at the station I was able to secure in the outskirts of Vienna a minimum-rate garret, which I tried unsuccessfully to convince myself was really terribly *gemütlich*. Europeans take all too literally a request for inexpensive lodgings. As Jeanne discovered when she found herself in Salisbury near Stonehenge in a renovated chicken coop. And as I should have remembered from my experience in Spain.

Having sensibly queried the government tourist office in Barcelona about the weather prevailing at Altamira, I took their advice about going instead to Majorca. Never was a hotel so idealized as that pictured in the brochure shown me by a waterfront travel agent. With its glass-bead portieres and dirt floor, the pension could have been the setting for a shoestring production of *Rain*. "Oh, no," I wailed to the concierge. "This will never do." The charge was only three dollars a day for a bed and three meals, but I lack the sporting instinct of a Sadie Thompson, any way you look at it.

The hall porter, who spoke a North African patois, detained my departure. "Me have fine room in ah-nex. Vairy good." Filled with misgivings, I trailed him a few blocks to the annex, his own three-room cottage, where he rented me his daughter's virginal bed. I also had ruffled chintz curtains, an attached chamber pot, and every morning a cheery "good night" from his plump, doe-eyed wife.

Although I have slept veiled—and unveiled—under canopies and great clouds of down, somewhat less silken were my initial diggings in the State of Madras. Because I arrived in southern India ahead of schedule, my room at the proper old English Club was still occupied. However, the manager telephoned the Midland Hotel in Madurai to let me have their *very best* quarters, for it might, she whispered over a cupped mouthpiece, "be a bit noisy." So off I bounced in a loose-jointed jalopy to a spider-webbed flophouse, where the desk clerk was all but inaudible in the blare of Dixieland and coarse laughter. Nor was his parting shot, as he handed me an eight-inch iron key, one to comfort a refined, single woman: "Be sure to bolt your door." Noting that the windows of my cell had maximum-security bars and there were companionable lizards on two of the walls, I took a tranquilizer, stuffed my ears with Flents, and snuggled into a bed that lacked only spikes to be fit for a fakir.

The memory of that night in a dive is appreciably dimming. But I shall never forget exploring, barefoot and awed, Madurai's Sri Meenakshi Temple with its ancient, childishly repainted sculpture, its bazaars, its Hall of a Thousand Pillars, and its shrines to the Hindu gods, their avatars and consorts, before which worshipers— their preference in deities smudged in colored chalk across their foreheads—bow or prostrate themselves in devotion.

And to think, if I had not been warned, I might have frittered my time away on water-logged cruises.

3

In the Black with the Green

Take lots of money. Nothing gives a woman more serenity. I suggest a third to double more the funds that you estimate you will need for routine expenses and souvenirs. Given any strength of character, you can leave the emergency cash untouched; in case of a crisis you'll be awfully glad that you have it. I know because I figured too closely on my first trip abroad.

I had what I was confident would be an adequate sum. My round-trip steamer passage was paid for, as were interim flight tickets. What could possibly go wrong? On short notice the steamship company canceled the return sailing on which I was booked. Although their Paris office tried hard to get me passage on another ship, no space was available. The alternative was to fly. Obviously. Except, the fact that I would be reimbursed for the cost when I returned to New York was academic; I was down to my last fifty dollars and had to be back at work the following Monday. This was Thursday.

In a panic I wired a friend for the plane fare. "Now, dear," Louise had insisted before I left home, "cable me if you run short of money." Her bank was sluggish about processing my SOS. I wired the traffic manager of the steamship line in New York to buy me a plane ticket and never mind the reimbursement. No reply. How could I know that he was in the hospital as the result of an accident?

Friendless in Paris, I started to have forebodings about being reduced to walking the streets. Even so, who could count on those

Continental lovers not getting their signals crossed over who should get paid?

Saturday morning, just as I was about to throw myself upon the mercies of the American embassy, Pan Am telephoned that the ticket I'd reserved had been paid for by the steamship line. Could I leave that evening? Could I!

"What exactly can an American consulate or embassy do for a stranded tourist?" I recently asked John M. Allison, former United States ambassador to Japan, Indonesia, and Czechoslovakia. "If a girl is robbed," he said, "or through carelessness loses all her money, the consul cannot provide funds to get her home. He can, however, be a big help. He can cable the State Department in Washington and ask them to get in touch with someone who can send money. Or, if this is impracticable, he may be able to get help from the members of the local American community, who often have an association which can take care of such matters.

"Public funds administered by the consul can only be advanced to indigent American seamen who have become too enthusiastic over the local beer or women and have missed their ship. It does seem a little unjust," the ambassador observed, "that a perfectly respectable American girl who has lost her money cannot be helped, while a bleary-eyed sailor can be sent home at government expense."

To cite another contingency, doctor and hospital bills overseas have to be paid immediately with cash, even though one carries medical insurance and the amount would be refunded later.

Of course, any American Express office will advance, on your personal check, up to $300 in traveler's checks—or $250 in traveler's checks and $50 in cash—upon presentation of your American Express credit card. It is also possible through the card to charge transportation on a number of foreign, as well as domestic, airlines. However, an individual has to have an annual income of about $7,500 and a good credit rating before she will be issued a card in the first place.

The best precaution is to arrange with your bank to send you promptly, upon receipt of a cable, funds to be drawn against savings, a personal loan, or securities. Peace of mind is worth the few dollars' interest on a short-term loan.

No matter how much of the trip you have paid for in advance, or how much you expect to charge on credit cards, you will need some pocket money. The most usual way to carry this is in traveler's checks, of which the best known are Cook's and American Express. The charge for issuing the former is 75¢ for each $100, for American Express $1 per $100. Both are easily negotiable anywhere in the world.

To keep the wad as flat as possible it is wise to get checks in $100 denominations for countries in which you will remain a week or more, in $50 denominations for those where you will be for three days—assuming you have not paid for accommodations in advance. The tens and twenties can take care of any additional money that is needed. With large-denomination traveler's checks you may also save on the exchange commission. For instance, in Iran the fee to cash each traveler's check is twenty rials (about 26¢)—twenty rials for a $100 check, two hundred rials for ten $10 checks.

In the major tourist centers expensive hotels, restaurants, and merchandise establishments will honor American Express and Diners' Club credit cards. Their modestly priced counterparts usually do not have business arrangements with credit-card firms. In a pinch a personal check will be more readily accepted—especially by enterprising vendors, who frequently suggest this manner of payment to a conservative shopper. Often they'll let you take the parcels with you without waiting to ship them until after the checks have been cleared—a couple of months later. I like to think this is due to the high esteem in which American integrity is held.

The problem of carrying funds is diminished by paying a travel agent in advance for lodgings, some of one's meals (breakfast and either lunch or dinner is the general practice), transportation, and local sightseeing tours. For these the traveler is given a booklet of vouchers, on which refunds may be made for unused portions, although not as a rule for meals. To avoid any misunderstanding, the tourist should have the agent's procedure clearly specified. Not to save any money on it takes some of the joy out of being wined and dined by a new beau.

The prepaid coupon arrangement is the only one possible in the Soviet Union and most of the satellite countries. Travel agencies representing such nations provide the visitor with a booklet of perforated scrip in various denominations of the local currency. These are presented when you are billed for lodgings and meals both at the hotel and restaurants. However, to cover additional expenses the actual currency may be purchased in the country.

I shall never forget how irked I was, when checking out of the Gellért in Budapest, to find that the manager was not empowered to reimburse me for the considerable amount of scrip that, thanks to the hospitality of a South American gentleman, I had left over. "Please, madame," the manager begged me, "take for it some of our excellent Hungarian Tokay and plum brandy." My pleasure over this amiable cultural exchange was dampened when the three flimsily wrapped quarts slipped from my grasp as I was climbing the wobbly ramp of the Polish twin-engine LOT plane to Athens.

For long periods abroad one may prefer letters of credit. More men than women, however, take a chance on carrying large sums in dollars; subject to theft, they do command better deals in exchanging money and making other purchases in areas where the currency is fluid. But only occasionally do you save by buying sizable sums of foreign money before leaving the U.S. Unfortunately, nations having a "free" or black market in money, which affords a higher exchange rate for dollars, usually have rigid currency controls and strict limitations on the amount of their money a traveler may bring in.

Ever responsive to a bargain, before going to Iberia in 1956, I took advantage of the fact that one could get pesetas 20 per cent cheaper in the United States than in Spain. Ten thousand were the limit a traveler was permitted to import, and I went it, figuring that the equivalent of $250 would be ample for a couple of weeks in the country. While I was about it, I also bought at Perera, a foreign-money broker in New York, $100 worth of escudos, simply as a convenience because I was arriving in Lisbon late Saturday afternoon and would be taking a bus early Monday morning for a week's journey through Portugal.

Since it was for the most part in crisp new bills, I did not shrink at stuffing all that exotic cash, along with the usual cushion of a hundred American dollars, into a dainty pink money belt that I strapped around my belly. True, I was uneasy about the bulge: instead of speculating that I was about four months' gone in a madcap pregnancy, would people guess that its nature was fiscal, not fetal? That this was my first extended venture from city to hamlet in a strange, non-English-speaking land on public rather than tourist conveyance heightened my sense of being surrounded by radar.

"There is absolutely *nothing* to be afraid of," I repeated to myself as I glanced with alarm at the jolly, snaggle-toothed farmer sitting beside me on the clean but shabby bus. I tend to equate character with healthy gums and white teeth.

"*Americana?*" he asked me. "*Sí,*" I unhappily conceded, for I had hoped in a faded seersucker dirndl to pass for an Iberian goose girl, unnoticed. Maybe I would have if I'd had the wit to put my camera into the flimsy, drawstring knapsack with which I was so lightly traveling, because surely my complexion was not foreign to his or that of his gaping compatriots. Catching in his next query the word "Nazaré?" I replied, "No, Obidos." And the anticipation of this eleventh-century walled village, the fief of the Portuguese queen Isabella, whose castle I was to occupy, shot a tingle down my spine. Fancy humdrum old me sleeping in a genuine watchtower.

The ride through the rose-covered countryside produced a succession of garrulous, stubble-chinned companions, whose insistent, unintelligible cant distracted my wonder at the incredibly large baskets filled with produce and fowl that the women, walking barefoot along the road, insouciantly balanced on their heads, a mode of transport pervasive among all but the aristocrats and males of the country. I was still watching for one who could top the nicely dressed young lady at the station who, gesticulating volubly to a friend as she strolled by, seemed oblivious of the two suitcases and laundry bundle perched upon her pate.

Shortly after 1:00 P.M. the latest of my seatmates nudged me and announced, "Obidos," as, when the bus stopped, did the driver, who, like most Portuguese I encountered, took seriously his responsibility toward greenhorns. At the roadside stand nothing that remotely resembled a castle was visible. "Castelo?" I asked a little boy. In response he mutely led me down the dusty highway into a tiny Arcadia, whose narrow, cobblestone main street culminated in a steep incline to the lower gate of the fortress. Peering through festoons of bougainvillaea, I saw at the top of the rock staircase what appeared to be an old-fashioned dungeon, seemingly window-less, and crowned with crenelated parapets.

The general factotum, a molten-eyed eighteen-year-old, asked in French, Portugal's alternate language, for my luggage. I responded with as much aplomb as one can muster with disheveled hair and glistening nose, "Voici mes baggage," indicating the knapsack. Clearly, he misinterpreted my endeavor to avoid ostentation in such an impoverished land as pure eccentricity, and when I saw how cravenly the wrinkle-resistance of my other dress had yielded to the pressures upon its folds, I couldn't but agree with him. Captivatingly medieval as the interior of the castle was, it was exceedingly difficult to play princess with the rump of my seersucker bulged from prolonged, humid sitting. Never again have I carried self-effacement to such lengths.

While I was signing the register—for once, no statistic more vital than name was demanded—the young major domo said that his name was Joachim and he would like to show me the citadel after lunch. He asked if by chance I spoke Spanish, perceiving how faulty was my French. I said, "Un poco," and he got that picture.

The village's tile-roofed, whitewashed cottages, decorated with yellow paint and geraniums, looked infinitely sweet cuddled inside the castle walls, on top of which Joachim and I were meandering. Romantically, we stuck our heads through the jagged lookouts where in olden days King Diniz's men may have searched the rolling hills for soreheaded Castilians and Templars.

When Joachim asked if I would like to attend the fiesta that evening, my cup bubbled high. "¿Te gustas bailar?" he inquired. "¡Sí, sí, sí!" I exclaimed, not unmindful of the intimacy of his verbs. Even though I am just a meat-and-potatoes dancer, there is little I like to do more than bailar. Pity, I reflected, that this handsome prince charming isn't in my age group. More's the pity I am not in his.

Joachim, having changed from his gold-buttoned brown uniform into a spruce blue serge, looked crestfallen when I showed up on the terrace after dinner in the same soggy seersucker. He should have seen the condition of its alternative. However, much as he would have preferred a more stylish date, he put a cheerful face on the situation, and we were soon companionably descending to the village. To my joy, at the onslaught of a sudden downpour Joachim pulled me into a candlelit hovel alongside the road where a marvellous old witch was cranking a spinning wheel. Graciously, the crone stopped to brew us some tea—a peppier potion than the saccharine pink punch we subsequently sipped at the outdoor tavern that was the site of the fiesta.

Fiestas and I never connect: in the clearing but two couples were dispiritedly dancing. Not so Joachim, who, getting a grip on my waist, spun me like a dervish about the dampened floor. "*Vamos a mi casa*" ("Let's go to my place"), he suggested, stimulated by the pirouettes. "*Mañana*," I came back, seizing my first opportunity to be a wag in tongues. Tomorrow! That'll tell him. Merrily, I savored the sally all the way back to the castle.

My first castle. It had been a day of milestones, and I had been rather highstrung throughout it. Nevertheless, probably I would have simmered down had Joachim not grabbed me in an impetuous embrace outside my bedroom door, and thereby agitated to an excited crackle ten thousand pesetas and contiguous capital in the money belt. So mortified was I at these vulgar noises issuing from my person that I burst into hysterical laughter.

Joachim looked shattered. But I simply couldn't explain to him, "Look, I am not laughing at your lovemaking, Joe. It's just that this money belt is such a gasser."

That was the last time I've ever put one on. Nor have I subsequently stuck anything down my neck more rackety than foam rubber.

Except for very short trips, it is wise to take about a hundred dollars in American currency, some fifty of which may be broken down into two ten-dollar bills, four fives, and ten singles. Although cab fares vary, one of the ten-dollar bills should easily take care of departure tips and local transportation to the air- or seaport, if you are not being driven by a friend. A ten-dollar bill could be spent for two cartons of cigarettes at the airport and perhaps a bottle of French perfume—both duty free. Orders for them, however, must be placed at the duty-free shop about forty minutes before flight time so they can be delivered to you in the plane. (A more limited choice of cigarettes, liquor, and perfume is generally also available for purchase aboard.) That will leave three or four dollars' change for incidentals and a cocktail or two before dinner (on economy flights they cost about fifty cents each in the aircraft).

Just be sure to retain nine or ten singles so that you can avoid cashing an extra traveler's check should you find yourself needing but three dollars, say, or six in a foreign currency when departing from a country. More than ten singles bulge the wallet and are, in my experience, unnecessary; agencies of American Express and Cook will always break one of their traveler's checks into fives or single dollars if they have them.

It's not fatal to be "stuck" with several dollars' worth of another currency, although to read some sources you'd think that dollars were the world's only negotiable money. Quite the contrary; the only one I have encountered that nobody would take—not even the Hotel Indonesia in Djakarta—was Indonesian rupiahs in 1963.

Small change is sometimes difficult to sell, but save in rare instances when there is friction between the two countries, you can at the international airport bank exchange all other leftover currency of the country you are leaving for that of the next place on your itinerary. When you arrive in a country, inquire at the bank what the practice is with respect to reconverting their money into dollars—and hang on to the receipts the bank gives you. I didn't do so for one exchange I made in Iran, and as a result, because of local regulations, I could only convert 7,500 rials into dollars—some ten. Rials at the time were selling for 780 to the dollar, so I took a loss of thirty rials, or about forty cents, on the transaction. It is seldom more on such a negotiation. With the balance I bought a Lebanese pound and felt like a woman of affairs.

At worst, Perera at Kennedy Airport or Deak at Honolulu, as well as their branches in various cities, or other money brokers will buy your excess foreign bills for a fee too picayune to worry about.

In Hong Kong one could quite easily pay for everything in American rather than Hong Kong dollars. There are travelers who also manage to do so in various European capitals—a practice that does not usually endear them to the host country since it implies an arrogance about our money that may be wholly unintended. Imagine, if you will, a Swede visiting the United States and offering only kroner—also a good stable currency—for services and expenses. We'd tell him pretty quickly where he got off. Other peoples are more polite, but be assured they will see to it that they do not lose by the transaction.

Before leaving the States you should purchase at least five dollars' worth of the initial foreign money you will need, if you are not being met, to take care of tips and transportation to your hotel when you first disembark, tired and eager to get out of the airport. In the event the foreign-exchange brokers listed in the classified directory of your phone book do not carry the moneys you need, they may be bought at the international airport from which you will depart, or from the purser of your ship.

The Perera and Deak offices have envelopes of prepacked currency in the most common foreign tender. Available in ten-, twenty-, and fifty-dollar packets, each contains one to two dollars' worth of small bills and coins, as well as an illustrated money converter and tipping guide. Perera suggests no less than the ten-dollar packet to ease your debut; however, I buy only the sum that I will need for overnight stays in various countries, unless there is a decided saving by purchasing additional currency in the U.S. It is not usually possible to secure in the States tip-size coins and bills in moneys other than those used in Western Europe and Mexico. Larger denominations, however, can be broken into smaller in the bank at the airport where you disembark.

Since the currencies of Western Europe have become stable, the broker's fee has varied from .005 to .03 per cent of the amount purchased. The prevailing free-exchange selling rates for bank notes in New York govern how much the dollar will buy. In the hard currencies of stable economies they vary little.

If you are interested in cutting costs—as I am—there are several ways to save money.

Although the airlines that are members of the International Air Transport Association (IATA) charge the same rates, economy-flight fares are approximately 25 to 60 per cent lower than those for first class, depending on the season. There are, furthermore, gradations in economy flights: the "twenty-one-day excursion" is the least expensive, the "regular economy fare" is about a third higher, and the "peak-period economy fare" costs 50 to 60 per cent more than the twenty-one-day excursion.

On the twenty-one-day excursion, travel must not exceed three weeks (excluding the day of departure), or be less than two weeks. The trip may commence eastbound only during certain periods: as of this writing, April 1–June 9, July 11–August 4, August 29–March 31. No travel may begin east- or westbound from 7:00 A.M. Friday to 7:00 A.M. Monday. The regular economy fare allegedly "applies all year"; however, one cannot take advantage of it for eastbound travel from May 22 through August 3, or westbound from July 17 through September 28, when the higher peak-period economy fare must be paid.

Because Icelandic Airlines is not a member of IATA, and thus not bound by agreed-upon rates, they consistently charge less for flights to the Continent. A privately owned airline, Icelandic claims they make more money than their competitors by operating the year round with a 70 to 80 per cent load factor, whereas the average plane is about 30 per cent full in the winter—hence the bargain inducements. Passengers going directly to Europe, with only an hour stopover in Iceland, will reach Luxembourg after a twelve-hour flight across the Atlantic. The planes, on which there are no first-class sections, accommodate 160 passengers in two rows of three seats each.

Innumerable fraternal, professional, political, and charitable organizations charter planes for trips—usually of three to four weeks' duration—to Europe, the Middle East, the Far East, Latin America, even around the world, at rates sometimes 40 to 50 per cent less than the lowest for commercial flights. The Civil Aeronautics Board insists that passengers must have been bona fide members of the sponsoring organization for at least six months before the flight, and that the club should not have been created for the purpose of low-cost travel. Advertising for membership is also forbidden. At this writing there is hope that the C.A.B. will permit the nation's so-called "supplemental" or "nonscheduled" airlines to extend their domestic chartered flights, for which no club membership is required, to jaunts outside the United States.

Most frequently the chartered flight carriers are KLM and Sabena. Although I have heard that the latter's flights are uncomfortable, I can testify that KLM's are superb. Some years ago I took a chartered flight on their craft conducted by the Volunteers of the Shelters, which sponsors orphanages all over the world. Although I have never taken advantage of their chartered flights, I maintain my membership in the Association for the Study of Business Economics, which is concerned with international as well as domestic affairs. A hands-across-the-seas organization of particular value to the traveler is the English-Speaking Union, which also has occasional chartered flights.

On all, an air of festivity prevails, with free cocktails, wine, champagne, and liqueurs bountifully provided. To the lone wolf their great advantage is that one usually stays with the group only to the first stop, then rejoins it on the return flight. So if you are not already a member of an organization that offers chartered flights, join a reputable one (there have been cases of fraud) and save money on your trip.

A minimum of fifty members of a social club, business organization, professional or cultural association may, if traveling together as an "affinity group," get a reduction from airlines on the prevailing economy-class fare. To qualify for rates that are competitive with those for chartered flights, one may through a travel agent or airline office join a non-affinity group, individual members of which must stay at the same hotel in each city on the tour itinerary and not deviate from the scheduled arrivals in and departures from intermediate stops. In addition to the fare, participants are charged $70, which covers a portion of their lodgings and sightseeing. Query airlines about the latest regulations: they change from time to time.

Inexpensive group and independent tours are open to students— high-school, college, and graduate—through the U.S. National Student Association and the Council on Student Travel.

Founded in 1947, NSA, a confederation of student governments of more than three hundred colleges and universities, is the largest official student organization in the world. It is a member of the National Advisory Council of the Peace Corps, is the only student constituent of the American Council on Education, and the only one represented on the United States Commission for UNESCO. Nonprofit, nonpartisan, and nonsectarian, NSA is associated with student organizations in over forty countries. The pre-college tours will take students fifteen to eighteen years old. College and special-interest tours limit the outside age to twenty-five for undergraduates and to twenty-eight for graduate students. However, one may be as old as thirty-five and still be eligible for NSA's "International Student Identity Card," which entitles holders meeting the educational requirements to price concessions in twenty-eight countries at student lodgings and restaurants, art galleries and museums, some theatres and stores, as well as on student transportation, including transoceanic ships and chartered flights within Europe. Complete data is contained in the booklet "Exciting Student Trips Abroad," available from U.S. National Student Association, Educational Travel.

The Council on Student Travel is a nonprofit federation of more than 150 North American schools and colleges, educational and religious organizations. The council arranges transatlantic passage for students and teachers, traveling independently or in groups, on chartered student ships during the summer and on regularly scheduled sailings and flights throughout the year. Any student or teacher may utilize council ships; for independent travelers there is a minimum age of sixteen but no maximum. The shipboard program includes political forums, art lectures, language classes, travel orientation, and recreational activities. Full information is provided in the "Students Abroad" booklets issued by the Council on Student Travel.

The "fly now—pay later" plans are seductive, but costly. In New York, as an example, the interest and service charge on them by the financing company is close to 10 per cent, whereas interest on a bank loan to cover the fare would be about half that.

Shop around for other angles in the air. For instance, passengers flying BOAC from San Francisco to Tokyo are treated by British Overseas Airways to overnight accommodations at the Royal Hawaiian or a similar hotel in Honolulu. Japan Air Lines will stand the cost of a night's lodgings at the Haneda Airport Hotel in Tokyo for JAL passengers going directly from Honolulu to Hong Kong. And, on the overnight flight from Tel Aviv to New York, Air France has been known to do the honors at a de luxe hotel in Paris. These breaks are, of course, governed by flight schedules.

Although their personnel may not remember to tell you so, the airline that has issued your ticket will probably pick up the tab for a meal and hotel room during a layover of several hours between connecting flights.

Always check what meals will be served in the plane; it's difficult to enjoy a filet mignon if you've stuffed yourself with hamburgers just before departure. Don't order any extras for breakfast at the hotel when taking an early morning flight; you will be given breakfast aboard. On Indian Airways it may be fried fish, curried meat croquettes encasing a hard-boiled egg, rice, sandwiches, and a banana.

Find out, too, if you benefit financially by passing up a meal. Pan American's "thrift flights" between San Francisco and Honolulu cost ten dollars less than the economy fare because passengers holding such tickets are not served the shrimp cocktail, pot roast of beef, unsalted carrots, unsalted stringbeans, cheese, chocolate mousse, and champagne. Instead they munch a one-dollar box lunch purchased in the airport.

Semicargo ships and freighters are not only inexpensive, but frugal too in their demands upon one's wardrobe. The best source of information on them is *Around the World by Passenger-Carrying Freighters,* published by Harian and distributed by Crown. One may also watch the newspapers in port cities for the sailings of freighters, then write directly to the steamship lines for information.

Many airlines, in co-operation with travel agencies, offer group tours to various areas of the world. Their itineraries are enticing, their quotations sometimes unbelievably low. It is wise to examine them carefully. What is the supplemental charge for a single room? Will you have a private bath? If breakfast and lunch are included, who's going to pay for your dinner? A new man, I hope. But don't count on it, because very few unattached males under the age of sixty-five go on group tours, and how much chance will you have to meet any outside the flock?

A folder picked at random characteristically reads: "The tour price does not include wines, liquors, mineral waters, after-lunch and -dinner coffee, tea, milk, etc., laundry, valet service, à la carte meals, excess baggage, personal tipping [for special services], baggage and personal insurance."

Only breakfast is included in the "Europe on $5 a day" plan, its $6.50-a-day ("The Big Splurge") plan, and, except when in Hilton hotels, the $10-a-day plan—all available through travel agents and IATA member airlines. In each plan the price is for double occupancy of a room. For a single room, there is a supplemental charge of $1.50 on the $5-a-day plan, $2 on the $6.50- and $10-a-day plans. A private bathroom costs another $1.50 a day on both the $5- and $6.50-a-day plans, but is included on the $10-a-day plan. Thus for a woman who wishes a single room and private bath the $5-a-day plan adds up to $8, the $6.50-a-day plan to $10. Nevertheless, since all include from one to eight sightseeing tours in each of the fourteen cities served, the packages range from good to excellent values, particularly in cities where prices are high; indeed, the $10-a-day plan ($12 for a single room) seems to me—after checking the prices quoted in New York for the Hilton hotels in Amsterdam, Athens, and Madrid—extraordinary.

Moreover, the operators frankly state: "It should be clearly understood that each $5-a-day payment includes a charge for the making of reservations and for the cost of planning these trips. A $5-a-day tour does not, therefore, offer the least expensive means of seeing Europe . . ."

Evidently it costs certain operators considerably more to handle their tours. As a cautionary example, on one of them the "two-night package" in Milan, for instance, includes transfers, bath or shower, Continental breakfast, morning or afternoon city sightseeing tour, routine service charges, and all taxes. Optional are "superior" or "standard" hotels at the respective rates of $37.50 and $29.50. The standard hotels used in Milan are the Cristallo and American, both in Class II, for which the rate set by the Ministry of Tourism in Italy at this writing is $3.50 to $4.50 a night, including all taxes and service charges, but exclusive of a small fee for heat in the winter or—if a Class II hotel has it—air-conditioning in the summer. The Continental breakfast, for which the cost with tip would be about 60¢, is extra. Add $3.52 for the city tour included in the package, and the highest price it would cost one on her own for two days, including all the components except transportation to the hotel, would be $13.12—as contrasted with the $29.50 charged in the professional's tour plan. In either case one would have to buy lunch and dinner, so that leaves $16.38 for the transfer, not from the airport but "from the air terminal, station, or bus terminal to the hotel and vice versa."

A person spending one night in Milan, before continuing her journey the next morning, would have been charged $15.50 on the professional's plan—or $11.50 for transfers and Continental breakfast. If, traveling alone and using standard hotels, she had wished to spend three nights in Milan, she would have had to add $9 to the basic $29.50 and pay a total of $38.50.

Should she have wished transfers and hotel accommodations, but no sightseeing tour, she could have combined the cost of the basic "overnight stop" with as many "additional nights" as necessary. Or pay $24.50 for the two nights, $33.50 for three nights, and so on.

The "optional excursions," says the tour operator's brochure, "can only be sold in connection with a package." The one to Lake Maggiore and Villa d'Este was priced at $16. The same trip, available locally, cost 8,000 lire or $12.80.

These charges however, are relatively reasonable because, after all, people are fairly familiar with rates in the popular tourist centers. Let's see what the same travel plan, which is by no means unique, proposes for Budapest. Taking the "superior" classification, we find that the three-night package comes to $106 for either the Gellért or Royal hotels, rated respectively by the Hungarian government "de luxe A" and "de luxe B" (while the overnight stop is $41 and additional nights $19 each). All meals are included, as well as a morning and afternoon guided tour in a private car.

Another agency's brochure reports that in Budapest a single room with private bath and full board costs $14.40 per day for de luxe A, $13 for de luxe B, which I verified. Sixty-two dollars and eighty cents is a lot to pay for seven hours' sightseeing and being taxied from railroad station or airport to the hotel and vice versa. Especially since a full day's sightseeing by private car with an English-speaking guide could be obtained in Budapest at a price of $21 for one or two persons.

Now, lest you leap to the conclusion that the latter plan has been offering bargains, note that their three-day Budapest package costs $101 for a single room with private bath, plus all meals at a de luxe B hotel ($13 a day, remember?), two half-day sightseeing tours by private car, and dinner at a "traditional Hungarian restaurant with Gypsy music." (Virtually all Hungarian restaurants and taverns ring with Gypsy music.) Moreover, the $13-a-day book of scrip for de luxe B accommodations, which an individual not traveling on a packaged plan would have had to purchase from a representative of the Hungarian government tourist office, would have paid for three meals a day in hotel or city restaurants.

Itineraries of all tour operators bear inspection before being bought. They may be fairly priced; they may not.

Once I asked a travel agent to reserve a houseboat for me for five days in Kashmir. Since at the time the de luxe class cost $6 to $10 a day with all meals and a couple of servants thrown in, I was astonished to receive a choice of three itineraries priced $135, $155, and $192, which included local sightseeing and a variety of excursions into the Himalayas.

"Those fellows have some rather inflated ideas about how much I'm prepared to pay," I remarked to the travel agent.

"But, dear," she said, "you'll find that it will cost you that much. I have just returned from Kashmir."

"Oh no, dear," I said, "I am not going to pay anything like it. I've checked the prices with the Government of India Tourist Office, and they're way out of line. Just reserve the houseboat. I'll take care of the entertainment when I get there."

It was off-season, so a houseboat "special class," for which I paid $8 a day, could have been secured upon arrival in Srinagar for $6, according to an Indian official in Banaras; but even at $8 a day, a breakdown of the $155 itinerary revealed that the bill was padded by at least $60. The agent was a friend, so obviously she was herself fooled.

The fact that we're accustomed to paying much higher prices in American restaurants and hotels is no justification for our being charged—usually by travel agents—more than the prevailing rates overseas. As the "Europe on $10-a-day" pamphlet explains: "The de luxe establishments charge remarkably standard rates the world over. But when one descends to the first-class level—to the still-elegant, still-luxurious first-class level—hotel rates become markedly lower than they would be in American first-class hotels."

To be on the safe side, always ask for an itemized bill. Even if they don't have all the prices on hand (and likely they do), few agencies would be so naïve as not to demand a breakdown themselves from the vague "foreign representative" who sometimes is alleged to have made the arrangements. This precaution alone can save a traveler hundreds of dollars. An agency is entitled to levy a service charge; a tourist is entitled to be told precisely how much it is.

Although the average American stays in de luxe or Class A hotels, there are many charming Class B hotels throughout Europe; the so-called "standard" hotels named in tour brochures are among them. Guidebooks that stress economy offer recommendations and additional lists are provided by government tourist organizations. Two of my globe-trotting friends consistently stay in YWCAs, where, they report, the accommodations are clean and in some instances quite grand. (Under any circumstances, they go to the de luxe hotels to write letters, have tea, and, not to rough it, collect ribbons of quality toilet tissue.) For specific information, write to the Young Women's Christian Association of the U.S.A. One need not travel with a group to take advantage of youth hostels. For the hardy, they are probably the least expensive type of lodgings, and only Bavaria and Switzerland limit youth to the age of twenty-five. Details are available from American Youth Hostels, Inc.

When motoring in Europe, the American Automobile Association and the *Michelin Red Travel Guides* (published here in English by Doubleday) are good sources of information on inexpensive hotels; moreover, most car-rental agencies in the United States and abroad provide motel guides.

Because Europeans prefer baths to showers, rooms with the latter are less costly. One can also save by engaging rooms without either. After all, the tub is usually no farther from your bedroom than the one at home, and the charge for each soaking is only about fifty cents. For that the chambermaid or -man scrubs and draws the tub to the temperature you prefer. I have even heard of their lining it with a clean sheet, the desirability of which is debatable.

Minimum-rate rooms in luxury hotels can be a bargain, and they are not too difficult to secure, since most people going to such places want handsome quarters. The only drawback here is that you're apt to get stuck with "extras" that fatten the bill. *Vide*, the time I stayed at the Grand Hotel Europa and Britannia in Venice, where the tab for two meals a day and an adequate little garret containing a purple chaise longue was $8.45, but I got hooked for having a telephone in my room. Never mind my bleats that I didn't use the phone; it was there for my convenience, and I had to pay.

In countries where the breakfasts are enormous (Britain, Holland, Scandinavia, Israel), one may as well eat heartily in the morning and lightly, if at all, at noon.

Don't be bashful about adding up the bill in either hotels or restaurants—or about querying items. Men do. And always sign bar bills right under the last entry if they haven't been totaled.

On the other hand, don't forget that railroad tickets, sightseeing tours, theatre and opera seats secured for you by the concierge will be on a separate bill at his post. The first time I was in Florence I innocently thought that the hall porter's reckoning represented the Excelsior's total bill and, checking out after paying it, congratulated myself on having been remarkably thrifty. They caught up with me at the Cecil in Alexandria with one of those letters beginning: "Dear Madam: We are sure you did not intend . . ."

Should you plan to travel extensively by bus or train in the British Isles or Western Europe, you can save money by purchasing ThriftRail Coupons or a Eurailpass. Vended only in North America, the former may be bought through a travel agent or at Los Angeles and New York branches of British Rail-International, Inc. Eurailpasses are available at travel agencies or offices in New York City of the French National Railroads, German Federal Railroad, Italian State Railways, and Swiss Federal Railways. A Eurailpass entitles the holder to reductions on trains, certain steamships and ferry boats, as well as on various motor-coach lines, including, in some areas, the superb Europabus network. When purchasing either ThriftRail Coupons or a Eurailpass, inquire about the latest means to cut transportation costs; new ones are always being introduced.

Take it as a rule of thumb that in lands where there are currency controls one can make decidedly advantageous purchases with undeclared dollars. In such countries there is also likely to be a great need for certain types of merchandise, which can be used as barter in the smaller shops. Nylon stockings are no longer as coveted as they once were, but as recently as 1963 I could have exchanged a beat-up cotton print blouse for the finest Balinese wood carving. The *objets d'art* I might have accumulated with a dozen white B-cup bras would have staggered me. A lot of the girls, shamed by the missionaries into covering their bosoms, could have used new bras for their dreamier strolls in the city.

It is also possible, if one plans to spend quite a time in countries where the currency is soft, to effect considerable savings by consulting a foreign-exchange broker like Perera. Because they buy up "frozen funds" at bargain rates, they can resell them to travelers at a discount. However, the economic situation is so mercurial in countries where this obtains that each traveler's opportunities will differ.

What is known here as the "free market" is called the "black market" when one is trafficking with unofficial local money-changers. The condition exists because there is a shortage of dollars needed to buy American machinery and products. In a number of Asian countries one may be approached on the street or in hotels and restaurants by a man who will ask if you wish to change money. He will offer a rate that is anywhere from 5 to 50 per cent higher than the official exchange. The bills he gives you may be bona fide; they may be counterfeit. He himself could be a government plant. Or a shortchanger. Nevertheless, my guess is that more people than not who travel in these areas take a chance on negotiations of this sort; certainly, tourists are anything but tight-lipped about them. It pains one to reflect—as did I when leaving Indonesia and Ceylon —that honesty may cost a traveler three to five times what she would have paid had she succumbed to sub rosa finance.

The discovery of falsified currency declarations or dealings in the black market can result in severe penalties. All the American embassy or consulate can do for the culprit is to see to it that she gets a fair trial.

There are times when it is perfectly legal to shop around for money. Until recently scores of Argentinian *cambios*, or money-changing stores, vied with each other in offering the most pesos for hard currency. The "Change" offices in Switzerland have given as much as $12.50 more in francs per $100 than the hotels, which nearly everywhere have a lower rate than banks and money changers, official or not. In Afghanistan the hotel gave me 55 afghanis for the dollar, the bank 63.25. "Do you," I asked an acquaintance in Kabul, "do better in the bazaar?" "Oh, sure," he said, "the bank itself changes money in the bazaar."

The first time I encountered a black market in money I turned up my nose. I had listened to the scuttlebutt about Turkey's inflation on the plane ride from Beirut to Istanbul (this was 1954), but had made up my mind to bypass that kind of bargain. Anyway, I thought, how do you *find* the black market? Like Switzerland and most free ports, Beirut would have been a good place to have purchased Turkish liras and other foreign coin advantageously, but I was too dumb in those days to know that, so I arrived in the country without a kurush.

The Air France limousine drove us gratis from the airport to the city terminal, where I asked a functionary if he could change a traveler's checks. He said it was against the law for him to do so; however, since he was going out of town he might take a chance. "But," he added virtuously, "I cannot give you more than the official rate."

"I do not wish you to," I replied. "Two-eighty [2.80] liras for each dollar are all that I expect." He looked at me as if I'd lost my marbles, and when I asked for a cab did not bother to tell me that the Park Oteli was a five-minute walk from the terminal. So I had a leisurely and circuitous ride to the Park, which at the time was considered the best hotel by Western standards. Who knew what the plumbing would be like at the more colorful Pera Palas?

The dining room at the Park was a bit starchy, and I was just unfolding a stiff serviette when the captain, handing me a menu, asked if I wanted to change any money. "Oh, no," I said, "I have just changed a traveler's check at the terminal." "How much they give you for it?" I told him. He all but spat. "I give you four liras to the dollar." "Thank you very much," I said, "but I am not interested in unsavory transactions."

That afternoon I took a city sightseeing tour, during which we sprinted through St. Sophia, the Blue Mosque, the Green Mosque —where Empress Theodora used to take the waters—through

Topkapi Palas (imagine an infant's cradle encrusted with rubies, emeralds, and diamonds the size of quarters) before arriving at Kapali Carshi, the Grand Bazaar. Just outside this colossal covered co-op, the guide in our bus asked matter-of-factly if any of the passengers cared to change money. "What are they offering?" one of them inquired. "Five-ten liras to the dollar for traveler's checks, five-fifteen for the green." I was getting some enriched arithmetic.

Most of my companions bought marked-down liras at a jeweler's to which the guide led us before embarking on the labyrinths under the lofty arches of this souk of souks, where, as traditional, we had been spared ample time to purchase keepsakes in the four to five thousand shops spread over ninety-two city blocks. I was brooding as I parted from the group, aware that guides shepherding tourists into emporia get a cut on jacked-up prices—roughly 10 per cent. I wasn't going to be a patsy about that.

In shop after shop I purposefully compared quotations on baubles and brass platters. The sell was hard, but I was determined to be shrewd. Meanwhile the day was darkening and the mud underfoot crusting to ice in the cold December air. Finally, I encountered a most persuasive vendor. "How much for the turquoise earrings?" I asked. "Five-sixty liras." "What if I pay in dollars?" I said, inspired. "One dollar." I gave him the green, happy about a canny deal. However, its potential gave me pause.

Lost in more than reflection, I now searched in vain for my party. Suddenly frightened, I rushed crazed from one exit to the other of the enormous rialto, hunting in the maze for one familiar mackintosh or coat. I only became more confused. Worse than that, all the big stray cats with which Istanbul was overrun—the dogs had been exterminated as rabid—seemed to have congregated at the bazaar; and I am an ailurophobe.

Now on the outskirts of the mart, I ducked frantically into the stall of what appeared to be a lumber purveyor. "Where," I cried, "is the tourist car?" He understood no English. I careened out and accosted a leather merchant. He spoke no English. Little did I realize that I might have muddled through in broken Spanish—if I could have remembered one word of it—since many of the bazaar's merchants are descended from Sephardic Jews who migrated to Turkey during the Inquisition and still speak fifteenth-century Ladino, a sort of Spanish counterpart to Yiddish.

The hides man tried to calm me. Indicating that I was to wait a moment, he waddled across the way to borrow a Turkish-English dictionary the size of an unabridged Webster. Fumbling shakily, I located the words *lost, taxi,* and *hotel.* Taksi. Oteli. Of course! Had I had the aptitude of a lower primate, I would have applied Turkish phonetic spelling to my problem.

Taking the curves of the narrow, steep streets on two wheels, like any competent Turkish driver, the hackie had me home in short order. The proceeds of my bargains at the bazaar took care of his fare.

The maître d'hôtel approached me as I was entering the cocktail lounge. Leading me to a table, he mumbled, "Would you like to change any money?" "What," I whispered, "are you offering?" "Five-twenty-five to the dollar." "Well," I hedged, "I'll think it over." Although I needed more liras, I was still squeamish about yielding to corruption.

In a mood too cerebral to go on the nightclub rounds available through Thos. Cook, I asked Ali, the afternoon's guide, if there were any concerts, dance recitals, or other ethnic entertainment that I could see in the evening. "I am particularly interested," I emphasized, "in the folk music and Oriental dance." He told me of a wonderful place featuring the latter, but cautioned me that, as a woman, I could not go there alone. However, for four dollars he would escort me through a lovely dinner, after which we could enjoy the Oriental dance and other worth-while diversions.

The guide, who had been unexceptionable in his beret, looked like the late Buster Keaton in the broad-brimmed felt "civilization hat" Ataturk had prescribed when he abolished the fez. The fact that he had primped for the occasion was troubling. Could I ingenuously have hired a gigolo? Since he was a far cry from the classic sleek Latin, I thanked Providence that in Istanbul I was unlikely to run into anyone I knew.

Ali suggested a nice German restaurant. I proposed that we eat at the famous Abdullah's. "I want to have dolma and shish kebab and Turkish delight!" "I will take you to an excellent place," he said. "It is run by a White Russian refugee—a countess." That seemed an intriguing enough compromise. I don't like to be overbearing.

Inasmuch as I was so receptive to local institutions, Ali remarked

I might find it instructive to ride there on a typical streetcar. That kind of conveyance falls outside what I regard as culturally enriching; nevertheless we made a dash for one and, with a strong assist from Ali, I managed clumsily to clamber up its rear steps as the vehicle clanged and began moving.

Dismounting in one of the gloomier sections of the city, we short-cut through a dark alley and arrived at a steep, rickety stairway on the outside of a ramshackle building that Ali said was the countess's café. I looked about in dismay. Ataturk had disbanded the harems, but who knew to what residual, bargain bagnio I was being enticed? (In stress I tend to be unrealistic about my allure.) I took a few tentative steps, then hesitated unhappily and looked down—into a dozen pairs of yellow feline eyes. Confronted with the alternative of threading my way through those cats, I decided that if dishonor was my kismet, so be it. But how tacky to go in a trolley.

The room that we entered was spartan rather than sultanic, its most satanic feature a table of chess players under a dangling unadorned light in one corner. Ali paid his respects to the countess in the kitchen, then conveyed her advice that I have *côtelettes de volaille Kiev*. "Order anything you like," he said grandly, "The price is reasonable." Studying the *icki listesi*, I chose as apéritif a Raki cocktail (half lemon juice, half anise liqueur). Ali said he preferred a small *bira*. Urging me to partake also of baklava and kaymak, he claimed satiety with his bowl of kasha.

Guaranteeing that he develop no carnal ideas, I said to him heartily, "Now tell me about your country's economy."

"You a schoolteacher?" he asked.

"No, but I am just terribly interested in your conditions and customs. For instance, outside of Monte Carlo, I have never seen so many banks. How come?"

"Well," he said, "when a fellow gets a few dollars together, he finds himself a corner and opens up a bank."

Not entirely enlightened, I asked about the black market. The fluid money situation existed, he said, because Turks were avid for American automobiles; European cars didn't stand up like those from the United States on their cobblestone roads. However, these had to be paid for with dollars. To amass enough, many Turks were willing to take a loss on the exchange against future profits. "I do not personally have anything to do with the black market," Ali assured me, "except as a service to help Americans who want to change money." If, he added, I wished to purchase some liras, he had a friend who would give me a good rate.

"Such as?" He repeated the afternoon's quotation: five-ten for traveler's checks, five-fifteen for "the green." "I can do better at the hotel," I lied, thinking quickly. "A waiter there is offering five-thirty."

"That is a very good rate," he said. "You should take it." But he looked pensive as we took leave of the bistro.

Our next stop was a large loft filled mostly with men clustered around simple wooden tables. They were nearly all drinking *bira*. Ordering one for himself, Ali persuaded me to have a banana liqueur. At one end of the hall there was a stage, on which several men were playing odd banjolike instruments as accompaniment to a succession of stout sopranos belting out Middle Eastern wails. Then a fleshy brunette came before the footlights and gyrated her jeweled navel. So this was the Oriental dance.

"Huh," commented Ali, "she thinks she is a very good dancer, but no man would marry her."

"Why not?"

"A man," he said, "would have to be of very thin character to marry such a woman. A woman," he explained, "is like a bottle of perfume; once the stopper is off, the fragrance is gone."

I declined the *konyak* Ali offered me. "But you are entitled to it," he persisted. I shook my head. I had noticed two tables away a conducted tourist party, several members of which had been on the afternoon's excursion. I averted my head, hoping they wouldn't recognize me—or, worse, my unprepossessing escort.

"Let's call it an evening," I suggested.

"But," protested Ali, "we still have to go to the modern Western nightclub. It is part of the tour." I said it was okay with me if we skipped it. Ali was conscientiously stubborn. "We will just stay a few minutes. You are to have a *wiski* and soda there."

At the top of another flight of dilapidated stairs we entered a small smoke-filled room, where a number of fat, kohl-eyed Turkish tarts in skin-tight black-satin sheaths were sitting in pairs and trios at bistro tables. Ali ignored them, but I have always been as intrigued as the next woman by daughters of joy.

Brightening, I urged Ali to tell me about himself. He showed me a yellowed snapshot of his wife and four children, for whom he was struggling to provide. As a guide, he said, his pay was low and his hours long—sometimes extending far into the night. He wanted very much to purchase a Dodge, but it took a long time to accumulate enough dollars. We passed the tourist party as we descended the stairway.

On our walk to the hotel from the *bôite*, I was silently calculating how much of the four dollars he had been able to pocket by sticking to buckwheat groats and *bira* when Ali cleared his throat. "If you want to change some money," he said hesitantly, "I think my friend will give you five-thirty-five to the dollar."

In recent years the official rate for liras has fluctuated between 9.25 and 10. What Ali's friend is offering I don't know.

4

Red Tape from Scratch

Red tape starts with a scratch: make sure that your most recent inoculation for smallpox was secured less than three years before the date that you plan to return to the United States. If its certified validity has expired by then, you will have to be vaccinated at your-port of re-entry to the States. Should this prospect not dismay you, remember that the health inspectors of many other countries insist upon proof of smallpox immunization before allowing tourists past their gates.

At least a month before your departure ask your doctor, travel agent, or airline what other shots may be required or advisable in the areas you will be visiting. You'll need time for those that require a series of weekly injections.

The dates of all inoculations are entered by your doctor in an "International Certificates of Vaccination" booklet. Smallpox, cholera, and yellow fever immunizations must be verified by your local board of health, to whom you may mail the booklet with a self-addressed, stamped envelope and a request for its speedy return.

"International Certificates of Vaccination" booklets are obtainable free from passport offices, travel agents, and international airlines, as well as most boards of health and doctors. They are also available for ten cents apiece from the Superintendent of Documents, Government Printing Office, Washington 25, D. C.

When visiting the Dominican Republic, Costa Rica, El Salvador, Guatemala, Honduras, Mexico, Nicaragua, Panama, Colombia, Ecuador, and Venezuela, one needs only a tourist card—obtainable from travel agents, airline offices, government tourist organizations, and consulates. Proof of citizenship is sufficient for the British West Indies, Bermuda, Guadeloupe, Haiti, Martinique, the Netherlands Antilles, Puerto Rico, the Windward Islands, British Guiana, and Canada. For all other areas not subject to United States jurisdiction, an American passport is necessary if you are a citizen of the United States.

An application for a passport has to be executed before a clerk of a federal court or a state court having naturalization jurisdiction— or before an agent of the Passport Office of the Department of State. Applicants for a first passport, or a new one after a passport's expiration, must provide proof of citizenship. A previously issued passport will serve for the latter. However, a native-born American applying for a first passport must, in lieu of a passport on which she was included, submit a birth certificate or facsimile of one with the application. If that is unobtainable, a baptismal certificate or a certified copy of the record of baptism will do. Should the applicant lack these, she may present census records, newspaper files, school records, or affidavits by persons having personal knowledge of the facts of her birth. With exhibits other than birth certificates, a notice by appropriate authorities (such as your state's Bureau of Vital Statistics) testifying that no birth record exists must be submitted.

Whatever the "secondary evidence," it must state the place and date of birth of the applicant. To be acceptable, birth and baptismal certificates must show that the birth or baptism was recorded shortly after birth. (It's absolutely impossible to get away with knocking off a few years.) All documents, save affidavits, will be returned by the Passport Office to the applicant unless further investigation is required. This, however, is unusual.

Anyone claiming citizenship by naturalization must attach to the passport application her certificate of naturalization. In case her citizenship has been acquired through the naturalization of one or both parents, or by birth abroad to a parent or parents with United States citizenship, she must submit the certificate of citizenship issued by the Immigration and Naturalization Service with the passport application. If this is unavailable, she should secure a Consular Report of Birth or Certification of Birth issued by the

Department of State. Failing either of these, she may present the foreign birth certification, evidence of citizenship of one or both parents, plus an affidavit from them specifying the periods and places of residence in America and abroad before her birth, as well as any service in the Armed Forces of the United States.

In the event an applicant's citizenship was acquired through the naturalization of one or both parents, she will have to provide her foreign birth certificate or copy thereof and evidence of admission to the United States, along with the naturalization certificate of one or both parents. If citizenship was acquired through the naturalization of a sole parent and the other is either dead or divorced, the applicant must also present the death certificate of the alien parent or submit the divorce decree proving that the naturalized parent received custody of her.

Finally, if a woman was married before September 22, 1922, to one or more aliens ineligible for citizenship before March 31, 1931, she should take a swig of Lydia Pinkham and discuss with the clerk of court or passport agent what will be acceptable as evidence of citizenship.

So much for proof that you are an American. Two duplicate photos, both signed by you and taken within the previous couple of years, must accompany your passport application. They may be in black-and-white or in color, but tinted black-and-whites are out. Retouching that eliminates aging lines and shadows is permissible. You should, however, be posed full- or three-quarters face before a light background for a head-and-shoulders portrait; our State Department, monolithically speaking, is not interested in the balance of your torso. The photographs—not less than 2½ by 2½ inches or more than 3 inches square—must be printed on a thin, unglazed paper base capable of withstanding the temperature necessary for gluing one of the pictures to the passport. Polaroid or vending-machine prints are unacceptable because they may fade before the passport expires; also unacceptable are snapshots and newspaper or magazine reproductions. Before ordering pictures, find out out how many you will or may need for visas in addition to the two required for the initial passport application. When traveling outside Western Europe, where no visas are required, it is wise to have extra pictures with you.

The Department of State asks that you print or type your full legal name on the passport application. If you use a different first name or surname and prefer that either or both appear on your passport, you may ask the clerk for two copies of the Supplementary Affidavit Regarding Change of Name, then get two relatives or friends to swear before a notary that they have known you for however many years by both your former and current names.

Three years after its issuance date the passport must be renewed to be valid for two years more. No matter when you apply for renewal, the expiration date is exactly five years after the passport was originally granted. Your original passport will cost ten dollars, the renewal five.

Although passport applications are usually processed within seven days, considerable time can be consumed acquiring visas. A travel agent will obtain those that are necessary or you may apply for them yourself—in person if there is a local consulate office, or by writing to the one nearest home. Consult the *Congressional Directory*, available in most libraries, for the addresses of foreign consular offices in the U.S. In Europe only the Iron Curtain countries demand visas. Since practices change, query your nearest Passport Office about visa requirements in other countries that you plan to visit.

Certain African nations have been known to require with the visa application proof that one has no police record; other nations keep out Communists and journalists, broadly defined. Some of Israel's neighbors won't let in Zionists or "Arab-hating Zionists," which they too emotionally infer from an answer "Jewish" to the religion question on the visa application—a query that as of this writing does not appear on the applications for transit visas at the borders between Lebanon and Syria, or the latter and Jordan. In their U.S. consulates, "no religious affiliation" is accepted only by Lebanon as a response. No travelers whose passports are stamped with an Israeli visa may enter Jordan, Syria, Lebanon, or the United Arab Republic. But if upon arrival in Israel you ask the immigration officer to issue the Israeli visa on a separate sheet of paper, removable from the passport, you may legally and safely cross the border at the Mandelbaum Gate (permitted once in either direction) between Jerusalem, Israel, and Jerusalem, Jordan.

This subterfuge is maintained because the Arab nations do not recognize the State of Israel.

With very little fuss I have gotten yards of visas—literally, because after the pages for them are used up, an accordion of additional blanks is stapled into the passport.

One year, infected with Carol's enthusiasm, I predicated the
balance of an entire Southeast Asian tour on my being in Rangoon
for the full moon. "The Burmese," she said, "get into wonderful
costumes and perform special temple dances. You'll simply adore
it!" This was during the planning stages in July; to determine when
the full moon would occur the following December, I telephoned
the Hayden Planetarium—which proved to be about as reliable as
consulting the entrails of a fowl.

I also wanted to be in Bali for the spectacular mass cremations,
having read that the elaborate rituals for the departed beggar the
American way of death. At enormous expense to the bereaved,
huge wooden animals are constructed, into which the exhumed
bodies buried during the wet season are placed and ceremoniously
set afire.

I was warned that I probably wouldn't be able to get into Indonesia, which at the time was peeved at the U.S. for threatening to
cut off foreign aid because Sukarno had nationalized certain American financial interests; moreover, the political situation was in general tumultuous. However, after satisfying the consulate that the
purpose of my trip was tourism, I was granted a visa. The Indians
also cross-examined me, but soon realized that I was no menace.
Nor were Ceylon and Cambodia thorny, although they, like Indonesia, were said to be nursing anti-American sentiments.

I didn't know enough about Burma to harbor apprehensions the
morning I taxied to their consulate. Still whistling a tuneless "On
the Road to Mandalay," I entered a modest building on a side
street shortly before 10:00 A.M., the hour most consular offices open
(they knock off at 12:30 or 1:00), climbed a flight of musty stairs,
and, seeing no one at the switchboard, approached a desk where
two acculturated Burmese girls were indolently chewing gum. Neither looked up until I coughed.

"I'd like, please," I said, "to make application for a visa."

"Over there," replied one of them, waving a languid, snaky arm.

I went back to the foyer and this time poked my head through the receptionist's window. In the recesses there was a girl absorbed in a crossword puzzle. "Pardon me," I repeated, "I'd like to apply for a visa."

"Just a minute!" she said. So I curbed my impatience and was shortly confronted by a sexily garbed TV-spy type.

"Fill this out," she said, handing me a form.

"What does this question mean?" I asked, pointing to a query that was new to me on such applications.

"Personal income," she snapped. "How much money do you earn a year?"

I gave myself a handsome increase, then pleasantly enough inquired, "Why do you ask it?"

"We are not," she said evenly, "obliged to explain anything to you." My eyes began to smart, but I bridled my gorge and completed the form, thinking fiercely, "These nasty little bureaucrats are not typical of the country; why, everyone says the Burmese are just darling!"

When I handed their slinky public servant the completed application, she asked for the letter from my travel agent testifying that I was in possession of an airline ticket out of Burma and would have with me sufficient funds for all my expenses in her country. Not having previously come across this stipulation, although it is not unusual with disadvantaged lands, I wondered how many American tourists had become a burden on their economy. In this instance, I supplied the telephone number of my travel agent, who verified that I had adequate means.

The next morning, when, as directed, I returned to the Burmese Consulate to pick up my passport, the dragon lady seemed more content. "I am sorry," she purred, "but the consul has not come in yet to sign your visa." Since she appeared anxious that I not wait around for him, I proceeded to my office in peppery disposition. I had no sooner arrived when he telephoned. And, with profuse apologies, reported that they were required to submit applications to Rangoon, which would take about two months and naturally that would be impossible inasmuch as I was leaving so shortly. Naturally.

Whether an earlier application would have been more fruitful of visa I don't know. Authorities speculated that Burma, in political turmoil, did not welcome Americans associated with the press. Even apolitical ones who just wanted to moon over exotic temple dances—and see if there really was a Mandalay.

Subsequently I learned that visas which suffer delays in the U.S. may frequently be secured a day or two after application at a nation's consulate in a nearby or contiguous country. Overseas airline offices can be helpful. When she applied in the United States for a visa to Poland, Harriet was told that it would take six weeks to grant it. In Nice a TWA official was able to get one for her within twenty-four hours.

The day for your departure has arrived. If you reach the airport by limousine bus from the city terminal or by taxi, a porter will immediately take your suitcases to the ticket counter of the line on which you are flying and place the luggage on the scale. He should be tipped twenty-five cents per bag. (Save for porters and washroom attendants, airline personnel traditionally do not accept gratuities.) If you are flying from your home town to one of the terminal cities and will a few hours later board an international line there, it is sensible to have your baggage checked through to your first overseas destination.

Before departing on your overseas flight, go to the counter of the line you are taking for validation of your ticket and inspection of your passport as well as, in some cities—New York, for instance— the "International Certificates of Vaccination" form. In Honolulu passports and inoculations booklet are inspected at a counter labeled PASSPORT. The clerk will clip into your passport a U. S. Immigration form, which will be removed when you return to the States.

If you decide to complete these formalities earlier in the day at the airline terminal you may arrive at the airport thirty to forty-five minutes before flight time instead of the usual full hour.

It's wise to carry purchase slips for any foreign-make cameras, binoculars, opera glasses, and transistor radios, or to register such articles with the customs official at the airport, to avoid being charged duty on them when you return. Allow a half hour for this and for last-minute purchase of foreign money.

Behind the ticket or passport counter there will be a bulletin board listing flight numbers, times of departure, and the gate number where you must go to board your plane. The clerk will give you a boarding pass. Sometimes a printed cardboard serves the purpose, sometimes the envelope in which your ticket and baggage claim checks are placed. The envelope will bear your flight and departure gate and probably your seat number.

Seating practices vary, but it does no harm to express your preference at the ticket counter one hour before flight time. If it's first come, first served, one is well advised to proceed immediately to the vicinity of the departure gate, where there is usually a small lounge. People at the head of the queue obviously have a better chance at a choice seat—assuming they step lively en route to the plane. However, if you don't like your location, once the plane is aloft you may ask the stewardess' permission to move to any empty seat in your class that you fancy.

I prefer the so-called "bucket-seat," which is located immediately behind the first-class section, or in the row nearest the engine room. This because it affords more leg room and is generally in front of the motors, so there is less vibration and a better view. It does, however, place one at the end of the line in quitting the plane—unless no objection is raised to your making a first-class exit. As a rule, the seats parallel with the emergency doors also offer extra leg room. In the hope of getting an unobstructed view, some prefer a window seat at the rear of the plane well behind the wings —on the shady side if sun causes wrinkles. There are planes, of course, whose windows have been mindlessly placed back of one's ears. This cannot be anticipated.

Any window or aisle seat is preferable to a middle one, although the first forces one to climb over two sets of legs to get to the lavatories, which are generally at the back of the section.

In economy class you usually cannot have your coat hung up but must put it folded into the rack above your seat, parallel with the length of the plane. No hand luggage may be placed there; hence, since at best leg space is snug, it is important to board with the minimum of parcels, flight bags, and other clutter, whether they are permitted in the cabin or not. Actually, overnight or cosmetic kits are superfluous; the washrooms of most planes provide more than enough toiletries with which to freshen up, including soap, towels, tissues, cologne, sanitary napkins, and sometimes even toothbrushes and paste.

Shortly after the aircraft attains cruising speed, the stewardesses in first and economy classes will demonstrate how to put on and inflate the life jackets. (On board ship, a lifeboat drill is conducted early in a voyage.)

Do not be alarmed by red flares from the plane's motors; they are normal.

Well before a plane is to make its first landing in a foreign country, the stewardesses will pass out cards to disembarking passengers. In general, the forms ask that you print in block letters your surname, first—or, at times, maiden—name (don't let the finer points of this trouble you), and occasionally your father's first name and nationality at birth. They also ask your port of embarkation (where you last boarded the plane), the number and date of your travel document (passport), when and where it was issued, and the same questions regarding your visa, if any; where you were born and when, nationality at birth, current nationality, marital status, occupation, address in city of disembarkation (the name of your hotel will do; if you have no reservation, say so), permanent (home) address, purpose of visit (you write in "tourism" or "holiday"), and duration of visit (which you may approximate).

Tuck the disembarkation card into your passport for presentation in the airport to the immigration official. Have your "International Certificates of Vaccination" booklet also in hand for the health officer. Their stations are the first you pass after entering the area for disembarking travelers. Don't fear you won't find them: the ground steward or stewardess at the foot of the plane's ramp will indicate the direction, and from then on just tag after passengers exhibiting qualities of leadership. You might also watch for signs, which in airports are always in English as well as the local and perhaps other languages, that read HEALTH CONTROL, IMMIGRATION, or PASSPORT CONTROL. Sometimes it widens one's social circle to ask questions of strangers.

When approaching countries where the political situation is jumpy, the stewardess may collect the disembarkation cards and the passports of passengers before they leave the plane. I am not sufficiently cloak-and-dagger-minded to figure out what this caution

forestalls. However, do not let it distress you; passports are returned promptly by the immigration official to everyone not suspected of tampering with the power structure of the nation's prevailing regime.

Once in a while the stewardess, being human, distributes the
wrong disembarkation card. The result is minor chaos at the immigration counter until, using your purse as a desk, you fill out a
substitute form that differs from the original only with respect to
typographical layout: *i.e.*, the questions are centered on the card
rather than flush left with the margin—or vice versa. The more
sluggish your adrenaline, the less this will age you.

Occasionally, before arriving in certain countries—usually Asian
or totalitarian—you also have to fill out a money declaration form,
a document on which you must dismember your kitty into the
amounts of U.S. and foreign currencies you are carrying in addition to traveler's checks. You may be asked to list as well such
locally scarce items accompanying you as a typewriter, tape re-
corder, transistor radio, camera, and jewelry, especially gold. This
presumably is to prevent enterprising tourists from selling them at
a nice profit in the native coin and thus helping to topple a shaky
economy.

One caution: before leaving the plane, if you have the slightest
doubt that you have heard the landing announcement correctly,
ask the stewardess to verify it. It's inconvenient to discover that
you have abandoned the plane in, say, Rawalpindi, instead of Peshawar.

The airport brass are generally fairly rapid readers, so once you
get to the head of the line it doesn't often take more than a minute
for the health and immigration authorities (sometimes they are the
same person) to glance at your inoculations card and stamp into
your passport the date of your arrival in the country—a milestone
you will need to remember for the exit formalities, which repeat
the entry red tape, with perhaps the additional nuisance of an air-
or seaport tax.

The procedure with documents is similar on ships. Tickets, vaccination forms, passports and any visas are scrutinized by officials at
the pier before embarkation. Sometimes, however, passengers must
turn their passports over to the purser, who keeps them during the

voyage. Immigration and health inspectors board the vessel as it is docking, and set up shop in a lounge. Finished with these formalities, their passports returned, passengers may disembark to go through customs on the pier, where luggage, alphabetized by surname, has been placed under huge identifying letters. If yours is not there, try the initial letter of your first name; my suitcases are put with the R's as often as the G's.

When flying, you have to go through customs in the baggage section of the airport. If you find no signpost, approach anybody in uniform or a couple close to a gentleman whose acquaintance you would like to make (this is always better finessed) and say, "Bah-GAHZH?" Only Americans or people with comparably appalling linguistic limitations will fail to understand and indicate the way.

Since my suitcases are always the last to be taken off the plane, I am grimly resigned to considerable delay in this quarter, and usually utilize it powdering my nose, pacing the floor, and, if I have not previously done so on the plane, asking around if there is an "out-o-boos" (airline bus) into the city. Only when I am despondently convinced that this time my luggage is really lost do I spot the small, fat valise bumping off the conveyor, to be followed at an interval by its more stately companion. Excitedly, I point them out to a porter, waving the baggage checks stapled to my plane ticket. That is, I do in airports providing such grace notes as porters. At Kennedy, Honolulu, and less affluent, self-service locales I, like other women without bearers, grumpily heave my suitcases myself onto the table for examination.

The routine overseas varies, but at some point one will be asked if she has "anything to declare" (presumably excess cigarettes and liquor, items for sale, or gifts for people in the country; I've always felt that if I kept myself underinformed on this topic I couldn't be accused of lying). "Just personal effects" is the password. The customs man will ask to see your ticket. Show it to him. And, like every other public servant outside the United States, he too will want to see your passport. They are absolutely mad about vital statistics. Okay, show him.

Most countries limit to two hundred the number of cigarettes that may be brought in duty-free, probably because they don't want to lose the high regional tariff on imported smokes. I know women who hide extra packs in everything from coat pockets to Tampax boxes, but that is unnecessarily sneaky. Travelers who will be leaving from the same airport may for a small fee have held in bond cartons exceeding the quantity allowed, to be reclaimed when departing. The same is true of liquor in excess of the amount that is permitted in duty-free.

Tourists entering a country for a brief visit are seldom asked to open their suitcases for inspection when they report they have nothing to declare. However, even if you're told to unzip your grips, the poking about is so perfunctory I cannot imagine what it would unveil beyond a broken bra strap. Satisfied that you're not smuggling in narcotics, gold bars, or munitions, the customs official will chalk an untidy, unintelligible hieroglyphic on your luggage and you may then flag a porter—if one is not even then hovering at your elbow.

He will inquire if you wish a taxi. Say no. Ask for the airline bus—if there is one. The cab will be much more expensive than the bus, which may be free but will probably cost $1 to $1.50. In the event there is none, and you don't want to dip into your principal, it's a good idea to find out from an airport attendant what a taxi should charge for the ride to the city. Don't rely on the porter's quotation; he may get a kickback from the hackie, who in general is not averse to gouging the unwary. Many cities have flat rates for trips from the airport to town. Having ascertained this from whatever source—perhaps in advance from the government tourist office or consulate—you needn't ask the taxi driver what he will charge; simply give him the correct fare upon arrival at your hotel. Otherwise, ask him the cost before you get in, and if that is out of line with what you have learned in the airport, say, "No, I will give you x number of francs" (or lire, escudos, rupiahs). Cabbies haunting airports know enough English to understand, and they will respect you the more for your assurance.

Some ten dollars is padded into a travel agent's bill for each time you are met in the airport by his foreign representative, "helped" through customs (*he* tells the official you have nothing to declare), and driven by private car to your hotel. Not even when I have been overcharged have I ever paid a cab driver as much as five dollars for the ride.

As an average, it takes about an hour and a half to dispatch the airport formalities and get to your hotel. Setting a world record, Hong Kong spins travelers through Immigration, Health Control, and Customs in three minutes flat; I've timed it, and this included a thirty-second colloquy concerning the extra cigarettes that I asked be held for me in bond for twenty-four hours. Rather than retard progress, the official said, "Never mind, take them along with you." In the British Crown Colony they are more concerned that you do not bring in firearms. Providing a unique voluntary service, a reception desk with three clerks greets foreign visitors individually and reports that they have confirmed your next flight. Two more minutes are required to buy a few Hong Kong dollars; and hotels have taxis waiting at the airport to whisk you to yours. Total time from plane ramp to bedroom and a cup of hot jasmine tea, courtesy of the house: twenty minutes.

In contrast, one is lucky to get through Calcutta's aptly named Dum-Dum Airport in two hours. Hot, humid, squalid, with tumble-down dusty furniture, and cranky, suspicious personnel, Dum-Dum delays the departure of the airline buses to the city until the last Pakistani has been interviewed in depth and his valises minutely examined. A lady is well advised in places like this to hang the cost and take a cab into town, assuming one is available.

There is always a bank in an international airport. Should you need local currency, stop there if it is open and exchange a couple of American dollars—no more, because the rate will be a few mills lower than that in the city—or break into small change a fairly large-denomination native bill that you foresightedly purchased in advance. Rare is the cab driver abroad who, hoping to pocket the balance, will admit he has change for the counterpart of a dime, let alone five or ten dollars. The bank is also a good place to check or doublecheck the cost of the taxi ride, the correct tip for the porter and the cab driver, if it is customary to give him any. Ask the bank clerk to indicate the proper coins for tips so you don't have to start right off doing fractions. Many travel guides, as well as airline brochures, provide this information, but in my experience, save for BOAC, most suggest the "rich American" rather than the going *pourboire*. With few exceptions—in Paris and Bangkok, for instance—if anyone advises more than the equivalent of fifteen

American cents for a bag (and in foreign countries even that is usually on the grand scale), you are being gulled.

In the airport there may be a ticket office for the line on which you will next fly; if so, reconfirm your reservation (this should be done at least forty-eight hours before departure). Although speed is of the essence if one is leaving the next morning, don't miss the bus by waiting for service, because this chore can be handled at your hotel.

Motor-coach tickets are sometimes purchased at the counter near the airport exit, sometimes from a conductor alongside the transport. Spotting neither, have the porter shove your suitcases into its baggage compartment, enter the conveyance, and relax; if there is a charge, an attendant will see to it that you pay. The airline bus driver need not be tipped, the largesse of some Americans notwithstanding.

If you should find the airport bank closed because of the extreme earliness or lateness of your arrival, and if you have no small change in the local currency, you may tip the porter a quarter or thirty cents in American money and pay the bus fare in dollars. You can always ask the doorman or hall porter at your hotel to take care of the cab and charge it to your bill. These fellows, however, have a tendency to tip the driver rather handsomely if the amount on one's chit is to be credited.

After driving leisurely through interminable, often exceedingly dreary outskirts, airline buses wind up at the city terminal. Some stop at junctions en route where passengers may take taxis to their hotels (tell the driver the name of yours, and he will let you off at the proper stand). But frequently even in big cities they go to the major hotels to discharge tourists. If not, one takes a cab from the terminal to the hotel. In this case, it makes sense to ask the porter who grabs your bags how far away your hotel is; it may be within easy walking distance and worth a fatter tip to him to wheel your baggage over. Personally, I don't care whether so unceremonious an arrival lowers me in the esteem of the doorman.

A third transit possibility from the airport is the cars that boni-faces in some areas regularly dispatch to meet planes and pick up guests, expected or importuned. Such automobiles are easily identi-fied by their chauffeurs, who surround one shouting, "Park Hotel?"

"Royale?" "Palace?" "Grand?" "Excelsior?" Be it gratis or added to the bill, and it usually is, this is a service that makes me feel cherished.

So do the flock of porters who rush out of the hotel for my luggage and usher me like a *grande dame* through the lobby to the haughty reception clerk. The tips they make eyes for also indicate they have mistaken me for Gloria Vanderbilt or Doris Duke. Asian countries tend more than Occidental to provide porters in relays, all of whom wistfully reveal their wish to be rewarded. Since my forty-four pounds of personal effects don't warrant a cortège, I customarily tip the last man on the caravan and, graciously thanking the others, leave it to him to split the take with his teammates. But that's after I've filled out the police blotter, been escorted to my room, and had the closets—clothes and water—deferentially displayed.

I've known a few hamlets and hill stations—in Portugal and Ceylon, for example—where one didn't have to register with the local *gendarmerie* within twenty-four hours of arrival, but that's iconoclastic. However, it is equally untoward to have to appear in person at some ramshackle precinct house—as required in Pakistan and Afghanistan. The prevailing ritual demands that transients or the presiding clerk complete at the hotel's reception desk a form repeating the questions on the disembarkation card. In some places you're on your honor; in others, perhaps to avoid falsification on the form, you must also temporarily relinquish your passport to the reception clerk, who will use it to fill out the police registration for you. Within the next several hours, or the following morning, it will show up in your mail slot at the concierge's bailiwick.

What the cops do with the tons of such documents they accumulate during a good season I don't know. I do know that for sensitive women providing this kind of personal history can be traumatic. Just as there are ladies who modestly wriggle out of their undies with back turned and slip on, so there are those to whom nothing is more private than their birth date. I, for one, would as soon display my bankbook as passport. Sooner. The State Department is said to be getting realistic about not asking women to describe on applications for passports anything as mercurial as hair color. Why not for ages something sanguine like "of consent"? After all, Form DSP-19, Application for Amendment of Passport, may be used to update other "descriptive data." But enough of this dreaming.

Let's assume your accommodations have not been prepaid. When you registered you were probably given a small card indicating your room number, the rate, service charge, and local taxes (I especially like the tax you have to pay in Italy for being taxed—by purchasing a tiny stamp that so testifies). If not, request such a card. To my mind, it is not up to the traveler to assume the labor payroll, so, save to the concierge and baggage porters, I am not one to offer the help more than token gratuities in addition to the service charge levied on the bill, which may vary from 10 to 22 per cent and will include extra fees for food or drinks served in your room. Indeed, to tip individuals is against the house rules in some British and Indian hotels, and I don't cross them unless I have received exceptional attention. Europeans don't. Why make it more difficult for them—or, indeed, for less-well-heeled Americans?

You have registered for your room and with the police, asked the concierge or hall porter if there are any messages or mail for you, secured a list of sightseeing excursions, and are now in your quarters —a bit bewildered about what to do next. You can buzz or telephone for room service and, while waiting for tea or a cold drink, freshen up (a woman alone has at her disposal twice the number of nice, fluffy towels, assuming she is not in ultima Thules like Katmandu or Hvar, where one is lucky to get even a raveled, discolored bathmat). Then you really must unpack something to wear for dinner. If it's as crumple-prone as my guaranteed wrinkle-resistant costumes, you'll either ring for the maid to have it pressed, give it a light sponging yourself, or if there is sizzling hot water in the bathtub, lock it in for a steaming. Cross your fingers about the fabric. I recall the bodice of a waltzing black chiffon that became a Boyishform Bra after such a sauna. Whatever your method, before leaving, hang the garment in an airy place to dry.

Unless you are staying for more than two days, straightway reconfirm the space held on your next flight. Never mind that it is distinctly marked "OK" on the ticket. The timetable may have changed, or perhaps there was a slip-up on the original reservation. Moreover, the host airline has to know where to notify you of delays. In non-English-speaking countries let the hall porter take care of it for you and spare yourself this typical telephonic exchange:

YOU [*briskly*]: Hello, is this Air So-and-so?

AIRLINE: Allo.

YOU: Hello?

AIRLINE: Allo.

YOU: Hello. Is this the Air So-and-so office?

AIRLINE: Allo.

YOU: Hello. May I speak with the reservations desk, please?

AIRLINE [*very faintly*]: Allo.

YOU [*on a higher register*]: Hello! I should like to confirm my flight No. ooo tomorrow morning to Erehwon.

AIRLINE: One moment, pleess . . .

[*Silence for ten minutes while you take a gulp of the drink you have ordered and strain your back reaching for a tourist brochure.*]

YOU: Hello. Hello. Is anybody there?

AIRLINE: Allo?

YOU: Hello; Is anyone taking care of my request?

AIRLINE [*after three minutes' static*]: Mhrdlu hrdlurf cmfwyp vbg ngoc.

YOU: Can *anybody* there speak English?

AIRLINE: Allo.

YOU: Oh, the devil with it . . .

When you are checking out, you may tip the concierge twenty-five to fifty cents, depending on the local economy, for this, and proportionately more for additional indispensable services.

No braver than the next woman, I confess that I have blanched before landing in certain outposts even though experience should have taught me that, however momentarily unpopular our government, or unstable theirs, individual Americans are seldom molested. Nevertheless, Indonesia in 1963 was unnerving. Bali-hai may have been calling, but my throat was getting tighter by the second as the Texan engineer alongside me on the JAL flight from Bangkok companionably described the daylight holdups in the streets of Djakarta and the perilous taxi rides from the airport.

"Worth your life to go there," he said, cheering me with yet another for the road.

I tried to take heart from the several families with children disembarking and was further buoyed by the generally good temper of the perspiring officials who, stripped to their shirtsleeves in the hundred-degree-plus heat, were languidly fanning themselves with our passports. After confirming my dawn flight down to Bali, I asked the friendly clerk at Air Garuda if he would be so very kind as to get me a *reliable* taxi—and before I knew it was cozily put up at the Hotel Indonesia, one of Pan Am's intercontinental chain and about as sinister as a Sheraton—the recently burned-down British embassy opposite it notwithstanding.

Ever sluggish in the morning, I had to check out without breakfast in a vain effort to be at the airport at 5:30 A.M. Halfway there the taxi driver inquired if I were flying to Singapore.

"No, Denpasar," I replied.

"That flight," he commented, "three hours late." Doubtful, I said to proceed to the airport; after all, wouldn't Garuda have notified me at the hotel of a delay?

Garuda, which is named for the giant bird in Hindu mythology, meant well, but its performance was eccentric. The clerk reported that the flight would leave at 11:00 A.M. What to do for five hours? I surveyed the waiting room. Bustling with insects, it was at 6:00 A.M. already uncomfortably steamy. The furniture was uninviting and largely occupied by pot-bellied, pajama-ed Chinese and their bundles, very few Indonesians being sufficiently solvent to fly.

Thinking to make the best of the situation, I asked whether it would be possible to hire one of the pedicabs I'd observed on the highway and thus see something of Djakarta and environs. It would soon be getting light. The man at Garuda emphatically vetoed the idea. Why didn't I, he countered, relax in the stewardesses' restroom? He summond Miss N'ophie N'ie N'ian Koen, who had a warm smile and beehive coiffure. She asked that I call her Sophie, N' being equivalent to S in English. She confided that she had studied hairdressing in Hong Kong and had her own "saloon" in Djakarta. She expressed a fondness for American cotton blouses, size 38. I said I was crazy about size 10 sarongs. We immediately took to each other.

The restroom had a bare bulb suspended from the ceiling, an

upended, three-legged table and some rubbish in one corner, as well as two lumpy settees at right angles to an enormous low table. Every hour a fresh pair of pert, teen-aged hostesses, introduced by Sophie Koen, sank onto the sofa, kicked off their pinching pointed-toed pumps, and assumed responsibility for my entertainment. Standing on the four-legged table, I snapped pictures of them until I ran out of flash bulbs. To get a line on the political situation, I asked them how they liked President Sukarno. They asked me about Elvis Presley.

Nevertheless, after eight hours in the airport I began to grow low in spirit. Having taken exhaustive inventory of the souvenir shop, I knew what was too much to pay for wood carvings in Bali—but would I ever get there?

At 3:00 P.M. the flight to Denpasar was announced. Never have I entered a plane with more misgivings, yet, curiously, I'd developed an affection for the entire Garuda crew, who were trying so earnestly to be a credit to their land.

As if in poetic compensation for my ordeal, even the runway in Denpasar was enchanting, a ribbon between golden rice fields where, oblivious of the Machine Age, high-cheekboned islanders in flowered sarongs were tying together fat bundles of glistening grain. Bali was well worth enduring a little initial discomfort.

So, too, in a different way was Budapest in 1960—though it came very close to melting my mettle. The flight from Amsterdam was five hours late, and a chilling October dusk had set in when we began to lose altitude. Nor was it bracing to be advised by mimeographed bulletin to secrete cameras in hand luggage, as KLM could take no responsibility for such equipment. This in contrast to JAT, on which, a few years previously, the courtly Yugoslav steward in the brocaded plush compartment helped me, two hundred feet above Dubrovnik, to select the most photogenic shots.

Standing in the Hungarian drizzle at the foot of the plane was a group of grimly armed police officers in long overcoats. To them all passengers immediately had to surrender their passports. As customary, those who were in transit were led to a special section of the airport. We who were disembarking—of whom I happened that day to be the only American—were marched across the muddy field to a barren room fitted with a long U-shaped, rough-hewn table. In its aisle stood the customs official; at its rump, sitting on countrified, plain wooden chairs, were three comrades, identically garbed in khaki trousers, military jackets, and visored hats: two men flanking a faded blonde, who needed a new perm and considerably smaller kepi.

How much money, she demanded, did I have with me? Confronting me publicly for the first time, this question seemed unrefined. Furthermore, I was embarrassed to appear to be so loaded (it was the beginning of my holiday). Before the attentive ears of a less capitalistic queue, I sheepishly confessed to what must have seemed like quite a purse. After the blonde jotted its components on the currency control form, my passport was returned, and I was told to proceed to the customs official, a fatherly man, who quickly dismissed me.

Muscular peasant women were stacking leather club chairs atop the sofas and sudsing the floors when I entered the big bleak passengers' waiting room. My fellow travelers had vanished and there were no attendants in sight. With a thumping heart, I searched for a sign reading IBUSZ, hoping a member of the tourist department might tell me how to get into the city. Eventually in the semidarkness I spotted one above a broad-beamed young woman with a sallow complexion who was sitting at a desk absorbed in what appeared to be a Graustarkian romance. Whether she really didn't understand English or simply resented interruption, she forced me to falter in foreign tongue.

"Out-o-boos *nach* Budapest?" I ventured. "*Omnibus*," she corrected me. "*Fünfzen minuten.*" I tried again. "*Dónde está*—no, no, that's Spanish. *Où c'est trouve* . . . How," I rummaged through my brain, "does one say 'where' in German—let alone Hungarian?"

In a state of aphasia, I got out my phrase book, flipped past chatter "For the Chambermaid," "On the Telephone," "Shopping." Aha, "Traveling—Arriving by Train." I adapted the question concerning the *Schlafwagon* to my problem: "*Wo ist der Omnibus?*" *Der* Omnibus, *die* Omnibus? For all I could remember, transit facilities might be feminine. She waved in the direction of the exit. "*Bitte schön*," I stalled, "*Ich möchte* . . . now, where is the phrase 'to change money'?" There was more ready-made conversation for use "At the Station," "At the Cloakroom," "Visiting

Friends," and "At the Dentist," but none for international banking. *"Bitte schön,"* I repeated, *"Ich möchte . . . Geld . . .* oh, yes, yes—*Hungarische!"* Pretty please, I need money Hungarian. One could not purchase it in advance, but if I had had the wit of an early hominid I would not only have rehearsed my lines on the plane ride from Amsterdam, but boned up on the local monetary system. Now—what was the value of all these coins and bills?

I rushed outside, fearful of missing the bus. A needless alarm. Forty-five minutes later a large rusted vehicle for suburban service creaked up to the airport. The plane's other passengers, who had been moping outside, clambered in. One of them mutely hoisted my luggage up the steep steps, and I selected a place in the double row of wooden kitchen chairs screwed to the floor. Another tired-looking blonde, in a navy male uniform, passed down the aisle collecting the fares. I couldn't understand her reply to my *"Wieviel?"* so I held out what I took to be a bill worth a couple of dollars and received a handful of change. At that time women who had been evicted from the brothels were being put to work in more civic pursuits, among them that of bus and trolley conductor.

For what seemed hours we rattled through wet, feebly lit roads and streets, pausing here and there to let off passengers. Along the route, typical of airport-to-city rides, nothing we passed justified Budapest's reputation for sparkle.

The terminal was dark and bolted when we arrived. I barked a shinbone dragging my suitcase down the perpendicular bus steps, then stood transfixed in the empty street. So I had to come to Budapest. Now what? The only other passenger, a middle-aged Mitteleuropean wearing a karakul-collared coat, had immediately disappeared. He came back. "Hotel Duna?" he asked me. "No, Gellért," I replied with as much radiance as I could muster, hoping for a lift. He shrugged amiably and walked off. There were no automobiles in sight. I hurried over to the blonde. "Tahksi?" I implored. "Tahksi?" she repeated, blankly. "Oh . . . tahksi!"—and sprinted into the night. I was now alone on the sidewalk. Melodramatic friends had warned that I would be trailed by the secret police. *Why* weren't they on the job?

All I knew about my hotel was that it was de luxe A, a former Hapsburg palace somewhere across the beautiful blue Danube in

the old city, Buda. We were certainly in Pest. I was so unstrung by
the time the conductor returned with a taxi ten minutes later that
I gave her three packs of Benson & Hedges. When she saw them,
a delighted-child's smile broke through her ravaged face—and I
daresay I looked pretty happy, too.

During that ride in a tiny black jitney through Gaborsville, all I
was conscious of was an effort to calm with extenuated sighs an
accelerated pulse.

The Gellért's urbane welcoming staff restored my élan, as did
the crystal chandeliers and Magyar melodies animating the elegant
dining room. In excellent fettle I strode in, charitably overlooking
the leers of a corner-tableful of peoples' republicans—Asian and
East European—who arrested their boarding-house lunges at the
poppy-seed rolls to swing around and stare lecherously at each passing woman—escorted or alone.

As if to mock their rough manners, the formally attired waiters
hovered over them with platters of rosetted *Oeufs en gelée*,
Gefülte Champignons Paradeis, and other viands of the *haute cuisine*, thus confounding the poor chaps, who had no idea how to
address such slippery *Vorspeisen*.

The string orchestra, which had been watching them obliquely,
struck up an impassioned "Ave Maria," thereby inspiring a thun-
derous ovation from the rest of the diners, who had accorded previous airs but perfunctory applause. Hmm, I thought, protest! How
edifying to observe these nuances of East-West relations. The vio-
linist gave me a bittersweet smile, glanced at the proles, then, tap-
ping his bow, led the other three musicians into a swinging "Ochi
Chornia." But the comrades were too preoccupied to notice the
tribute, what with wolfing the *Fasan Smetana*—not to mention the
tomatoes.

Giddied by the czardases and waltzes, I myself was soon engaging in intercultural dialogue with the Argentinian hidalgo at the
next table, who, overhearing me converse with the waiter, asked
rhetorically if I spoke English.

Olé! For the next four days it was Gypsy fiddles and Tokay with
Ricardo.

5

Ready-to-Wear on the Wing

Without a man, travel light: there are stations without porters. Ergo, the criteria for ready-to-wear on the wing are versatility, suitability, comfort, and heft. At this writing, forty-four pounds of luggage are permitted in economy-class overseas flights and sixty-six in first class. An increase may be authorized in each, as well as on the "flying buses," or supersonic planes. But short of going via spaceship, it is how much you can, in an emergency, haul yourself that should govern what you will take. Fortunately, by switching about sweaters, skirts, and blouses, eye-catching baubles and stoles, two or three thoughtfully selected, becoming suits or jacket dresses can be multiplied into numerous attractive costumes.

For fall and spring temperatures two suits and three dresses, or vice versa, plus refreshing changes in accessories, are enough. I carried that amount for sixteen days in Morocco plus a short voyage home, and as usual had one dress too many. It was so unseasonably cold that I lived in the suits. More clothes are necessary for journeys that will embrace both cool and hot weather. Departing in late autumn for a six-week, round-the-world trip spent principally in Southeast Asia, I wore a navy wool suit with a printed jersey blouse (drip-drys crease irreparably while napping in a plane), and carried a red cashmere coat, later buttoned inside a plastic raincoat to keep it clean and simplify the toting. I packed a cardigan sweater, two seersucker and two late-afternoon dresses, a wool stole for evening, and five cotton blouses that could be paired variously with the suit and two dacron skirts. In addition to the navy pumps I was wearing, I took red straw and black patent leather, as well as a pair of rubber-soled canvas wedgies, in which I could walk in comfort and safety for miles over pebbles, ruts, and slippery stones. I also had a head scarf, six pairs of stockings (superfluous in the heat), three changes of nylon undies (they rotted in the tropics), two pairs of pajamas, and a silk crush-proof robe that doubled as a housecoat. (For those who sleep nude, this caution: chambermaids and men the world over charge into one's bedroom ten seconds after they have banged on the door.) A flat, black suede evening purse and a light-weight, collapsible umbrella completed my wardrobe. It weighed thirty pounds and provided fifteen changes of costume, variously complemented by navy blue, black, or red accessories. Nobody mistook me for the Duchess of Windsor, but even so I could have eliminated the umbrella and one of the cocktail numbers: that U.S. Army colonel on Waikiki Beach would never have known that I had worn the same flowered print in Bangkok with a Yul Brynner, so long as I hadn't dribbled it with *Tra Pla Turd*—a sauced Siamese fish.

It is possible on a trip to get along with less—as one American airlines stewardess could attest. Ironically, her single suitcase was not put on the plane when she crossed the Atlantic; nor did it catch up with her as she good-naturedly perspired in a two-piece wool dress through Egypt, Lebanon, Syria, and Jordan. "The camels are beginning to nuzzle me," she said, "but aside from that I really don't mind."

There are others who like to have with them a gamut of apparel, particularly if their clothes are ever a conversation piece and they will be partied a lot. For her three weeks in London, Paris, and Rome, Lyn took this eyeful: sable and mink stoles, a black raincoat, one cashmere sweater, eight street dresses, two knits, two full-length evening gowns, three cocktail frocks, two silk suits, six pairs of shoes, Emilio Pucci slacks and shirt, a bathing suit, shorts, assorted gloves and handbags, plus twenty-two hats. Well, Paris had a right to see *her* hats.

Lyn conserved on lingerie, but she still had to pay excess-weight charges. At the per-kilo (2.2 pounds) rate of .005 per cent of the first-class propeller fare to Rome—or $4.69 per kilo—they came to about $40. But then in Paris she purchased four hats, seven skirts, four pairs of shoes, six pairs of gloves, a vicuña sweater, and eight bottles of perfume. She might have sent part of her luggage air-freight, for which she would have paid $1.30 a pound.

Those not mingling with the *haute monde* will find one hat sufficient—and that preferably of a soft fabric that can be stuffed without injury into a bag. During the summer hats and gloves are disdained by the women of the country even in the capitals abroad, though sunshades are used in the tropics. Both long and short evening gowns are worn on cruise ships and ocean liners. But unless you plan to be seated with society at the grand opera, or know in advance that you will be entertained at night spots, or have a history of attracting affluent men, the more dazzling dresses will probably languish unused during the average brief trip. A simple sheath or cocktail skirt and blouse will be chic anywhere formal garb is not *de rigueur*.

First-class passengers on liners used to get into evening gowns every night but the first, last, and on Sunday; now, except at the captain's dinner, for which a short one will suffice, as many women wear cocktail dresses as more chichi attire. Thus on my voyage on the Italian Line's stylish *Raffaello* I felt not at all drab with only a décolleté chiffon dinner dress and three-piece brocaded silk suit that can be worn with or without its jacket and disguised with diverse glamorous tops. A baroness at my table nightly varied a well-cut sheath with an assortment of beaded sweaters.

Though it be summer or your destination tropical, take a sweater and a coat—one reasonably wrinkle-proof and water-repellent. Because in hot weather a wrap is easily forgotten on a plane, train, or motor coach, hook a luggage tag round one of the buttons so you may later retrieve it. The cloak's warmth depends on the climates to be encountered, its style on whether you will be concentrating on rural or metropolitan life. Save in winter, a wool stole or small fur can serve for night outings, and either packs well.

For early spring, late autumn, as well as winter, you may find bed socks and warm nighties a blessing; during those months, indoor temperatures abroad are much lower than those to which Americans are accustomed.

The air with which a woman wears her clothes and their fit count more than the garments themselves. Appropriate dress, however, is important abroad. If on an American street we were to see a woman from Bali in a topless sarong, or an Indian matron with a breast casually exposed, our sense of decency would be outraged. Yet sometimes we are unintentionally equally *outré*. Consider that in most countries where there is no dairy industry and bosoms are regarded as merely functional, female legs are completely covered, and waist indentations are padded out with cummerbunds. Nowhere in such lands—or, indeed, those where native women wear pajamas—will one encounter a hint in a woman's costume that beneath it are buttocks—trim or plain wobbly—so often offensively evident in the adhesive slacks and shorts blindly worn in the United States and some spas on the Continent. Not that American women are uniquely ignorant of the conventions that can be violated: a young Belgian on a tour about Sicily, I noted, was unable to still the hisses that complimented the comeliness of his little bride's behind—half-bared in skimpy shorts.

At resorts there is usually a good deal of latitude in attire. But not always. Feeling my way in Lucerne, I wore a cotton dress. All the German and Scandinavian girls had on those cheeky Continental briefs. The next day in Interlaken I put on pedal pushers, and before sundown was so abashed by the clucking of the Swiss *Frauen* I felt like Godiva with her head shaved.

"Why must those girls visit Notre Dame in pants?" a postman asked a reporter for the New York *Times*. The wearing of slacks and shorts in cathedrals and mosques also drew the most censure from representatives of foreign governments whom I queried concerning exceptionable dress in their countries.

I have never been more conscious of too short skirts than in Nepal, where the staring at my legs—and they're not all that good —was obsessive. I might have been flattered had I not also been aware, as I threaded between the smirking carpet weavers in a center for Tibetan refugees, that the comments the fellows were passing were not entirely genteel. Before I go there again I'll be letting down some hems.

Dress is most puritanical in devoutly Catholic and Moslem lands, principally Spain, Mexico, and the Middle East. A respectable American matron with whom I shared a car between Lebanon and Jordan learned this to her revulsion when her sleeveless arm was spat upon by a Bedouin boy while she was gazing at the desert. To him she was shameless. The same attitude would have obtained in Israel's Orthodox sectors, where, whether she entered a synagogue or not, she would have to cover her head, arms, and back. Mandatory in Eastern Orthodox and Roman Catholic cathedrals, modest garb is an expression of courtesy in other houses of worship as well. One is taken inside a great many historic churches on almost any foreign itinerary; thus, separate jackets or cardigan sweaters are useful.

Although even the Soviet Union and its satellites object to insufficiently covered female visitors, by and large American women may wear overseas what would be appropriate in comparable areas and social situations in the States, remembering that slacks and shorts, which appear on our city streets, draw frowns on their counterparts abroad, even in such resort areas as Nassau and Bermuda.

Full skirts are necessary for modesty in countries like Japan, where one frequently sits on the floor; they also allow more leverage in ascending and descending the too-long steps which much of the rest of the world seemingly constructed for giraffes. In torrid climates loose, opaque cottons that demand neither girdle nor slip would be more comfortable than fitted synthetics. In fact, since Indian women bare their midriffs to catch a vagrant breeze, I see no reason why during a heat wave Americans on the Subcontinent shouldn't follow suit.

Nevertheless, when in doubt about what to wear, it is better to err on the conservative side. Having said that, I think if I had it to do all over again I might not have worn the canvas wedgies for tea with the Maharajah. It all happened because I dropped into the local government tourist office of Varanasi—or Banaras, as we know this holiest of Indian cities—to find out if there was some way to get to its sights other than by means of the outrageously expensive tours conducted by a travel agency in the hotel.

The tourist department manager—in his white tunic and dhoti, a dead ringer for the dancer Uday Shankar—suggested that I engage a cycle rickshaw to drive to the Bharat Mata, the Monkey and Golden temples, the Sacred Bull and Well of Knowledge, the buried Buddhist city of Sarnath and the Ganges, where, from a simple barge, I could observe the purification rites and cremations at

the burning ghats. The conscientious Mr. Wabhawan also provided an exceptionally fine guide, Vijay Kuman Ranka, who has
since opened in Banaras his own travel service for visitors interested in covering India economically.

"Would you like to see the Indian ballet?" Mr. Wabhawan
asked, explaining that it was a depiction of the *Ramayana*. Perhaps
I'd like to meet the Maharajah, on whose grounds the performance
of the great Hindu epic took place? I sure would. He rang up the
palace. The Maharajah, he reported, would be pleased if I came to
tea. He was, moreover, putting an elephant at my disposal.

Consternation. *What* does one wear on an elephant? More precisely, can you climb one in high heels? I'm a pretty awful climber
even when it comes to horses. Mr. Wabhawan had remarked that
the Maharajah was an exceedingly pious man; in fact, he drank
water only from the Ganges. Reasoning that my scooped-neck
print might seem immodest to him, I decided to play it cool. As
cool as I could in humidity so high my clothes were getting mil-
dewed.

The little handle-bar-mustached Maharajah wore a fluffy white
turban wrapped around a maroon cone, which matched the pajamas under his sheer white, embroidered trousers and jacket. He
had jewels on nearly all his fingers and a topaz in his nose. I was
pure wash 'n' wear.

His sweetmeats were ambrosial, but his glances at my feet made
my toes curl. The Maharajah's slippers were gold spangled silk and
their toes, too, were turned up. Even the little Balinese stewardesses had commented that my sensible shoes were "funny." I was
in agony. And it turned out that you use a ladder to scale an elephant.

What, I later asked an Indian lady, should I have done—faced
with the alternative of sports clothes or an afternoon dress too
décolleté to be worn in the company of people affronted by low
necks? In principle, she said kindly, I was right to be considerate of
the taboos of other cultures. However, because—like most Indians
by whom an American is apt to be entertained—the Maharajah
had traveled in the West, he would make allowances for foreigners.
"Besides," she added a little impatiently, "he is a man. You should
have dressed up for him."

My humiliation notwithstanding, I regret that the manufacturer has discontinued the canvas wedgies, for nothing contributes to the buoyance of a journey like a well-mattressed foot. Extremities swell in the heat and humidity and during flights and long walks, so be sure your shoes are a width wider than usual or well broken in before you depart. I'd forgo another dress any day to take extra pairs.

The traveler is permitted to carry unweighed into a plane an overcoat, raincoat, pocketbook, umbrella or walking stick, binoculars, camera (even two), reading matter, and a "rug"—by which I suppose they mean a lap robe, an unnecessary item since airlines provide blankets for the chilled. Nevertheless, a warm blouse or sweater is nice to have in the summer for the lower temperatures aloft.

Planes have Dramamine available, as well as aspirin, for passengers afflicted with motion sickness and headaches. On jets the former is exceedingly rare. JAL, some chartered and many first-class flights supply slipper socks; for all others take soft folding slippers into the craft. To assure slumber, carry a light shield for your eyes and ear stopples (Flents are fine). I used to need a sleeping pill, but now I find the movies that are shown an adequate soporific.

It's sneaky but possible, when flying from one climatic extreme to another, to put inside your coat a dress more suitable for the terminal temperature. Madras was so torrid I wore cotton aboard, then changed into wool in the washroom before landing in New Delhi.

Within the baggage weight limitations must be packed toiletries, drugs, film, and cigarettes (unless the last are purchased on the plane or at duty-free shops to be delivered abroad). Astonishingly these can add up to more than ten pounds for a longer than four-week hiatus.

Some foreign hotels provide tiny soap cakes, but one cannot be sure of finding them all over. At best they have more souvenir than sudsing value. So bring along your own. I find that a bath-sized bar of soft-milled soap is a sliver in ten days. Maggie swears that one-third of a hard-milled cake lasts her a full fourteen. She is not compulsive, however, about bathing.

If you use washcloths or sponges, take them as well. You will not find any in bathrooms abroad, although there is usually a plenitude of towels save in occasional out-of-the-way places. For such emergencies I always pack a small, elderly towel that can be discarded at the end of the trip.

Sanitary supplies as well as tissues may be purchased in all modern overseas cities; sometimes the texture is even superior to ours. However, the time spent shopping for them might be more interestingly employed. Count how many cleansing tissues you average a day and take somewhat more.

As departure approaches you may suffer misgivings, become vaguely apprehensive. This is caused by a subconscious guilt over spending so much money. To assuage it, pinch pennies. Instead of buying cartons of purse-sized packaged tissues, get boxes of two hundred for less than half the price. Place about forty into each of five plastic bags, thereby eliminating the weight of the cardboard in individual packets.

Similarly, hoard empty plastic pill vials for your cosmetics: they may be filled with sufficient face powder and foundation, hand, face, or other creams for the average journey. For longer trips duplicate the contents. They're lighter and occupy infinitely less space than conventional plastic containers. Scotch-tape identifying labels on all receptacles and seal them with adhesive tape to avoid spillage in transit. Even so, bottles should never be more than two-thirds full during flights. However sealed, perfume or cologne in plastic sprays always evaporates and leaks. Little glass bottles are the only solution.

Although many women prefer leather cosmetic cases, the best toilet kit, to my mind, is the simplest—a small, unfitted but capacious satchel with a zippered pocket for a wet washcloth. In it one may have handy her everyday needs: toothbrushes, paste, soap in plastic container, tiny hair and nail brushes, comb, hairspray, emery board, nail file, tweezers, deodorant, pills, tubes or vials of sunburn lotion, face cream, foundation, mascara, shower cap, and mirror.

If you always have trouble locating toiletries in your suitcase, try grouping related items in clear plastic food bags. The following paragraphs suggest a sample breakdown of what various bags, dependent on individual needs, might contain:

Extra washcloths (ten-cent-store quality, which may be discarded to cut weight on return trip); Wash 'n Dri or similar packets (don't overload with these; one can replenish from the washrooms of various planes that supply them).

Emergency pills and medicines not in everyday use; cold-sore lotion; insect repellent.

Band-Aids (assorted sizes); corn plasters; corn and callus remover; foot powder; roll of one-half-inch Air Vent adhesive tape.

Shampoo; hair tint and peroxide (each in triple plastic bags); applicator, rubber gloves; Pliofilm garment cover for sink protection; small towel; razor.

Tiny clothes brush; shoe brush (a small nail brush works well); chalk spot remover, Spotchief, or similar product; leaf or two from a packet of leather shoe and handbag polishers.

Extra soap.

Match books (not free abroad); flints; lighter fluid (forbidden on planes, although operating lighters in the craft provokes no rebuke—much in the spirit of the "No Smoking" signs and ashtrays in the washrooms).

Eyewash powder; half-pint plastic bottle; eyecup; eyedrops; contact-lens wetting agent; small bottle of concentrated mouthwash.

Talcum; extra face powder, puffs, and lipstick; face cream (if it's a sometime thing).

Nail-polish remover pads or liquid; Q-tips and cotton; nail polish; extra emery boards; cuticle nipper or scissors.

Sewing kit: a typewriter-ribbon container or a plastic box about three inches square is ideal for thimble, tiny spools of thread to match each garment, and large-eyed needles; large and small safety pins; scissors.

Bottle opener and cork; penlight; candle (for the times—fortunately rare—when fuses blow out); sink stopper (for Eastern Europe).

One-half cup per week of travel of laundry powder in triple plastic bags (spilled, it's murder to get out of surrounding items and the lining of a suitcase); coarse sponge and a half-cup of scouring powder, again in triple plastic bags, for occasional tubs.

After years of trying all manner of capsuled detergents with, at the end of three weeks, only tattletale gray undies to show for the bubbles, I found my problem solved when Louise, who works for Lever Brothers, gave me a handful of Rinso Blue washing-machine powder packets. Each packet took care of three basinfuls, and everything that wasn't faded to begin with stayed pastel or snowy white. I felt like a singing commercial. Because the envelopes in which the powder was wrapped were easily pierced, the next time I went abroad I poured from a soapbox what I needed into the tougher reinforced plastic bags—and saved another few cents.

Clothespins, plastic clip-hooks, inflatable or, if weight permits, multihooked lucite hangers, along with a few wire ones, are best for drying wash. You can always find something from which to suspend one or the other, whereas portable clotheslines make a bedroom look like a Neapolitan alley. An allergy-proof, zippered, plastic pillow case makes an excellent laundry bag either for soiled garments or still-damp ones that must be transported.

Women get very arch about toilet paper, and there's no question that it's a good idea to tote at least half a roll, smashed flat. Although one still encounters some with a glazed finish (the purpose escapes me), generally the quality is improving. However, chambermaids and w.c. attendants—particularly in the East, where tissue is not looked upon as vital for tidiness—frequently forget to reload the spindles. Paper towels are, I think, more important since they are rarely available in washrooms, which at best have a single cloth towel on a roller. There are travelers who rely upon tissues, but for their absorption, resilience to fraying, and kindness to tender skin I prefer Doeskin paper towels, which may serve a dual purpose. A few perforated leaves folded in the purse will meet a normal day's demands.

Except on planes, toilet-seat covers are seldom in evidence abroad. One cannot when traveling be neurotic about such matters.

Many roadside restaurants apparently consider napkins at breakfast or luncheon effete; hence, if blotting your lips is a reflex action, tuck a quantity of paper napkins into a pocket of your suitcase. One for each day should be adequate.

People always ask, "Do you take a travel iron?" I don't. I don't care that they can be fitted with transformers for foreign current; I resent their weight. Moreover, a good pressing job presupposes a proper ironing board, and even the collapsible sort adds pounds. The Galle Face in Colombo is the only hotel I've been in that will lend guests both boards and irons. However, submitting a dress or suit to valet service seldom costs very much, and in hotels garments are usually returned pressed within four or five hours.

Since I've never owned a travel clock without a capricious alarm, I always ask the hotel to call me when early rising is necessary. Now I save weight and leave the clock home.

One wakes up feeling like a baked meringue under the fluffy featherbeds and comforters found in many European hotels. Often the head of the couch is elevated with a bolster and huge, luscious pillows, which are great props for reading and eating, but too high for one unaccustomed to sleeping in a chair. Against that contingency or its opposite—the occasional bean-bag-quality headrest—I always take an infant's down pillow, which weighs a few ounces and assures peaceful slumber.

A strong, generously proportioned string bag is useful for overflow parcels of mementoes purchased abroad, as well as for breakable camera equipment that might not survive the brutal banging suitcases suffer from baggage attendants at air terminals and other depots. Suggested photographic accessories are listed in Chapter XI. For the occasional parcel too large for a shopping bag or suitcase, take one of those wooden handles that can be hooked onto the string.

Ignore what follows if you already pack with efficiency and speed. Though months in advance I have added what I wish to take with me on the current trip to my perpetual list of staple travel needs, I am lucky to finish in two hours if I haven't had a dry run with a scale. (That, incidentally, is the time to note in your diary or address book the weight of soap, tissues, cigarettes, and the like, so that as they are used up you'll know roughly how much may replace them without excess-weight charges on the return trip.)

The challenge in packing is how to avoid wrinkles, and I make no pretense to having completely met it. I used to reduce creases by using a twenty-six-inch nylon-covered suitcase, in which skirts need but a single fold in the center or none, and dresses but two, the second being at the waist. It's more economical of space and

cuts down on crumple to line folds with acetate jersey or nylon
tricot garments. Blouses can be laid out flat with the sleeves em-
bracing a stole, scarf, or sweater. Tissue paper tends to shred and,
light as it is, increases weight. To balance the humps that folds
make, alternate the direction of garments. This will eventually
create cavities in which a purse or shoes stuffed with socks, stockings, bras, or panties can be gently inserted, covered, of course,
with shoe socks. Jamming too much into a suitcase will always
cause wrinkles, as, one is redundantly warned by experts, will excessive space in a suitcase. Cotton blouses that are heavily starched
stay crisp longer than those starched but lightly. However, if there
is anything that can withstand the crushing effect of extended humidity, I'd like to hear of it. Some women have good luck with
drip-dry fabrics. I don't. Knits are the best, and, for cool weather,
tweeds.

The last items to be needed should be the first placed into the
suitcase; by the same token, the initial change of clothes, a robe,
and nightie are at the top.

Toiletries and drugs are more easily located if you pack them in a
small suitcase or satchel, which will also hold film, camera accessories, a sewing kit, maps, books, scratch-pads, address book, diary,
extra ball-point pen, and miscellaneous supplies, including a couple
of coin purses to keep from confusing the small change of various
lands. Your nieces and nephews will for a time find the residue a
tolerable gift.

The most commodious catchall and, indeed, the best receptacle
for clothes that I know of are both manufactured by Lark, whose
garment bag is the nearest thing to a portable closet and bureau.
Unzipping its fifty-inch length, one can pack two skirts, blouses, or
dresses to each plain wire hanger (rather than the inadequate ones
provided by Lark)—enough changes for six weeks. There are three
spacious zippered pockets, two on the outside of the bag and one
on the inside, which also has two shallow zippered pockets. The
bag folds in half to be strapped together near the bottom. When
open, a hook at the top permits clothes to be hung without un-
packing. The bag weighs four pounds. Its matching valise weighs
three and has two deep, inner, zippered pockets, as well as two
large ones on the outside. Between the two bags one can travel

supremely uncluttered and even find things without becoming violent.

At first their lack of locks worried me. However, I flew around the world with them without noting any evidence of snooping, let alone theft. After all, anyone wishing to pick a lock is generally nimble enough to do so. Just be sure that you are insured for loss or damage to personal effects.

While it is possible to travel with but one suitcase, it is wise to have a small bag as well for short excursions from your headquarters hotel, which will usually store the large one while you are gone. As in the United States, luggage may be checked through in foreign airports and railroad stations to one's ultimate destination.

Before my first overseas trip I heeded the advice of a travel guide that urged one always to carry candy to fend off starvation should a meal be missed due to delays in transportation. So, dutifully, I depressed my suitcase with two pounds of fruit drops, never dreaming they made candy in Europe. Subsequently it became my more conservative practice to collect sweets offered in the plane. Then came the day that I absent-mindedly put into my pocketbook two Hershey bars thus acquired. Three hours later, sitting in a torrid air terminal, I reached into my bag for a snack and came up with a handful of brown syrup—a sight that widened the eyes of the others in the lounge. A stuffed handbag in transit is enough of a strain without ineradicable stains; since then I've stuck to candies that melt solely in the mouth.

To lessen the wristload, remove from their ring all those keys to old trunks and vacated apartments and reduce to the necessities the contents of your purse: passport, a vaccinations booklet, traveler's checks, transportation tickets or vouchers, calling cards, credit card (if you plan to use one), cosmetics, and money. Passport cases add to the burden; once through entry and exit formalities, put your passport into a zippered pocket of your handbag and leave its handsome, heavy leather folder in the hotel, or get a light one that serves also as wallet.

Let those sturdy enough carry satchel-sized handbags. Enough can be packed into a moderately large purse and even a single suitcase to keep anyone *soignée*.

The only real grooming problem abroad is the increased need for shampooing; hair gets dirty twice as fast on a trip. Luckily, there are beauty parlors in many first-class and nearly all de luxe hotels. My hairdresser, Emily Maurer, gave me this tip: when your locks are a fright and neither beautician nor shower is at hand, massage a very little talcum into several portions of your scalp, rub your hair thoroughly with a clean turkish towel, then brush until not a vestige of powder remains. Touch your scalp with cologne, and the treatment is finished, coiffure intact. In desperation one may also cleanse the hair to some extent with Wash 'n Dri pads. Both measures, however, should be given a rehearsal at home.

Before the first few exposures to the sun, apply grease paint or a heavy foundation to your nose and suntan lotion to the rest of your face; thus you will look rosy but not alcoholic. Beyond that, most cosmetic aids are superfluous: the sheer excitement of seeing exotic places gives any woman a glow.

6

Victuals and Vins

"Well, how do you like living in America?" I recently asked an Asian acquaintance who has been residing in the States since the early 1960s.

"Oh, I like it very much," he replied. "I am beginning to get used to the food—although I can't quite bring myself to try the water." I felt stabbed. And suddenly I realized how the rest of the world must wince at our squeamishness about their cuisine—to say nothing of water. At times this is carried to extremes of tactlessness. One of Nehru's sisters has had American guests who would not eat green salad in her home—thereby implying that her kitchen was unclean. Imagine if the tables were turned.

It's a shame that travelers are often so fearful. There's high adventure in exotic food and drink; nobody not restricted by doctor's orders should deprive herself of it. To ward off stomach upset, one should, of course, eat sparingly at first of unfamiliar or highly spiced foods and those delicious sauces that are so seductively concocted in Europe. Americans are not accustomed to them or to the multicourse lunches and dinners prevalent on Continental menus.

For those who like to cook, it adds to the anticipation of a trip, and gives the digestive tract a workout, to prepare dishes containing the ingredients that will be encountered on location: chili peppers, cardamom, saffron, turmeric, coriander, and ginger; mustard, poppy, caraway, and sesame seeds; cumin, basil, oregano, and anise; not to say garlic. In *The Complete Round-the-World Cookbook* (Doubleday), which comprises recipes gathered by Pan American

Airways, Myra Waldo briefly describes the cuisine of eighty-four countries. Titles offering more detailed information about the cuisine of individual countries appear in the "Cookery" listings of the *Subject Guide to Books in Print.*

I admit though that there have been places where I've eaten with trepidation. In Quito I quite forgot the advice of Señor Chiriboga, a most helpful Panagra official, to have a box lunch prepared at the Humboldt Hotel before embarking at 7:00 A.M. on a fourteen-hour jog by autoferro to Guayaquil. By eleven the jiggling of this bus on tracks had churned my gastric juices to such a demanding pitch even the *mandarinas* hawked through the windows by Indian vendors during halts couldn't blunt it. At one o'clock, when we stopped for an hour at a dingy station house, I, like the Ecuadorian passengers, dashed over the trestle to the dining room, famished. "Dysentery," I thought, "here I come!" Fasting is not my forte.

An apple-cheeked Indian child raced to my table with a huge bowl of broth bright with diced garden-fresh vegetables. As I was sucking the last drop the boy hurriedly replaced it with a dish containing a strange rubbery-looking object. Gingerly, I nibbled a corner. It was a corn croquette and delicious. I sighed. In lightning succession the little *camarero* chased back and forth with course after course of the most succulent, and fortifying, meal I had in all South America. No mean praise, when you think of *serviche*, Peru's pickled fish, and that Argentine beef.

In Knossos I hesitated to taste a Greek salad with a young Cretan under a dusty grape arbor busy with flies. I had said I was hungry; he was being responsive when he returned to the unsteady little table with a platter of tomatoes, olives, hard-boiled eggs, feta cheese, sardines, and lettuce, which he set down between us.

"Aren't *you* going to eat?" I inquired.

"Oh, yes," he said, diving in. Well—of all the pigs, I thought with indignation; he didn't bring any for me! "Do have some," he urged, handing me a fork. "There is plenty." This was something new to me in folkways. I crossed my fingers and speared a tomato on our community plate. He was adamant about not letting me share the expense. Cretans are at once impoverished and proud

"I'm dying to have some real Nepalese food," I groused to Mr. B. K. Rijal, my guide, en route to a Tibetan lamasery. "All they have at the hotel is the usual bland stuff they insist on serving in this part of the world to Americans."

"Please come in here with me," he said, entering a hut nine feet wide by seven feet long, containing a hard narrow bed parallel with a wall kitchen. I looked about uneasily, having had in mind something more sybaritic. Mr. Rijal, who augmented his meager earnings as a guide with lectures on Nepalese culture, spoke briefly to the cook. "Please sit down," he said. "While the *mamu* is being prepared, would you like to try the *chang?*"

"Oh, sure," I said, not too sure. "What is it?"

"Tibetan rice beer." It tasted like exceedingly sour sake, but I persevered. Alcohol is reputedly germ-free. Now if that *mamu* was sizzling hot, I might emerge uninfected. "Can you use these?" asked Mr. Rijal, indicating a pair of thick chopsticks. "Nepalese eat with their fingers," he added.

"I'm a little out of practice," I said, "but I'll try. With the chopsticks, I mean." I managed to clamp a lukewarm *mamu* between them, and chewed a bit, thoughtfully. It was ground mutton enveloped in a white, semi-solidified paste. Mr. Rijal poured me a cup of Tibetan tea, which, he explained, was whipped with yak butter and salted. "Very interesting," I said without conviction, or indeed relish. These viands in the land of yeti (the Abominable Snowman) and yak probably wouldn't kill me, I thought, but, just to be on the safe side, I spun a few Buddhist prayer wheels at the next stupa we passed. Counterclockwise, as is the custom.

The Royal Hotel at Katmandu eventually came up with schnitzel of wild boar. At the Palace Hotel in Hvar the schnitzel was pure wiener—noon and night. "I would like typical Yugoslav food," I complained to the waiter. He looked blank; then suddenly his eyes widened. "Fortunately, madame," he said, "tonight we have the national Bosnian dish." "Splendid." He arrived with a casserole of ground left-over veal smothered in diced potatoes. Very enlightening. The next evening the waiter greeted me with an anticipatory smile. "Tonight, madame," he said, "we have the national Serbian dish." "That's nice," I said, "but I think I'll settle for the wiener schnitzel." "We have only one portion left," urged the waiter, still pushing the Serbian *specialité.* I gave in. He arrived with a casserole of ground left-over veal smothered in diced potatoes. Well, first of the month, when my father was fussing about the bills, my mother used to give us this type of home economics cookery. But she never had the showmanship to present it as the national Bosnian or Serbian dish. Which it may even be.

If the indigenous Dutch food is also about as exotic as Yankee Doodle (and why not, considering the influence on the Colonies of Peter Stuyvesant and that crowd), Amsterdam offers a better Javanese *rijsttafel* and *nasi goreng* than I was able to find in Indonesia.

To savor the delights and surprises of Japanese dining one should stay at Nipponese inns, where the eye is exquisitely nourished along with the palate. Fancy yourself wrapped in a commodious cotton kimono, arranging your legs as unstiffly as possible on the tatami-covered floor before a very low, beautifully grained table. On its lacquered trays are oddly shaped, tiny porcelain dishes, no two alike in decoration, yet each complementary, containing a variety of hors d'oeuvres, or *zensai*. A servant in a gaily flowered kimono (hers is prettier than yours) shuffles in, bows, drops to her knees, and proffers a damp, lightly perfumed, tightly rolled fingertip towel with which to wipe your hands, and face too, if you wish. You return it to her basket and take a pair of chopsticks —usually of the wooden, half-split variety known as *waribashi*— from a miniature fish or animal rest. Which of the tidbits to taste first is the quandary. There are vegetables cut to resemble delicate flowers and fans, pink-tinted quail's eggs, seaweed cakes, and at least three kinds of raw, thinly sliced, absolutely fresh fish. Dunked into *shoyu* sauce spiced with mustard or grated ginger, it is delicious, and not in the least pungent. Bowing again, the girl places before you a covered lacquer bowl filled with clear, piping-hot soup that tastes like chicken broth but is actually made of seaweed. They call it *dashi*. Chicken itself comes later, along with rice and hot tea. Or perhaps you're having wine, a slim vial of heated sake, which the servant, on her knees beside you, will add to an elfin cup each time it's put down. For dessert, if you can even face any by this time, there is a crisp, juicy pear. After that it is easy to topple over to sleep on the thick pad unrolled on the floor.

Although I missed having *manna* in the Fertile Crescent, I did try *sangat*, an unleavened Persian bread that looks like wholewheat matzo and tastes like damp ones. Isfahan bakeries festoon their fronts with them—evidently not to dry out. In Egypt, as an appetizer, one dips folds of *pita*, a similar pancake, into *homos*, which is a paste of chick-peas diluted with one of *tehina*, and that's sesame seeds puréed with water. In India there are wonderful meatless curries, to which vegetarian Hindus credit their dazzling white teeth; the Egyptians hold that chewing sugar cane is the secret of theirs.

The whole Middle East has marvelous kebabs, which means any grilled meat (the "shish" is the skewer). The Iranians distill the petals of the damask rose and other blossoms to flavor their puddings and sweets, and are fond of throwing cherries, apples, nuts, and a variety of dried fruit into their *khoreshes*, or stews. One of them—*Mullah Ghas Kardeh* (Swooned Priest)—is said to be so succulent that the *mullah* fainted from the joy of eating it. The Turks, who claim to have invented the kebab, have a dish called *Imam Bayildi* composed of the same ingredients—eggplant, onions, and tomatoes—that *their* prayer leader, the *imam*, liked so much he also fainted. (I get a bit of vertigo myself from eggplant.) Regardless of who was its innovator, the Turks win hands down with the most sensual-sounding victuals: e.g., a typical dessert, *Kadin Göbeghi*, or Lady's Navel, and *Kadin Budu*, Lady's Thighs, which is meatballs.

It's not true that there are no good restaurants in London; try the upper floor of those seasoned-looking pubs, where they know how to roast beef. It's also not true that there are no poor restaurants in Paris; beware of bistros excessively kind to your budget. Nevertheless, France houses some of the world's greatest kitchens; theirs is a most varied cuisine, represented virtually everywhere. In Rome and northern Italy, most particularly Bologna, the *ristorantes* offer continuing evidence that the French cuisine was inspired by the Italian cooks Catherine de' Medici took to the court of Henry II—which may surprise those who associate Italian cooking with spaghetti, ravioli, and pizza.

Although a history of Baalbek by John Awad states that one of the bas-relief busts in the north portico is of "Cleopatra pierced by an aspic," surely she would not have so suffered in Bruges, an enchanting medieval Flemish city in Belgium, where one can go berserk trying to choose among the *plats du jour* at the Beenhouwery.

A superdelicatessen, it displays *tripe à la mode de Caen, aspic de homard et crevettes, côtelettes d'agneau à la gelée, médaillon de foie gras, poulet en aspic au foie gras, pigeonneau en casserole, galantine de veau* . . . A like madness seizes one confronted with the hundreds of tiny open-faced sandwiches that comprise the *smørrebrød* in Copenhagen and its counterparts in Norway and Sweden. But for pure bliss one should wander through the alimentary bazaar in Bangkok, sampling the savories simmering on the braziers, or recline in Oriental languor on the cushions of a traditional Thai restaurant like Salinee, weighing the merits of adding lemon grass to *Pu Ca* or a chicken curry.

A girl might simply be nostalgic for a steak, yet not recognize it on a menu that lists *tournedos, entrecôte, bifteck,* and *chateaubriand*. If so, she would do well to beef up her vocabulary with Martin Dale's *How to Read a French Menu* (Appleton-Century).

Usually, however, the dreariest food that one encounters is ersatz American, and that goes as well for our popular cocktails. I've heard of a Danish bar that cools the martinis with a little electric fan and, from their mean temperature abroad, I wouldn't be surprised if that were the prevailing practice. Moreover, if you don't specify a "dry martini *cocktail*," like as not you'll be served a glass of dry Martini vermouth. Martinis are princeling size in England, and most everywhere peaked. "Four parts vermouth to one gin?" a waiter in Biarritz typically misunderstood my conservative directions. The frustration of getting their drinks properly mixed all but gives some Americans a seizure. Finally, Scotch and martinis are expensive overseas; they cost just as much as they do here.

So be merry with the indigenous quaffs. Try tequila and pulque in Mexico, schnapps and akvavit in Scandinavia, ouzo and that awful resinated retsina in Greece, the powerful pisco sours in Peru, slivovitz and *prošek* in Yugoslavia, Irish whiskey in Eire and Santory in Japan, the regional wines in Morocco, Chile, Lebanon, Italy, Germany, Switzerland, Portugal, and France, ales and stout in Britain, and the excellent beer in Britain, Belgium, Denmark, Holland, Germany, Mexico, and Japan—all of which claim to have the globe's best. Sweden has the worst. One can grow fond of the medicinal taste of Italy's Campari and, not surprisingly, sherry is a delightful apéritif in Spain, although in a misguided effort to please the Americans it is sometimes served on the rocks. In a holiday mood one needs less sedation than in workaday life.

Fear of having to dine alone and then face an empty evening probably deters more otherwise intelligent, self-reliant women from traveling alone than any other concern. To that, some prefer even the dullest of companions.

Everybody who travels by herself has some quiet meals alone. The bright girl takes advantage of them to jot down details about people and locales that have struck her as arresting or amusing, even sad; attitudes she has found surprising, remarks that were funny. They'll make her postcards and letters entertaining and will refresh her memory when she starts polishing up the anecdotes that will be turning her circle green when she gets back. All of a sudden she will realize she has been too engrossed in the extraordinary world about her to be lonely. And that is a glorious and triumphant moment—one that can metamorphose a personality. Mine needs an annual going-over.

Many travelers innocently get themselves saddled with full- or demi-pension arrangements (also known respectively as American or modified-American plans—as contrasted with European plan, or no meals included). Doing so may effect a slight saving, but it has disadvantages: the meals are table d'hôte, the menus are likely to be unimaginative, the hotel dining room may be gloomily empty. Exploring foreign restaurants is vastly more diverting. If elegance awes you, go to the modest. Europe is full of family-run bistros with excellent food. Their friendly atmosphere is relaxing, and the waiters can give you an insider's view of the country. Just ask what they think about some current event—local or world—and they become as gassy as cab drivers in Gotham.

In the *SAS World-Wide Restaurant Cookbook* (Random House), Charlotte Adams offers, along with recipes, ideas on where to eat, as, on a grander scale, does Charles H. Baker, Jr., in *The Esquire Culinary Companion* (Crown). Guidebooks to individual countries suggest restaurants, and still others will be listed in the brochures available at most foreign hotels. The names of less costly cafés may be secured from local tourist bureaus, hotel per-

sonnel, sightseeing-tour guides, and airline offices. New acquaintances are always exchanging recommendations. I've even gotten
tips from the tellers in banks. You needn't be timid about asking
the natives of the country to direct you to a good inexpensive restaurant, one to which they themselves might go. Ascertain if unescorted women are welcome. At night, except for exceedingly
short distances, it is usually wisest to go and return in a taxi. Get
the hotel or restaurant doorman to summon one for you—a service
for which he should be tipped the local counterpart of a quarter.

Before leaving the hotel, inquire what dishes the area or restaurant is known for, so that if the waiters don't speak English,
and you cannot decipher the menu, you may request one of them.
Failing that, the words *"la specialité de la maison"* would be
understood by almost any restaurateur in a country where at least
some French is spoken. Add a "please" in the local tongue, or
French, German, or even English, smile, and you can dispense
with the verbs. Braving foreign restaurants gives one aplomb. If
you're too tired or timid to venture to one at night, go in the
daytime.

It's important, however, especially for a woman alone, to enter a
room with her head high and the best possible posture. Wait at the
threshold of the dining room for someone—the maître d'hôtel or
captain (in an expensive place), a waiter, or the manager—to approach you. If you spot the fellow who seems to be seating people,
beckon with a slightly raised finger. Tell him, in English if you
must, that you wish a table for luncheon or dinner.

It's nice to be able to speak other languages. I have tried but I
can't seem to retain any, yet I have never found it an insurmounta-
ble problem in a restaurant. They get the idea. And if one is gracious won't regard one's speaking English as arrogant.

Don't, if you are alone, be too distressed if the table at which
you are seated is not particularly desirable. Restaurants the world
over defer to known big shots and spenders or attractive couples.
That's a fact of life. It can sometimes be circumvented by handing
the maître d' the equivalent of fifty cents or a dollar when you are
explaining where you would like to sit. Men do it all the time.
Even so, if it is the right kind of establishment, don't expect a
ringside or prominent table; the best that can be hoped for in a

chic place is a location a reasonable distance from the dirty dishes. And this is just as well, for otherwise your motives might be misunderstood.

Now perhaps you would like some wine. Again, in the event you are not *au courant* in viniculture, ascertain in advance what is the most popular local beverage and ask for it. In places where French is understood but English is not, *"du vin rouge* (or *blanc) s'il vous plaît"* is sufficient to get a carafe of the everyday red or white wine, which can be quite good, if occasionally too *ordinaire*. Traditionally, red wine is drunk with red meats and hearty dishes, white with fish, poultry, and delicate fare. However, white Burgundy has sufficient body to cope with the former, and a light red won't overwhelm the latter. Rosé wines are preferred by many people under any circumstances. Order what you like best—sweet or dry—and enjoy yourself.

If there is a wine steward—*sommelier*—on the precincts (he always wears a heavy chain with a large key as pendant), don't be shy about asking the waiter to send him over to help you select your wine. It's much easier to get a half-bottle abroad than in the States, although vintage wines are not usually served by the glass or carafe. However, Americans make more to-do about good vintages than do most Europeans.

The bus boy will bring a wine bucket, into which your selection will be placed. When the *sommelier* thinks it is sufficiently chilled, he will take it out, remove the cork, sniff it, and, after the wine has had a chance to "breathe," pour a small portion into your glass. He will watch anxiously while you taste it, so reflect a moment before you say, "Hmmm. Excellent." One has to be awfully sure of her ground to venture any other opinion. For this service the wine steward should be tipped 10 to 15 per cent of the wine bill.

The first time I went through this ceremony abroad was in Nice, where I was choosy about settling on a Haut-Médoc '49 to contend with sautéed veal flavored with Cointreau, Grand Marnier, and Vieille Cure. Halfway through the meal I noticed that the waiter had slipped me a mere Médoc '49, but I kept my peace until I saw on the bill that I was charged for the more expensive grape. The next couple of hours I congratulated myself for having corrected the error—until I realized that I would have acquitted my-

self even better had I remembered to drop the aitch when discussing that Haut.

If you are having several meals in your hotel, you may order a
large bottle of wine and ask the waiter to store it for you to be
finished on subsequent days.

"The bill, please" are words worth learning in any foreign
tongue (the peculiarly American "check" puzzles even the English), but failing them, *"l'addition, s'il vous plaît"* will probably be
understood. If not, miming the act of signing one's name is universally comprehended.

It is customary in one's hotel to sign for all meals. The cost,
together with service charge, appears on the final bill. If you are in
doubt whether a service charge has been added to a restaurant
check, and can't speak the language, say to the waiter, "Service?"
or "sair-VEES?," which he may understand better than the American pronunciation. When the service charge appears on the check,
there is no need to fatten it with more than the smallest coins that
come with your change. However, in cities like Paris an additional
5 to 15 per cent may be expected. Let the attention you have received govern your largesse. Wherever you are, if the service has
been indifferent or surly, have no qualm about leaving the minimum. In most places this is 15 per cent, but you may wish to verify
the local practice with the hall porter. Only once have I been told
by a waiter that he wished no gratuity—and this, if you please, was
in Sodom. Of course, it's changed a lot since the old days.

There are restrictions on the sale and service of alcoholic drinks
in certain countries, principally Britain (during specified hours),
India, and a few of the Moslem lands. If you enjoy a drink before
dinner (or a nightcap, for that matter), it is wise before entering
such prohibitive states to check the latest regulations. Some of
them are even quite stuffy about bringing in a bottle—for instance,
Saudi Arabia, where Virginia won the right only by insisting her
doctor had prescribed it.

In London, most people make a beeline for theatre tickets. On
my last visit, feeling like a stroll, I elected to purchase them from
one of the vendors along Piccadilly rather than through the hall
porter. It was after hours, though, and the agent had just closed up

shop. Disappointed, I asked if he could recommend a good restaurant. "You can't go wrong at Hatchett's," he said. "Cross the road and walk north about twenty yards." I crossed the street and, while trying to figure out what that was in blocks, came upon Hatchett's understated sign.

At the foot of the thickly carpeted stairs leading into the dining room I was greeted by a maître d' in tails. Curbing an impulse to bolt, I asked for a table for one. Several couples were foxtrotting to "Roses of Picardy" as I, the only unescorted woman, was led to a banquette. Everyone was in dancing attire, whereas on the plane a few hours earlier I had finally succeeded in wrinkling my theretofore virtually unbendable tweed. At least I wasn't necklaced with cameras.

The maître d' handed me a menu. Noting that any way you viewed it, in both calories and price, this was going to cost me a few pounds, I decided I might as well have a fling. We had a lengthy colloquy about the wine. A couple across the dark narrow L in which I was seated smiled. Another to my left inquired if I were an American; was I on holiday in London; what was I planning to do there? I said I hoped to see some plays—among others, the then-current hits *The Boy Friend* and *The Entertainer*.

"You may have difficulty securing a ticket for *The Entertainer*," said the man. "If you do, ring me tomorrow. I may be able to help." The lights were too seductive to read what he scrawled on the paper that he gave me.

The Entertainer, in which Sir Laurence Olivier was starring, was a sellout. Excavating the gentleman's trump card from the rat's nest in my purse, I gasped at my good fortune; it read: "R. Hiley in Sir Laurence's office." My affection for Britons burgeoned.

If I got a stall, British-theatre version, crashing Hatchett's, I got the good old American type when I decided to dine, on my last night, at Prunier's, the London branch of a celebrated French seafood establishment. I had been sloshing around in the rain all afternoon hunting for bargains in cashmere, and, admittedly, arrived a bit spotty.

The captain directed me to the oyster counter. "I prefer a table in the dining room," I said. "You may eat here," he said. "I *prefer* to eat in the dining room," I said. "Madam, there are no tables."

"I don't mind waiting for one. I have several hours to kill before going to the airport anyway." The manager came over. I repeated my request. He repeated that there were no tables. "Where is the ladies' room?" I asked. "I'll freshen up and then have a cocktail while I'm waiting for one."

After forty minutes they gave in and brought me a menu. To make it worth their while I ordered grilled *loup de mer*, a Mediterranean fish, nested on a thicket of fennel blazed with Pernod. "Madam," said the anguished waiter, "that dish takes twenty-five minutes to prepare." When he brought it to my table the flames soared like a blow torch, riveting the eyes of the other diners. Leisurely, I relished it, then ordered coffee and a Martell. The help looked apoplectic, but it was amazing how they dimpled when I passed out the tips.

I asked Ivy, an English friend, why they'd been so sticky. "But," she said, "they don't serve unescorted women." I don't see why not. It wasn't a nightclub. I wasn't being flirtatious or coarse. Perhaps it's up to us girls to integrate some of these places.

For those less crusading, restaurants preponderantly present no problem, and fortunately there are few countries that frown upon women tourists dining out alone. The independence of the American female is widely appreciated. It may be pleasanter, though, provided she's good company, to recruit another woman.

This possibility did not present itself in Marrakesh, where I had to wait until after the crowded Christmas and New Year's holidays for available hotel space, then found it in such abundance that I enjoyed the ministrations of the Koutoubia's entire staff, bent on coddling their solitary guest. Even so, I'd have lit out for more populous surroundings had I not paid a travel agent in Casablanca for mine in advance. The dining room, particularly, was less than *très gai*. Instead, with its traditional Berger songs and dances, the Arabic restaurant Dar es Salaam, described in a tourist brochure, sounded precisely my dish.

The cab driver stopped just inside the native quarter, or *medina*, opened the door, and instructed me to go *tout droit*, then *à gauche*. I looked at the dark alley before me, reluctant to proceed. "Dar es Salaam is *là-bas?*" I stalled, unable to believe that a typical old Moorish palace would be located in such a slum. He said,

"*Oui!*" and slipped into gear. "Well, okay . . ." I muttered. "I just hope this is going to be all right."

The lane's pits and pebbles were hazardous to high heels. I had picked my way but a few fearful paces when, darting like mice from an alcove, a pack of ragamuffins surrounded me and, hands outstretched, began screaming, "Mone-y, mone-y!" In common with most Moroccan small fry, they were wearing identical white Bata sandals, and even in the dim light their hair reflected henna. "Oh, go away!" I said fretfully, myself again before this evidence of convention. Give to one, and you have to give to all. I faltered on.

A black man in the ubiquitous ankle-length, hooded robe—the jellaba—overtook me, occasioning a coronary spasm. "Dar es Salaam?" he inquired. "*Oui*," I squeaked, quickening my tempo, though it was a toss-up in which direction I should spurt. "It is around the corner to the left," he said, leading the way. I followed —several feet behind, in case a sudden retreat seemed strategic.

Still trembling, I entered a lounge where, seated on narrow, yellow-and-black brocaded-plush benches, a number of Europeans were hunched over mint tea served on low, intricately tooled, solid-brass trays. I speculated on their price as the alley scout escorted me past them into the dining room. Similarly furnished, it too was walled with blue-and-green tiles beneath scalloped arches of gracefully arabesqued plaster. Dreamily, I pictured it in my apartment. I could, however, do without the mishmash of Moorish carpets; color schemes have yet to preoccupy Morocco.

I propped a couple of stout cushions stiffly behind me, since, without an escort, reclining is rather silly. A waiter in a red fez and pepper-and-salt jellaba asked if I wished to order the couscous.

"What kinds have you?" I asked, feigning authority. "*Viande*," he replied, leaving me incompletely enlightened. By that time I had sampled *la soupe de Ramadan*, a hearty potage with which during the ninth month of the Islamic year the Moslems daily break their dawn-to-dusk fast. And I had sweetened my tooth with *bstila*, the huge strudel pie filled with pigeon, almonds, cinnamon, and honey. Pausing at le Mick et Pat Café for a comfort break on the bus trip to Essaouira, I'd even grabbed a kebab-burger, famished after a six-hour journey during which I had had but an orange, albeit one the size of a Texas grapefruit. Now I wanted something more eupeptic than semolina crowned with boiled carrots. However, the waiter responded so irrelevantly to my questions, I decided to explore the possibilities no further. After all, I'd come there principally to have a look at the symbolic dances of a pastoral culture.

"*Et du vin*," I said, adding just to show I knew my way around, "*le Chaud Soleil rouge*," the red Hot Sun wine I had been enjoying all week. An orthodox Moslem, he informed me, nostrils distended, that the restaurant served no spirits. Mine drooped.

A maidservant wearing a bright bandanna and long-toed yellow babouches scurried over with a big brass teakettle and basin. Having noted the practice of other diners, I casually thrust out my palms. She poured warm water on them and handed me her damp Turkish towel.

A half hour later a clay casserole was carried over in a round plywood container covered with an enormous straw cone, designed to retain heat. No utensils were provided; the ones nature gave me had been cleansed. I recalled having read that it was proper to twirl the cereal into tiny dumplings and pop them into one's mouth, but I wasn't about to try it the first time among strangers. I asked the waitress for a fork. She brought me a large soup spoon. It worked fine with the mush but wasn't up to the *viande*. With chicken, couscous can be pretty good. At Dar es Salaam, with an old lamb shank, pretty bad.

But the ethnic dancers were coming on, and I was eager to see these High Atlas maidens. Their grace had been rhapsodically described in a local tourist magazine by a journalist who had happened on "a delicious little idyl, at midday, not far from an Ait Telti village, in a well-hidden spot," where, standing in a brook, a group of girls were taking a makeshift shower with earthenware jugs. "They throw the water so adroitly," he reported, "that two or three aspersions are enough to wet all their body."

Giggling, big-bellied, with *beaucoup* gold teeth, each, for her appearance at Dar es Salaam, was wearing her Friday-best caftan—a floor-length, brocaded housecoat—and snood, under which she hid her hair and what might easily have been curlers as well. Shoulder-to-shoulder they circled before us, stamping and clapping while in weird, high-pitched voices they chanted tales of tribal trysts and tribulations.

Then, quickening to their men's slaps on the *guedra*, a regional tom-tom, they began jerking their pelvises to an increasingly animated rhythm—maintaining the while a good-natured mien. When the drumbeat reached a frenzy, they sank as one to the dining-room carpet, where, spread-eagled in a supine daisy chain, those Atlas Mountain maids continued to simulated paroxysm an ageless fertility rite.

All this fun with curious customs and comestibles is, of course, predicated on your remaining in good health. So before leaving take the necessary inoculations, have a physical checkup, and get your eyes tested if it's time they were. The vigorous scrubbing Indian peasants give their teeth at daybreak with the twig of a neem tree is said to be excellent for the prevention of caries. Americans not having access to one would do well to see their dentist before departing on a journey.

There is space in the "International Certificates of Vaccination" booklet for the traveler's doctor to note down her blood type and group, known sensitivities, the medical treatment she is taking, and general physical condition. Below that may be entered the prescription for eyeglasses or contact lenses.

Carry on your person at all times a tag, bracelet, or card specifying any physical condition you have that may require emergency care.

Take sensible precautions and don't be neurotic about water and salads; both are usually safe in the better restaurants and hotels. If cabbage, for example, is your poison, don't eat it. It will be just as flatulent overseas as at home. I have suffered *tourista* but twice: in Provence, a gourmet's paradise, where I wolfed down huge helpings of cassoulet (I never could eat beans), and—again out of stupidity —in Kashmir. (Anybody knows rancid butter is physicky. It can go bad at home, too.)

In the tropics and areas without adequate refrigeration, stick to food that is hot enough to have killed any germs. Pass up iced beverages where you would fear to drink undistilled water and don't, of course, drink water from spigots labeled "nonpotable."

Inspect the thermos bottle in your bedroom containing the boiled water. Glancing idly into one at the so-called "first-class" Balihotel in Denpasar, I was revolted to see slime. For the balance of my stay I brushed my teeth with orange crush.

Many hostels and cafés press one to buy mineral water when it is obviously unnecessary. The Aviz in Lisbon was one. A former ducal palace, the tiny hotel had stained-glass windows, petit-point-covered chairs, and a dining room so *cordon bleu* that I didn't complain when the bill for luncheon carried prices steeper than those on the menu. But I refused to pay the few cents added for mineral water that I had asserted I did not wish. A principle was involved, and I chose to be tedious.

Swim only in chlorinated pools. Try to get plenty of rest and don't overexert in unaccustomed heat and high altitudes. Visitors arriving in Mexico City or Cuzco, for example, are advised to lie down for a few hours before doing any sightseeing.

If you become ill or have an accident abroad, the name of a qualified doctor can be secured from the American embassy or consulate, the local government tourist organization, or your hotel. Intermedic provides a directory of English-speaking, participating physicians in more than a hundred foreign cities in some fifty-five countries—with emphasis on regions most visited by Americans.

Have your own doctor prescribe the nostrums you may need to arrest minor upsets. The possibility of serious ailment is slight if you are in reasonably good health. Wear sturdy heels on cobblestones and step high over such pitfalls as drain holes in the bathroom and elevated thresholds between it and the bedroom.

There are no worse overseas hazards.

7

Carriers Away

Never worry about having transportation problems if you travel outside a group or alone. In the event difficulties arise—and they're rare—a native of the country, an official, or another traveler, usually male, will come to your aid. Delays in flights, the longer the better, are a godsend, drawing passengers together in shared irritation. In this respect I have found Alitalia productive.

But you can also count on, among others, Avianca. For hours scores of us sweltered in the Bogotá waiting room pending our flights to Quito and Lima. At first we paced the floor, separate and aloof (a good ploy), and during luncheon pretended to be perusing the Spanish gazettes, since, unlike the resourceful Colombians, we hadn't thought to bring along our guitars. At 5:00 P.M. the flight for which we'd dragged ourselves out of bed twelve hours earlier was announced. These bound for Ecuador rushed into the plane, only to circle the city and return disgruntled to the airport. The Lima passengers, who were still grounded, greeted us with good-natured guffaws, and suddenly the group fused, trapped in the same tedium. It was a festive evening after Avianca packed us all off to the chic Club Militar for cocktails and dinner.

Intercontinental transportation, of course, is limited to ships or planes. A woman may pamper herself by going overseas on a luxury or even single-class liner, and I'm all for it if her time and wallet permit. The food is usually epicurean, and, although an extensive wardrobe is no longer a must, endless parties afford many occasions to wear pretty clothes and make friends. Furthermore, in proper season the ocean air is tonic.

On a recent mid-January voyage from Gibraltar to New York aboard the Italian Line's opulent turbovessel *Raffaello,* the "Good Morning!" bulletins for the five-day crossing read:

"To-day at 8:00 o'clock the outside temperature is 61F. It is raining. The sea is rough."

"To-day at 8:00 o'clock the outside temperature is 60F. It is raining. The sea is rough."

"To-day at 8:00 o'clock the outside temperature is F. 56. The sky is overcast. The sea is smooth."

"To-day at 8:00 o'clock the outside temperature is 52F. It is raining. The sea is rough."

"To-day at 8:00 o'clock the outside temperataure is 35F. It is raining. The sea is rough."

If, therefore, one was unable to pace the deck, let alone sunbathe, or swim in any of the pools, ample activity was nevertheless engendered. As typical of large liners, passengers were straightway invited to sign up for tournaments: ping-pong, deck golf, and trapshooting (for which the pitching sea was no boon), bridge, canasta, and gin rummy. Chess players found each other, as did those needing an eye-opener at ten in the morning, when the bars began serving.

At 11:00 A.M. there was a stereophonic concert, at noon a complimentary dance lesson by the directors of entertainment, whose services could also be employed "to learn, improve, and modernize your favorite dance rhythm." Indeed, the day was continuously melodious with tea, cocktail, and evening musicales. After dinner, cabaret performers and orchestras enlivened the ballrooms, where groups of singles as well as couples found diversion until the early hours of the morning. There were news broadcasts; TV, Hollywood, and foreign films. For churchgoers divine services were provided; for readers, a library of solemn leather-bound classics. If anyone landed feeling peaked, it was a triumph of the night life over solarium, sun, and infrared treatments, gymnastics, massages, and cabinet baths.

Shortly after embarkation on a voyage passengers are assigned by the chief dining steward or maître d'hôtel to the tables at which they will eat. Usually there are two sittings—early and late—either of which may be requested. Single women, however, are likely to find more sociability at a large table during the late meal. Contrarily, single men frequently prefer their own solitary tables, to which they may invite guests. In contrast to the average cruise, the *Raffaello* (and I cannot generalize from it) attracted quite a number of ostensibly unattached males. A few chose to remain so; most couldn't get themselves attached often enough, for ships have a devil-may-care atmosphere that seems to inspire dalliance in spinsters, matrons, divorcées, and widows.

Liquor, tax-free, is inexpensive aboard ship, so early in the voyage the cocktail parties begin—in the passengers' cabins or one of the lounges, where, by advance arrangement with the dining steward, canapés can be served without charge. Sam, a veteran social director on ships, advises a girl to give a cocktail party as early as possible in the voyage—so much the better if in response to hospitality, but not necessarily. Convivial couples and single women are always available in abundance, and extra men may be recruited at her own table, as well as from the officers and entertainment staff. Or the traveler may ask the ship's hostess to help her gather a group of people with congenial interests for the party. Particularly on cruise ships it is not considered foward to invite passengers whom one does not know. They will retaliate with invitations to their parties, thus widening a woman's circle geometrically. All in all, an excellent course for one not too shy to make the first move.

Most girls are more relaxed, and thus fare better, being themselves. Others find it fruitful to vary their guises: they may be demure at breakfast or radiantly healthy (if that can be managed), matter-of-fact at lunch, glamorous at dinner. Whatever the role, they will meet more people if they participate in at least some of the ship's activities. Hostesses on the United States Line make a special effort to introduce passengers with similar interests.

To my mind, the best place to shop for Atlantic liners is *Fielding's Travel Guide to Europe* (Sloane); for the Pacific, *Olson's Orient Guide* (Lippincott). If you wish to make friends with the nationals, it is sensible to travel on the ships of the countries you will visit.

Although the *Raffaello*, amiably, was fairly permissive about the mobility upward of passengers, most liners with more than one class limit the run of the ship to those booked in first or de luxe class. Not so with freighters, which permit total freedom of the craft.

There are other differences. Freighters and cargo-liners often provide better cabin accommodations for less money. But they lack the beauty parlors, gift shops, therapy and hospital facilities of the large passenger ships. They are also slower, and their schedules erratically geared to the loading and unloading of cargo. Moreover, a passenger list of twelve may comprise ten or eleven bores. One of my more gregarious friends recalls a dreary two-week voyage during which she was trapped with, but not accepted by, clannish, beefy Babbitts. Another has taken potluck at freighter tables with tots who massaged their scalps with the scrambled eggs and, in exuberant mimicry of Moby Dick, spouted lemonade.

After each of her sixteen solo sailings to La Ceiba, Honduras, Lesley has glowingly reported having had a ball—sometimes as the solitary passenger, with all the officers to jolly her. An inveterate party-giver and -goer, she finds traveling alone on the banana boats a tonic—and thereby exemplifies an important point: it's not what you see but how much you enjoy it that counts.

The main thing to avoid is giving any impression of being a clinging vine. You make your own fun on a freighter. "We don't exactly samba before breakfast," Doris wrote me from a Brazilian vessel, "but the music is playing then should we want to. Of an evening, there is a wonderful small band of disparate ingredients (each member is a master), and they perform with much joy. The main hit is a lively tune, 'Ave Maria of the Hills'—about Rio— with words like 'It can be very sad in skyscrapers; we on the hills are nearer to heaven.'

"A passenger ship," Doris observed, "is more like a resort; a freighter is a piece of life. It can be very lonely; one must be independent. One's relations with people have to be like those in a city apartment house. The crew are not geared to take care of tourists, yet they can be as friendly as one's neighborhood store. More so, because this is a floating world.

"If one is lucky, one makes true friends on a freighter because the problems show—the character. Yes—one needs character on a freighter."

On ocean liners and freighters, gratuities in lump sums are customarily dispensed—discreetly in envelopes after the last meal. On cruises 50 per cent of the tips are distributed midway on the voyage and the balance at its conclusion. Even the major guidebooks disagree on the sums, although there is unanimity that, with the exception of the deck steward, one need not reward anyone who has not performed a personal service—and must never tip any of the ship's officers.

On cruises tip the dining-room steward one dollar a day, the cabin steward one dollar a day, and the cabin stewardess fifty cents a day if she serves breakfast in your bedroom. American ships are unionized; hence the help is not dependent on tips for their wages. The reverse is true on foreign liners, where service is apt to be much better in the hope of earning greater gratuities. The following are conservative working figures for a five- to seven-day voyage. Increase the amounts proportionately for longer journeys or extra attention, such as meals served in the cabin.

	FIRST CLASS	CABIN CLASS	TOURIST
Maître d'Hôtel or Head Dining-room Steward	$3–$5	$2	$1
Dining-room Steward	$5–$8	$4–$5	$3–$4
Cabin Steward	$5–$8	$4–$5	$3–$4
Cabin Stewardess	$0–$5	$0–$3	$0–$3
Wine Steward	$0–$2	$0–$1	$0–$1
Deck Steward	$1	$1	$1
Bath Steward	$0–$1	$0–$1	$0–$1
Cabin Boy	$0–$1	$0–$1	$0–$1

At the end of the trip, the bar steward is tipped 15 per cent of the liquor bill, exclusive of the wine ordered in the dining room. Each waiter at your cocktail party should be tipped five dollars. One waiter is usually enough for up to fifteen people, two for fifteen to twenty-five, three for more. In the event the cabin steward and stewardess have shared the room chores, split the *pourboire* between them or let them divide it themselves. The same holds true if you've been hovered over by two dining-room stewards. If you have left your shoes in the corridor outside the cabin at night to be polished, "boots" should be tipped a dollar.

For cargo-liners and freighters, *Travel Routes Around the World* suggests that a sum equal to 5 per cent of the fare be set aside for gratuities, which is a reasonable kitty also for passenger ships. On cargo-liners, "out of every $10," advises the Harian publication, "give $3 apiece to your room and table stewards and $1 to each other steward who may have served you. . . . On freighters . . . you can split a sum equivalent to 5 per cent of your fare between your room and table stewards. If you receive service from any other steward, give him up to 1 per cent of your fare. . . . If service seems poor, decrease your tips. And if you seem to have a surplus left over out of your tipping budget, pocket it yourself."

Many travelers simply consult the purser about the practice prevailing on his particular ship; it varies from one to another.

There is no tipping in the air. And if one needs character on a freighter, courtesy is all that is necessary on a plane.

First-class accommodations offer roomy seats and plenty of space in which to flex one's legs at a cost roughly 30 to 50 per cent higher than economy class, depending on the season. Airlines lavish "free" cocktails, champagne, wines, and brandy on the haves or expense-account travelers before, during, and after superb à la carte meals, which may be ordered in advance and are served to them first. Swissair, whose menu is three feet long, in addition donates slipperettes and hankies. Other lines, too, evidence their appreciation with tokens: slipperettes, cigarette boxes, pencils, and pens (BOAC); slipperettes, toothbrushes, lotions (TWA); slipperettes, stationery, Irish liqueurs, and pens (Aer Lingus); slipperettes, playing cards, Spanish fans (Iberia); perfume, liqueurs, and cigars (Finnair). The VIP lounges in airports are for the elite ticketholders, who are also presented with a handsome airline flight bag that would cost anybody else a couple of dollars. Moreover, first-class passengers are permitted to disembark before the others, giving them a head start on the red tape.

Because the economy sections were oversold on my flights between Osaka and Hong Kong and again between Rangoon and Calcutta, several of us were moved to the upper-class section, where I tasted this lofty living gratis, and it's lovely. But is it worth the difference in fare? Not if you're paying for it out of a modest salary.

True, on a long flight you can feel rather claustrophobic jammed next to or between two other people, both of whom have bulging thighs and their elbows on your armrest. The bald head of the gentleman in front may be lowered to your lap. And, cramped against overnight bags and parcels, legs grow precociously rheumatic.

Nevertheless, economy class is still short of steerage. On off-season flights it is often possible to have three seats to yourself, to lower the arm rests between them and recline at will. Stewards and stewardesses are attentive, the meals range from fairly good (on American planes) to excellent (on certain foreign lines, among them Swissair, Alitalia, Air France, and JAL), the drinks are inexpensive, and the washrooms thoughtfully appointed. Economy- and first-class passengers have access to the same bargains in duty-free perfumes, liquors, cigarettes, and sundries available aboard. I don't know how much Ma Griffe, Miss Dior, and Diorissimo gets unloaded, but I have yet to take an international flight on a foreign line when they weren't being peddled. Another of the staples is Johnny Walker Red Label Scotch—a real buy. For both classes there are racks filled with newspapers and magazines.

Of the jet birds, JAL is the most generous with souvenirs for the economy class. A plastic case contains maps of air routes and Japanese cities, cabin scuffs, a pair of fans, the bill of fare, and assorted tourist tips (especially on where to purchase silks, cameras, and pearls). Many agreeable hours may be consumed toying with these keepsakes, which are rather more peptic than—typical of American lines—a grim, solitary vomit bag tucked into the seat pocket before one.

Taking JAL's lead, a number of lines on the Orient route are now serving hot or iced fingertip towels shortly after take-off, along with the candies and chewing gum to ease the pressure on your eardrums. To alleviate serious pain Flent earplugs are better.

The one time I flew Air France, we were scarcely buckled down when the stewardess circulated among us with a pint of Lanvin's lavender, with which the ladies dabbed their wrists and ears and the gentlemen sloshed their faces. We were fragrant all the way from Istanbul to Athens.

Wild monkeys roam the roof of Palam Airport in New Delhi

and sweet little lizards cling to its walls. Nevertheless, the most glamorous international airport is our own at Honolulu, what with a Japanese garden and pagoda and Polynesian lounge, where a Eurasian waitress in an epidermal cheong-sam with thirteen-inch slits serves refreshments to lei-den passengers and bon voyagers, among whom are barefoot American matrons in muumuus and kooky muus carrying orchid maribou beach baskets. *Aloha.*

One can gain quite an insight into a people by their airline's conduct. The Czechs, for instance, seem like a jolly folk. On the flight from Djakarta to Pnompenh we had no sooner finished our breakfast of wieners and beer when, to commemorate the crossing of the equator, the pilot burst from his cabin dressed like King Neptune and merrily doused us with water. Then he opened bottles of champagne and schnapps. It was a real nice party, and I got a certificate testifying to the milestone, which I treasure along with my diplomas for crossing the international dateline and climbing Mount Zion.

Stewardesses on Indian Airlines wear turquoise and gray saris with bare midriffs and serve anise seed to help one cope with the abrupt change in altitude; the girls on JAL slip into flowered kimonos with obis outside city limits. Using only real china and silver, the no-nonsense Swiss put on bungalow aprons when they start messing around in the empyrean with trays, and the El Al stewardesses distribute recipes for blintzes. There are no sarongs on Garuda, but the dashing red capes on Avianca hostesses and the slinky, tight-torsoed pajamas on the Vietnamese are absolutely celestial. As are the latter's croissants.

Cruise ships range from luxurious, round-the-world, floating hotels to those conducting tours of a gamut of seas. The cabins are apt to be cramped, but there are social directors to keep the passengers peppy aboard and guides at ports to shepherd them to the monuments and marts. The traveler is sheltered against the pitfalls —and windfalls—of the unexpected. She will, however, save considerable money on the shore excursions if, instead of arranging for them through the purser, she and a few other passengers hire a car at the pier to take them to the points of interest listed in the purser's brochures.

The last cruise that I took was aboard a chartered yacht that sailed the Saronic Gulf, stopping for a half day, more or less, at each of various Greek islands—Aegina, Poros, Hydra, and Spetsai. Although the pretty girl guide was amenable to the wishes of the party (there were six of us: two elderly couples, one elderly spinster, one ageless spinster—all, save the last, amiable, affluent California Republicans), it was difficult to feel one was more than rubbernecking the temples of Poseidon and Aphaia or, for that matter, the orange groves to which we were also ingenuously led. I hungered for leisure to poke alone along boats festooned with sponges, anchored at quays draped with red-ocher and gold nets. Leisure to mosey up rocky hill paths and perhaps get lost in the tangle of white cottages shuttered with blue to match the sea and the sky. Most of all, I wished I could repeat the lark I had had in the Cyclades.

The hall porter at the Olympic Palace Hotel in Athens had bought me a round-trip steamer ticket to Mykonos, told me which trolley to take to the port city, Piraeus, and handed me a card on which he had written in Greek, "Please show this foreigner the way to Pier X." I didn't walk more than a half mile in the opposite direction.

After being blown to a froth on deck, I went into the lounge to read *Zorba the Greek* and immediately fell asleep, as is my wont with Kazantzakis. When I jerked chin from chest I was chagrined to face the quizzical smile of a patrician white-haired lady, who remarked that she shared my torpor toward her country's celebrated novelist. The roasting we gave him forged a warm bond.

"Oh, there's Aleko," she exclaimed, waving at a man of about forty who was approaching. "Did you have a good nap, Aleko?" she asked affectionately, adding to me, "We're getting off at Tinos"— her worldliness notwithstanding, she to make a pilgrimage to the miraculous icon in the Church of the Blessed Virgin, he to transact some business. I grew in volubility, particularly when another man joined our circle.

After a lively dinner together we agreed to rendezvous in Tinos for our return passage. Buoyant with anticipation, I proceeded on to the island of Mykonos, where the next morning I took a caïque, a long, narrow skiff, to Delos, the birthplace of Apollo. The resident guide on the rocky, nearly deserted island didn't even know Eng-lish by rote. And although I can sometimes catch the drift of French when overpronounced by people to whom it is foreign, his wasn't much more intelligible than the alternate, Greek. Thus it was some time later that I caught up on the full story about Leto, Apollo's unwed mother.

The gods, however, were with me, for I struck up an acquaint-ance with a young woman from Paros, who agreed to distract the spinners and Orthodox priests whose pictures I wished to take un-posed in the doorways and lanes of the chalky white town.

The climax of the excursion was my reunion with the Athenians, who, taking advantage of a couple of hours' anchorage in Andros, took me to dinner at a waterfront taverna in which the bouzoukis were not playing Greece's new anthem, "Never on Sunday." Doing as the Greeks do, we walked directly into the kitchen, where for my gastronomic education Aleko selected from the huge steamy caldrons lemon soup, fried Kaskaval cheese, and mounds of tiny crisp cuttlefish, which, as is proper, I ate heads and all—to the disappointment of the wistful cats underfoot. A box of Turkish delight completed mine.

One may travel in and between countries by conducted tours, train or motor coach, which at times make the most sense. The European are extremely well organized. Pausing en route at his-toric landmarks and scenic splendors—indeed, frequently detour-ing to them—the spacious, comfortably upholstered buses are skill-fully driven round the hairpin turns, with which the Continent abounds, by baritones and tenors who burst into melody as the day wanes—"O Sole Mio" and "Cielito Lindo." The passengers rejoice that they know the words, and join in.

There are multilingual guides—usually girls—who parrot the lore about monuments in English, Italian, German, Spanish, and French, but understandably are a little weak in basic colloquy. "Excuse me," I asked one when we stopped to admire the sharded Hellenistic columns at Selinunte, "could you tell me, please, where is the ladies' room?" "*Una birra? Una* Coca-Cola?" she replied briskly.

That was in Sicily, where I took a five-day conducted tour of the island, all efforts to find practicable means of proceeding alone having failed me. It was just too complicated—and dangerous. Sicily is one place where a woman should not go unescorted. It is a harsh and excitingly beautiful country with striking contrasts in terrain, and, in its architecture and inhabitants, reflects the rape and issue of many conquerors: Greek, Carthaginian, Arab, Norman. Outside of Palermo, Sicilian women are seldom seen on village streets; they are doing the work while their men gather on the sidewalks in packs, idling away the day. Even a beggar child to whom I gave a coin thanked me the only way that he knew—with a leer and lewd gesture. They're not effeminate; I'll say that for them.

The group with whom I traveled was more or less motley: two Frenchmen and their wives, a young Belgian couple, a few German girls, a retired American businessman and his bride, along with several blurs whom I don't remember. The American gentleman said he was crazy about music and kept asking one of the Frenchmen, a concert pianist, to play the album of "Moonlight Melodies." He seemed surprised that the Frenchman didn't know them.

One may write to government tourist offices for the names and brochures of companies that conduct bus and train tours, which travelers may arrange to join either through an American travel agent or the hotel concierge upon arrival in the country. Such information is also available in guidebooks. The motor coaches, which have compartments for luggage, pick up passengers at the major hotels. If you want a window seat, be sure to try in advance to reserve one.

At the conclusion of both extended and half-day conducted bus trips, it is customary to tip the guide. If he has gone to especial pains for you, the amount may be as high as 10 per cent of the cost of the excursion, though it could gracefully be less. But you need not give him anything if the service has been indifferent or poor.

The apogee of land luxury is the chauffeur-driven car and native guide. Where gasoline is dear and skilled mechanics (who also serve as drivers) rare, the price may be as high as $35 a half-day. Even so, it is usually a great deal less costly to hire a car and driver through your hotel than to let an American travel agent reserve them in advance. However expensive, when inevitable I enjoy them.

Ideally, one should enlist a kindred soul or two and share the charge—a happy solution for me in La Paz, where the travel agents' programs were priced for plutocracy. "Why," I sputtered to the clerk, "a person could hire a private taxi for less." One of two Frenchmen at the counter alongside me said, "Well—shall we?" Chemists who had attended an international conclave in Rio, they had been at Macchu Picchu when I was, a day or two before, and were having a final fling in the Andes before flying back to Marseilles.

Getting an early-morning start, we headed for our first destination, Lake Titicaca—at 12,500 feet the world's highest lake and, I suspect, the bluest. By motorboat we visited the island in its center, reputedly the birthplace of the first Inca, then followed the Indians in balsa canoes bringing in their catch. Jack-knifed like their husbands over the smoking fresh fish were Indian women in stiff bowler hats, brown and red-striped ponchos or chartreuse and turquoise dresses belled out behind by the multitude of petticoats (*polleras*) underneath. They seemed oblivious of our clicking shutters until we took our last shot, then matter of factly stuck out their hands for the pervasive *propina*, or tip.

The Frenchman who had four cameras could have found no carmate more *simpática* than I. Between us we ecstatically took hundreds of pictures—of snow-covered Mount Chacaltaya, said to have the world's highest ski-run; of open-topped trucks jammed with impassive standing Indians; of solitary alpacas staring narcissistically into the water; of herds of llamas, their vain, snooty faces flanked by bobbing red and blue earrings. We snapped Indian markets displaying Heinz cartons filled with vegetables, multi-hued feathers, and the dried fetuses of llamas, which are so good for warding off the Evil Eye—and sad little cemeteries in the barren gravel, where graves were marked by askew wooden crosses and tin cans holding dead mountain flowers.

In Nepal, the road to Kirtipur—a Shangri-la only four miles west of Katmandu, but isolated on a plateau—was so eroded that the chauffeured jeep I hired took thirty-five minutes, listing the while, to traverse it. Twice we nearly overturned in muddy ruts two feet deep. There is in this former capital of the Malla kings a brick pagoda temple a thousand years old, and many ancient customs endure. A small boy was beating a bongo to his buddy's conga down the steep stone steps of the town when I arrived there, and the entire village was bestowing gifts on a couple's first-born. Across the way a fourteen-year-old girl was shyly smiling, dressed for her wedding.

The women of Kirtipur, a mixture of Mongol and Indo-Aryan stock, are delicate-featured and nearly every one a beauty. I was told that once upon a time the village was attacked by unfriendly neighbors, and after all Kirtipur's warriors had been slain, their mothers and wives and sisters and daughters put on the men's clothes and fought off the invaders. Then, to perpetuate the species, it is said, they cohabited with, but did not marry, their man-servants.

In Bali, I engaged Njoman (Second Son) Oka, an extraordinarily sensitive and intelligent guide, who as operator of Balitours in Denpasar, provided a car and driver. Appreciative of my interest in the island's customs, he brought me close to the rites of a people whose religion—Hindu since the seventh century A.D.—retains animistic features.

"In Bali we have many gods," Mr. Oka's assistant frequently reminded me—the whole Hindu pantheon, including its trinity of major deities, Brahma the Creator, Vishnu the Preserver, and Siva the Destroyer, their incarnations and consorts; the goddesses of the lakes, the gods of the mountains, the spirits of the forests and the winds and fire. Before a Balinese matron can get on with her chores, she must prepare offerings to the hungry household gods, the spirits of the ancestors and the newly deceased. Early one morning the assistant took me to the compound where he lives so that I could watch his "oldest mother" arrange the petals and rice in the tiny dishes that she placed on an altar of their family temple. The other mothers whom his father had married were not on the premises.

Putting on ceremonial sashes and headache bands, Mr. Oka and I went to the courtyard of a family that had been having a lot of bad luck, for there are plenty of evil spirits in Bali. When we arrived the family were circling their patio, purposefully stomping with the *sengguhu*, a priest whom they had called upon to exorcise the spirit. The *sengguhu* halted the march periodically while he whacked the ground smartly with a broom, raising a great cloud of dust—and pure hell with the devil.

After a big candlelight feast on place mats made of fresh, plaited flowers, a party of us attended an outdoor performance by the extraordinarily beautiful Balinese dancers of episodes from the *Ramayana*. One really should be familiar with this literature before traveling in Hindu and Buddhist lands, for its story is ubiquitous in architectural decoration as well as the dance.

Then two men and I drove with Mr. Oka to the torchlit village temple, where a large gathering of Balinese, separated into groups, were beseeching the gods to speak to them through a priest working himself into a trance on a dais to our right. The chanting grew more excited each time he put his face closer to the brazier of smoking incense and breathed deeply of its fumes. Suddenly plunging his nose into the burning coals, he let out a yell and began crying like a child in falsetto. The gods had entered him all right, but they weren't forgiving the people their trespasses, and there was much weeping throughout the congregation.

Preparations were being made in the village for the purification of the ashes at dawn, twelve days after the last mass cremation, and I wandered through the square dazzled by the thatch-covered bamboo altars hung with streamers—yellow leaves from the young coconut palm and green from the sugar palm—and, incredibly, bacon and rinds. There were fringed umbrellas and canopied tables on which red and orange flowers and fruit were intricately paneled into high, cylindrical offerings to the sun god.

As he was illuminating the beach the next morning, throngs of Balinese gathered with their priests on the sand, before runners laid with bouquets, food, and holy water, to pray for their dead, whose bodies and souls were represented in effigy by flowers placed in a lacy white paper-covered *wade*, a ten-foot reliquary composed of three platforms designating the underworld, this world, and the heavens. The men who carried it to the shore set it ablaze, and when the flames had subsided, they waded with the tower far into the ocean, followed by the quite cheerful mourners and musicians, who returned to Vishnu, the god of the sea and the source of all life, the souls of the departed.

Moved by the ceremony, I splashed right in, too, and would have tagged after them to the horizon had not Mr. Oka shouted to watch out for leeches and pits. It took days and days for my shoes to dry out.

Driving a rented car oneself is considerably less costly than hiring a guide and chauffeur, but for one person more expensive than using public or conducted-tour transportation. Some of the added cost may be defrayed by the opportunity an automobile opens for staying at low-priced out-of-the-way hotels and inns. And incalculable are the insights into a country thus afforded.

With an intrepidity extraordinary in a tenderfoot, Pearl, traveling alone, rented a car on her Maiden Voyage. Upon her arrival in Paris she went to an automobile rental agency, where she secured a Simca, then drove to the office of the American Automobile Association, which mapped her trip through the Loire and Rhône valleys.

"Their directions were so precise," she says, "that I never lost my way once. I stayed at hotels recommended by the AAA and they were nearly all very good." Typical of country folk, the people outside Paris were friendly. "If you made an effort to speak French, they tried very hard to help and understand."

Gasoline is sold almost everywhere overseas by the liter (there are 3.785 to the gallon), and in some countries tourists may purchase at a discount gasoline tickets for presentation at filling stations. At the conclusion of a journey, refund is made for leftover coupons. "Occasionally," recalls Pearl, "a rural garage will pretend they don't know anything about gasoline tickets. Insist. They'll understand."

Gasoline, however, must be paid for in cash; credit cards are rarely accepted.

For the first few hours the clutch shift on foreign cars may seem strange. Pearl quickly became accustomed to that on hers. She also learned to read road signs giving distances in kilometers; soon she had quit dividing the number by eight and multiplying the quotient by five to approximate the mileage and was gauging herself entirely by kilometers. Save when she got behind a typical peasant oxcart, traffic was no problem; nor were the warning signals, which follow an international, easily interpreted code.

Details about renting or buying a car abroad, leasing one, or using the repurchase plan are available in guidebooks, from local automobile clubs, travel agents, government tourist offices, the United States National Students Association, and American car-rental agencies, among them, Car-Tours in Europe, Europe by Car, Kinney System, and Auto-Europe. The last has a Women's Travel Division devoted exclusively to assisting and advising unescorted women who will be driving on the Continent. With the exception of government tourist bureaus, the foregoing organizations will make advance rental, leasing, or purchasing arrangements. They also supply motoring guides, road maps, and miscellaneous information about campsites, hotels, motels, and inns. Similar data is obtainable from Caltex (California Texas Oil Corporation), the Esso Touring Service, and Shell Oil Company service stations through the United States. The same oil companies have service stations in numerous Western European countries, as do British Petroleum and Gulf Oil Corporation. All provide motoring and general travel information. More advantageous deals may, of course, be made locally than through American go-betweens.

For short distances by train many recommend second class; it's less expensive, and the difference in compartments is usually more a matter of décor than comfort. In Europe most first- and second-class compartments accommodate six passengers, three on each of two facing seats. There is frequently a windowed corridor running the length of the train where, when tired of sitting, one may stretch her legs and yet watch the passing scene.

Regardless of class, it's important when traveling alone by train to keep one's wits about one, particularly if none too familiar with the local language. Whether the ticket is purchased for you by the hotel concierge (and in some cities this can spare you a great deal of time standing in line) or you buy it yourself in the railroad station, jot down the track number from which your train will depart and where you must change trains, if necessary. Then get a clearly detailed map of the area through which you will be traveling (available at newsstands) so that you can check how close you are to your destination. It's difficult enough to understand public-address announcements in American English, let alone Babel, especially where there is a discrepancy between our Anglicized versions of place names and the originals: Munich for München, Florence for Firenze, Constance for Konstanz, Vienna for Wien, and so on.

Lacking a knowledge of the country's language, it is essential to learn and be able to recognize the word for "track." In some stations you may simply give your train ticket to the porter who carries your luggage and follow him. In others, porters proceed to the trains via a different route from that of the passengers, whom they meet on the correct platform, in the area where the Class I or Class II cars will stop. Watch for signs with numerals so indicating, particularly if you are not using a porter.

It's more nuisance than disaster to board a car in the wrong class, since one can walk through the corridors within the train to the right one. If confused about the direction, sit down in any free seat until a conductor comes by. When traveling second class, and thus less likely to encounter English-speaking people, it is good manners to be able to ask in the local language, "Pardon me, is this seat free?" The occupant may be taking a turn in the "wagon-restaurant" or washroom and resent usurpation of his space.

Boarding a train from the wrong platform can be a major blunder, as I learned during a *Walpurgisnacht* in West Germany. I was headquartered in Zurich and daily fanning out on excursions in different directions. One trip was to Freiburg im Breisgau at the edge of the Black Forest. After inspecting a thirteenth-century cathedral, I climbed a hill to a restaurant affording a panoramic view of the city, dined, and returned to the railroad station with just sufficient time to catch the train to Zurich, but none to waste while the ticket agent investigated certain irregularities he discerned on my return stub.

"*Nach Zürich?*" I asked nervously, pointing to a train that was coming to a stop outside the station door. "*Auf Gleis zwei,*" he retorted. "Well, I know I'm going class *zwei*," I said huffily, rushing into the second-class car as the doors were slamming shut.

While I was still catching my breath in the corridor, a nice English-speaking gentleman asked me how long I was going to stay in Hamburg. "I don't plan to go there at all," I said. Plan to or not, I was on an express train to Hamburg.

The conductor seemed annoyed until the nice gentleman explained to him that I was an *Ausländer* and asked what could be done. He was told that the train would make a brief stop at a junction midway to Hamburg. There I could board a train bound for Basel, where there were many for Zurich. He pulled out a time-table and showed me the schedule.

Although the conductor was quite gallant about handing me down the steep trestle and leading me between the tracks to the small junction depot, the trainmen there were tight-lipped during the half hour I awaited the train to Basel. Indeed, I had to humble myself and ask for a hoist in climbing from the roadbed to the platform four feet higher.

Everyone in Switzerland speaks, at the very least, English, French, and German, so in Basel there was no problem in understanding that I had missed the last train but one to Zurich—and that one was leaving from the other station across town in ten minutes. The cab driver said we couldn't possibly make it, but I insisted he try. Again I slipped in just as the doors were closing—and found myself in a crack *Zug* that got me back to Zurich before midnight, only slightly wiser for the experience.

Because I pulled another stupid stunt en route to Kyoto. My Japanese travel agent had written out explicit directions for getting there from Kashikojima, but when the bus stopped at Uji-Yamada, where I was to take a train to Kyoto, I decided on the spur of the moment to stay a few hours for a look at the Great-Heaven-Shining-Goddess in the Daijingu Shrines. The ticket agent said I would have to change trains en route to Kyoto. Not entirely sure that I had understood him, I worriedly asked a Japanese opposite me if the train we were on went directly to Kyoto. He nodded, but ventured no further comment, evidently not wishing to lose face by admitting he did not understand English. According to my map we appeared to be proceeding in the right direction, so I was astonished to see all the other passengers quit the train at Osaka. As, with some concern, did I when the cleaning folk started to sweep up.

"Is this," I asked the stationmaster, "the end of the line?" With a polite giggle over my predicament, he said that it was. Too tired by this time to follow his advice and take another train to Kyoto, I threw monetary caution to the winds and joined the queue for the small taxis, which, in many countries, are cheaper. Nevertheless, I arrived at my hotel several thousand yen poorer, and it was some hours before I could contemplate purchasing any of the Satsuma or cloisonné vases displayed in the boutique.

I have had good and bad experiences going by train second class. The first time I tried it was on the *rapido* (express) from Florence to Naples, a six-hour ride, during which I was stared at unblinkingly the entire way to Rome by the sallow, all-male cast of a whodunit. They were straight out of Charles Addams, and I had forgotten a cardinal rule of travel: always bring something to read.

In Rome we exchanged one of the characters for a handsome blond Atlas who immediately began rustling and rearranging papers in his SAS flight bag. He looked so much like a Scandinavian counterpart of a pompous but harmless Joe Doakes whom I know that I relaxed. Perhaps I even smiled, for he asked if I were American, then switched the conversation to interesting channels. He told me about his work and extracted from the flight bag stills of himself costumed as Mark Antony in a Cinecittà production of *Cleopatra*, starring Hedy Lamarr. There's no question his legs looked better bare than in the puckered homespun trousers hemmed by what turned out to be his Neapolitan mama.

Once I had a lively journey through the Austrian Tyrol on a train whose second-class passengers were first-class *gemütlich* farmers. Cordially, a bosomy fräulein in a billowing dirndl invited me to sit with her and her fellows, and before long, caught up in their ebullience, I, too, was shouting *"Wunderbar!"* at the *schlosses* and *kirches*. Those Austrian castles and onion-topped churches are absolute *Himmel*.

In contrast, I had the uncomfortable experience in France of sharing a compartment with three ribald workmen, who, taking literally my *"Je ne comprends pas français,"* howled with laughter as they joshed me from Paris to Marseilles with prurient suggestions, which I comprehended all too well.

On the whole, I prefer entraining first class. One is accosted by more refined men.

Just one more caution about trains: be sure to save your ticket stubs; in many places they have to be shown at the turnstile when leaving the station.

Even a modest trolley ride in a foreign land is more exciting than being coddled and herded in tourist buses. In cities like Rome, London, Paris, or Hong Kong, where it's a breeze to get about on the local transportation, it's foolish to limit oneself entirely to organized sightseeing. Some of it, yes—to get oriented and for covering a great many, sometimes distant, monuments in a short time. Afterwards, go out on your own. For every taciturn person from whom you ask directions, there will be a thousand graciously extending themselves to be helpful. I have found no country where this is not true. However, in many locales passengers wait for transportation in orderly queues and will look unkindly upon anyone usurping their place, which is often established by the numbered ticket each takes from a machine where the vehicle stops.

A rung higher on the adventure ladder is to travel between cities on the buses used by the local people. Why it should seem more glamorous than taking a Greyhound to Trenton I don't know, but it is.

When I learned there was a "desert bus" from Alexandria to Cairo, I eagerly took it, visualizing oases and nomads and flashing-eyed sheiks on spirited stallions. Certainly, it sounded more exotic than the diesel. And thus I had the singular adventure of seeing it rain in the desert, which any Egyptian will tell you is impossible. We stopped only twice on that vast desolation—once to wait for a camel to meander across the road, and midway for comfort at a gasoline station, which proclaimed on pylons in Arabic and English: "Chevrolet, Pontiac, Cadillac."

It was gloaming as we approached Giza on the outskirts of Cairo, and, being an excitable sort, I nearly went to pieces when I caught sight of the Pyramids, having always thought them most likely a myth. On the broad boulevard into metropolitan Cairo we passed theatrically garbed dragomen astride Assyrian-nosed dromedaries, fellahin in ankle-length nightshirts on asses, bicycles, and afoot, balancing great trays of produce on their heads. Sailboats were loafing on the Nile, paled by the glimmering lights and neon Coca-Cola signs, while along the avenue was a graceful white mosque with a delicate minaret. Cairo is an amalgam of the exotic and the modern.

However, in Portugal, using the people's transportation, I had the unnerving experience of being let off the motor coach in the middle of the night on an inky black highway by a driver who had forgotten to unload me at Aljubarrota, but pointed helpfully in the direction of my *estalagem*, a mile or so down the road. Stiffening my knees, I plodded along stiltlike—in terror of satyr and beast. The ham *sahndweech* I got upon arrival at the government inn barely retarded my pulse.

Nevertheless, in Ecuador I succumbed again to the lure of mingling with the people of the country on their very own transporation, and thus found myself one morning running to catch a bus for Ibarra. The next day I would go on to Otavalo, where, I was told, the Indians set up on Saturdays a most colorful market. I was a bit tardy, but a Rumanian artist, to whom the cooperative Mr. Chiriboga of Panagra had introduced me, had stalled the vehicle's departure from Quito until I caught up.

He sat with the driver—always a choice spot—while with every left swerve of the lumbering bus I was smashed against the window by the heavy, swaying body of an Indian woman, who had fallen soundly asleep with the first shift of gears. Blockaded by her bundles it was impossible to reach down and scratch the lumps that were beginning to balloon on my legs from the flea bites. "Señora," I thought again and again in anguish, "surely you have napped long enough!"

Yet I have seldom been more rapturous on a ride, for the Ecuadorian Indians are among the world's most picturesque people. Clusters of them—uniformly dressed in either deep blue or maroon knee-length wool ponchos, white pedal pushers, and broad-brimmed felt hats—unconsciously formed choreographic patterns in the forest as we passed. Even the pigs they urged along the winding mountain road seemed uncommonly beautiful.

By the time we arrived in Ibarra, the muscles in my calves had lost their elasticity, and the Rumanian, impatient with my painful, lagging steps, strode hastily ahead that he might see the colonial architecture before nightfall. No woman is at her best looking tortured. During dinner he announced that he would take the 3:00 A.M. bus to Otavalo, the better to sketch the Indians assembling at dawn; probably I should depart a couple of hours later.

So at four-thirty in the morning I gathered my duffel bag and waning courage, paid off the night clerk, and set out for the *zócalo*. My heart pitched when I noted in the moonlight a sinister, solitary Indian, who appeared to be following me. Well, he had to be following me; there weren't any other girls strolling about the square at that hour. I quickened my pace, thinking if he gets really close, I'll take refuge in the cathedral. Fortunately, the Catholic world is full of such sanctuaries.

I made it to the bus before he did and promptly forgot the pursuit, if it was one, in the commotion at the stand. Like New Yorkers besieging subways during rush hours, the Indians ahead and behind me clawed their way into the conveyance. A tiny woman carrying a huge bundle lost her footing and fell flat against the steep steps, which did not deter a big man from using her as a ladder. She let out a shriek and, when she had pulled herself together, gave him a good piece of her mind, and he deserved it.

For an hour we pumped up and down the corrugated road. My camera shook off a screw, and I was glad I had not eaten. When the bus halted at Otavalo, the passengers poured out. The Indians were clustered nearby as I stumbled off the high bottom step and took a belly flop into the mud—a comedy turn that convulsed them. A raisin-eyed Indian boy helped me up, slung the strap of my flight bag over his shoulder, and said to me in Spanish that he would be my guide. He told me his name was Manuel Dias and that he had eight years. I blotted up as much of the mud as I could with a tissue, smiled at the Indians to show that I, too, liked a good laugh, and, heigh-ho, we were off to the fair.

One may make tracks in a gondola, rickshaw, trishaw, samlor, pony cart, shikara, droshky, buggy carriage, motor scooter, jeep, junk, gig, or jitney—and if using the last in New Delhi, watch out for your head: on a sudden bounce, it can be cracked by the iron bars on the roof. More simply, one may go places by bicycle—

overwhelmingly the most popular mode of transport in Bermuda, Amsterdam, and Copenhagen, where, last time I took a census, there were one million people and six hundred thousand bikes. Sweethearts ride side by side, their arms around each other's shoulders, and whole families pedal as one—father with baby in a basket up front, his hand stretched out to steady a little girl on a little girl's wheel alongside him, mother and grandmother spinning tandem in back. Stiff-spined executives clenching stern pipes in their teeth ride swiftly past, seemingly oblivious, if not of their black briefcases, of their rapidly rotating legs. For a few kroner a day you can rent your own bicycle in Denmark; the hall porter or local tourist association will arrange it. As undoubtedly would their counterparts in many of the countries represented in the International Youth Hostel Federation, which also offers tips on hosteling independently abroad.

But the best way to savor the essence of a place is by walking. One can find one's way with a detailed city map purchased from a newsstand (those provided at hotels usually omit many streets) and by asking directions en route. Merely pausing to look at a map will frequently attract assistance—particularly from students studying English.

Concentrating, as is typical, on the cathedrals and museums, none of the conducted tours that I took in Seville, for example, revealed the city's character as vividly as an afternoon's stroll with a young Spaniard, who, noting my bewildered expression, had asked if I were lost. And though I usually am, being lost is enlightening. There's nothing like a confused ramble along the back canals of Venice to give one a perspective on the *palazzos*. One gets a different view of Paris ambling about Place Pigalle with the sub-bourgeoisie and pausing at a clearing to watch a shill bet the crowd that a bare-torsoed carnival strong man can't break out of the heavy chains in which he appears locked.

Of course, a woman can wander too far from the hub: I witlessly did in a search for Paris's big produce market, Les Halles. Coming upon a street sign reading RUE ST.-DENIS, I said to myself, "Now, that rings a bell," and walked happily along it while I raked my memory why. In a minute I was in the very capital of Gomorrah— a shiny-nosed, earnest American confronted with a line-up of trollops invitingly arched against a wall. Ruffians lunged at me and hissed in my ear—in many lands the mating call of the male animal —and, far from displaying any heart of gold, the girls glowered over my invasion. I panicked. Running catercorner across the nearest intersection, I collided with a truck from Les Halles. There was nothing loving in the lip I got from the driver.

8

At Sea with the Language

"Don't you have a language problem?" people are always asking a monolinguist like me. Sure I do—sometimes. "Of course," they complacently remark, "English is spoken everywhere"—at best a half-truth. In areas where Britain has ruled, it is indeed the alternate tongue, at least among educated people. English is spoken by a great many Europeans; it is being widely studied in the Soviet Union, Japan, and elsewhere. If one sticks to hotels and shops catering largely to American tourists, there is little difficulty. However, as is immediately apparent when you strike out into areas off the beaten path, even in Western Europe, English has a way to go before becoming globally pervasive.

I admire people who have the perseverance in adulthood to master a foreign language. I haven't, although I've made sporadic attempts. I took sixty dollars' worth of French at the New School, but in Intermediate Conversation the class started discussing Rimbaud and Baudelaire, and I can't cope with those fellows in advanced English. So I studied with an album of Living Language records, and graded myself A plus on the final examination. I'm great with theory, but, like so many of my compatriots, have a tin ear.

Trouble is, even with strenuous effort it is virtually impossible for mature American vocal chords to gargle a Parisian *r*, hawk an Arabic *h*, or strangle a German umlaut. Then there's all that nonsense of investing inanimate objects with sex. It's as booby-trapped as if English were pitted with whom's. Not that my backwardness

138   *Maiden Voyages*

about gender makes me feel too bad; throughout Asia I have been addressed as "sir."

One's always being told how endearing it is to foreigners if you say at least a few phrases in their own language. And I have observed, resentfully, the killings made by girls with foreign accents— particularly French, Austrian, and Oriental. Only once have I been in that enviable situation. Having forgotten most of the Spanish I studied at school, I spent the entire summer before I went to Spain in assiduous review—again with Living Language discs (Crown). (Long ago, in a burst of optimism I obtained them in French, Spanish, German, Italian, Portuguese, and Russian.)

Then, to guarantee that I'd have to speak Spanish, I stayed at a small neighborhood hotel in Barcelona. The waiter seemed enchanted when I ordered the paella, but waiters are always looking for a little gigoloing on the side, so I depreciated his reaction. When I asked a policeman for directions, an expression of tenderness crossed *his* face. It was the same with everyone I approached. Puzzled, I asked myself, "So what's making *me* Miss Rheingold all of a sudden?" Then it dawned on me: I had one of those accents. For three weeks you couldn't shut me up.

That, however, was my only triumph. The same enunciation was unintelligible in Peru, Argentina, and Chile. Pothibly becauth they found my Cathtilian acthent a thuperannuated bore.

The year that I went to Sicily, Italy, and the Dalmatian Coast, I studied Italian recordings for six months before breakfast, thinking it would be an all-purpose tongue for lands bordering the Adriatic. Tuned up loudly so I could parrot it in the bathroom, the talking machine progressed from *Al-FRAY-do, Ahn-TOE-nio, CARRR-lo* to *"Dovè un buon ristorante?"* (an excellent question; one's always looking for a good restaurant). I also learned superfluous comments like *"Compiro ventiquattro anni in settembre"* (I will be twenty-four in September).

However, the meaty dialogue about the eccentricities of the American drug-STORE—where *"Lei può anche ordinare una bistecca"* (you can even order a beefsteak)—widened my social orbit. For, like an aging Romeo beneath my balcony, each morning the gentleman in 2-D stood, refuse in hand before the incinerator, mooning about the Dark Lady in 3-B, who, like him, had reached that lesson in Living Language Italian, the cadences of which were clearly audible in the stairwell.

"I'll buy you lunch at Alfredo's in Roma," he dashingly promised me. "Dinner," I said. "Lunch." "*Dinner.*" And many *bisteccas* later he did.

Although I wish I were brighter about them, I don't let my ineptitude with languages deter me from traveling where I wish, and neither should anyone else capable of pointing to a map and sounding out the phonetics in a phrase book. I never go anyplace without one—plus a small dictionary, because phrase books have their limitations, even inaccuracies. Under any circumstances, unless you can understand the answers, there isn't much use in being able to ask the questions. The advantages, too, of having at hand "easy dialogue" like the following from a Portuguese manual are debatable: "What figure is that, Papa?" "That is a centaur, my son! A creature half horse and half man." "Then where does it sleep? In a bed or in a stable?"

The main thing is to try to remember the values a particular language gives to consonants and vowels. In times of confusion—not to say ignorance—I have a regrettable tendency to mouth foreign words as if they were English, thus rendering myself incomprehensible. Yet through some alchemy, Sally, by recourse to any Latin-root word that comes to her quick mind, makes herself understood wherever Romance languages are spoken. In accents pure Pennsylvania, allotting each clearly enunciated syllable equal stress, she asked for soap in Granada: "Por fa-vor, key-air-o sal-a-vay la vis-ah-go"—and nobody spat in her face. Nor was breaking a sandal strap in rural Italy any disaster for the contagiously amiable Sally, who simply stated to a passer-by, "Key-air-o ash-eh-tay san-dahl-ay as necessary-o com-prar las no-vee-tas." Within an hour she was shod to order *à la* Capri. Whereas others are stricken dumb by fear of mispronunciation, Sally communicates.

It is, however, important to learn how to pronounce correctly the names of foreign dishes, one's hotel, and, I discovered in Iran, the street that it's on.

Hailing a cab, I asked to be taken to the Teheran Palace near Avenue Pahlavi. I knew it wasn't far, but I was too bushed to walk any more. We drove and drove, and eventually I observed that we seemed to be in the vicinity of the airport. "No, no," I said, "Avenue Pahlavi." The driver stopped by a curb and consulted a countryman, who stuck his head into the window. I repeated the address. The man reflected a moment. "Oh," he said, "Pah-la-VEE!"

It is also wise to bear in mind that idioms emerge as gibberish when literally translated into another tongue. At Angkor the driver of my samlor (a bicycle-drawn carriage) spoke only Cambodian and French. At a loss how to ask him to pick me up the next morning, I rendered the Spanish *mañana por la mañana*, into *demain pour le demain*. Although until then the young man had been exceedingly reserved, he burst into delighted laughter, revealing a mouthful of teeth blackened with betelnut. Indeed, he appeared entertained for the next several hours. When he deposited me at my hotel, his mirth again bubbled up. "I . . . weesh . . . you . . . vairy . . . good luck!" he said, shaking my hand vigorously. Blunders are unimportant if they don't hurt anybody's feelings.

There are those who would vote for German, but I hold that French is the most useful language to know abroad. Surely few would quarrel that *the* important phrases for women travelers are: "Where is the ladies' room, please?" (or the usual, less prissy version thereof). "Please, is there a porter here?" "Pardon me." "Thank you." "Waiter." "The bill, please." "Good morning." "Good afternoon." "Good evening." In Israel *shalom* takes care of the last three, while—still kind to the memory—*shalom, shalom!* serves for "Get lost!"

Although its vocabulary is still meager, there is a universal tongue unrelated to Esperanto. Besides scientific terms, it includes such useful internationally understood words as *aeropórt, autó, bar, cigarétte, Coca-Cola, cocktaíl, photó, hotél/otél, okáy/hokáy, pardón, taxí, toilét,* and *traveler's checks.* Add for comment the words *good* (meaning it's interesting or nice) or *véry good* (it's great), and you will do hokay. At any rate, it will be simpler than planning as far ahead as one has to with sentences in languages like German.

People the world over use the word or words for "please" much more often than we do. Even "thank you" is frequently acknowledged with "please!" Which I imagine is meant as an abbreviation for "please don't mention it"—a phrase that practically all foreigners who have studied English employ where we would say, "You're welcome."

Tongue-tied in their language, I have as a stranger experienced innumerable expressions of friendship from the inhabitants of foreign countries through which I was traveling. Many times from the simplest people.

One occurred during a couple of hours in a cavernous garage in Nazaré. I had spent the afternoon dawdling along the ocean front of this most vivid Portuguese port, watching the fishermen bring in their catch. Swarthy descendants of Phoenician sailors, they are fierce-looking men who wear stocking caps with long tassels, plaid shirts and trousers. The multi-petticoated women, barefoot like them and the ragged children, not only balance large jugs on their heads but oil- and ashcans as well. At dusk they hurry along with tubs of fish on their pates and an eel or two swinging over their wrists.

Because the restaurant that had been recommended was busy with flies, I decided not to eat dinner but to go directly to the depot even though my bus was not departing from there until 9:45. I was a little nervous, too, about the fishwives, who, my drab cotton dress notwithstanding, had jeered at me on the beach and mimicked, hand on hip, what seemed to them my sashaying. I just have rubbery ankles.

When I had done all the powdering I could in *o toalete de senhoras*, I sat down on a long bench in the yawning garage, looking to a young Portuguese woman at the other end for protection from possible annoyance by the tattered, barefoot mechanics. To my dismay, she was soon surrounded by five of them—as was I when she left. There were no other passengers about.

Taking the lead, a long, lean, snaggle-toothed man started asking me questions, but I opened my phrase book and recited, "Eh-oo FAH-loh saw eeen-GLAYSS." Whereupon he sat down beside me, and with the greatest patience tried to teach me Portuguese. Slowly, slowly, and with numerous graphic gestures, he told me (and, curiously, I was able to understand him) that conditions were very bad for the poor people in Portugal, and many Nazarens had gone to "Californy." A kinsman of his who went there made one million escudos! When he returned to Nazaré he was wearing a fine cravat and—the garageman said, pulling me to my feet and taking my arm—strutted proudly with his lady, like this, up and down the street. The other fellows nodded their heads vigorously in support of his tale of wonders achieved in Californy.

Although they smelled a bit gamey, they were all nice chaps, and when I boarded my bus we exchanged Portuguese and American cigarettes as emblem of our friendship. They waved and waved as the motor coach pulled out of the huge, grim garage.

On other occasions I have been surprised in remote regions to find that seemingly preoccupied people have been watching out for me. In a southern Indian village, the only English-speaking person at an arid junction, I was pacing about forlornly, worried that I would make the wrong bus connection to Mahabalipuram (because who can pronounce it accented on the second syllable?), when suddenly half the peasants in the vicinity rushed over to me and excitedly pointed to the approaching vehicle I was supposed to take.

In contrast, even though I was waiting in the airport at Lahore without certainty that a "no-show" would permit me to fly on to Peshawar, I was thoroughly enjoying the panorama of Arabian Nights turbans, robes, and crook-toed sandals. And when the plane to Rawalpindi and Peshawar was announced, I sat on impassively. However, a short, rotund Pakistani sage with an imposing white beard evidently thought I was woolgathering. "Your flight," he said tersely. I tried to explain that there wasn't any space for me on it, but he did not understand. Just then the ticket agent beckoned and said, "Hurry, hurry! The plane is leaving." I got to it so tardily the steward had to shove me in through the baggage compartment.

Many, many times there is rapport without speech, a sense of mutual understanding that requires no words. I found the epitome of this in Japan.

Since I'm obviously not what even a prejudiced parent would call a quick study with a foreign phrase, I decided to forgo the drudgery of echoing a set of Japanese language records. After all, nobody has understood a single word I've ever hazarded in Serbo-Croatian, Hindi, or Greek. Moreover, the phrase book I toted in-

spired cheer; in general, vowels appeared to alternate with consonants with a reliable precision, and one was advised that the former
maintain inflexible Latin values. I didn't take too seriously the caution that there is scant syllabic stress in Japanese, and confined my
frets to the paucity of memory-building English associations—
biiru, uisukii, and *burandē* notwithstanding.

However, I don't wish to appear too self-effacing. Because I
managed to become fluent with *ohayo,* the impolite form for
"good morning"; *yen?*—"how much?"; *moshi-moshi* or *mosh-mosh*
(pronounced, with an utter lack of respect for Latin values,
"mushy-mushy" and "mush-mush"), which on the telephone is
equivalent to "hello"; *hai,* meaning "yes," and that marvelously
onomatopoetic *aiie!*—"merciful Buddha, no!"

I had long been acquainted with tempura and sukiyaki, so the
problem of nourishment didn't trouble me: I felt that at worst I
could subsist on them. Nevertheless my confidence was badly
shaken in a resort, or national park, north of Sendai called Matsushima. I could have eaten at the Matsushima Park Hotel, an ex-
pansive establishment with pagoda roofing and large, bosomy bay
windows, but the white linen, eyelet-embroidered slipcovers and
absence of other guests made it a real Meiji mausoleum. Besides,
the food was pure roadside American. Instead, I slipped into a
modest village café—well past noon to avoid slurs about my table
manners, since at the time I was still knitting and purling the
chopsticks, and there was quite a bit of droppage.

After perusing the menu, printed entirely in Japanese, I
reached a decision. "Sukiyaki," I said. "Aiie," responded the waitress. "Ah, well," I said amenably, "tempura." "TEHM-pur-uh,"
she corrected me. I shrugged, adding, "And *cha,* please." "*O-cha,*"
she contradicted, getting tedious. Perhaps it's just as well that I
remained serene, because I later learned that *o-cha* is the bowl of
green-tinted hot water served with a sweetmeat the moment one
arrives at an inn, average restaurant, or any kind of appointment,
while *koh-cha* is black tea, and *koi-cha* is the powdered ceremonial
tea that is whipped with a coarse-haired, balding shaving brush into
the consistency and color of pea soup.

Trains in Japan usually have dining cars, but the stewards pretend to Westerners that they serve only Yankee food. I found it

both piquant and less pauperizing to scamper after the Japanese, who, heeding an unintelligible public-address announcement, would take advantage of a three- or four-minute station break at mealtimes to rush to the platform newsstand, purchase a small, plywood-boxed luncheon, then dash back to their seats. In this way, for forty cents I was introduced to a lapful of lovely regional dishes: broiled eel, rice decorated with caraway seed and a pickled cherry, bean curd, custard, rouged ginger slivers, a medley of marinated and fresh vegetables, with a vial of the ubiquitous *shoyu* sauce. Crowning the spread was a solitary shrimp. Teams of slacks-clad girls trundled tea and soft-drink carts through the train to assuage the subsequent thirst, and shortly thereafter an attendant swept from under the seats the remains of the repast. People are always sweeping in Japan—on the streets, in the parks, stations, and buses; one becomes very tidy about disposing of the butts of Peace and Hope cigarettes, two brands dispensed by the sanguine Japanese.

Lest I give the impression of being anti-Caucasian, may I credit a venturesome Australian with having advised me, en route to Nikko's spectacular shrines, not to miss the paddy fields and plumed trees in Aso National Park in Kyushu. I had not planned to spend more than one night on the island, at the conclusion of the rather overtouted Inland Sea voyage, since the attractions of its terminus, Beppu, are principally hot springs and mud, and I'm too healthy for that kind of loafing.

Instead I entrained for Mount Aso, one of Nippon's active volcanoes. It wasn't the Australian's fault that we caught the tail end of a Nagasaki tempest, and I was swung by cable car over a teeming canyon, ultimately to weep with disappointment at the sight of a quenched, soaking wet crater.

It was cozier at the inn, where in semi-Western style I was provided with a small table and two chairs on a balcony overlooking a fragile bridge and water wheel nestled in the cool green and gray of the rock garden. In fact, concern there for one's creature comforts knew no bounds, for sliding panels revealed a pair of closets equipped respectively with American plumbing and floor-level Japanese *benjo*—enough to drive a burgeoning Orientalist like me into a fidget of indecision.

However, sensitivity is not unusual in Japan. There was, for instance, that modest hostelry in the city of Nagoya run by a pair of plump, merry sisters and a bent old man, who scurried fore and aft, bowing to his knees and smiling. Right after four o'clock *o-cha*, they figured I must be wanting my bath, but when I scribbled on a scratch-pad "10:00 P.M.," only the briefest of glances were exchanged—even though only swine have dinner without prior submersion in blistering water. Perhaps they realized that this was my crafty puritan way of avoiding community in a coed tub.

When I indicated by phrase No. 320 that I should like a cab, they summoned a lad of fourteen, who drove me in the family car to the cloisonné district. I wasn't concerned about finding my way back, because taxis are plentiful in Japanese cities, and one can choose between handsome sedans with lace curtains or less prepossessing bantams charging ten yen less for the first mile and a quarter. As it happened, I stood so long on the wrong corner trying to flag one that a twenty-year-old, taking me perhaps for the Statue of Liberty, came over and said, "Please, may I have English conversation with you?" The large number of students now studying the language have been instructed never to shirk an opportunity to be of assistance to Americans—which can be a boon to one incapable of Japanese conversation.

That's in the cities. Miming does it in rural areas like Gora, a village located in Hakone National Park on the legendary Tokaido Road, about an hour's ride southwest from Tokyo. Gorakadan, my *ryokan*, or inn, was exquisite—set high in the mountains near Fujiyama and with a view so exciting I almost forgot to kick off my sneakers before entering the inn's portals. (The eight million gods of Shinto help you if you step over the threshold with your shoes on; from the stricken looks I got the couple of times I so blundered, I gathered that it means *endless* purification.)

It was at Gora—early in the trip—that my love of Japan had its birth. Exhilarated by an excellent night's sleep on the floor pad and a hearty breakfast of cold ham and eggs—efficiently prepared the previous evening—I had set forth immediately thereafter for Mount Fuji. But by one o'clock, after three changes of bus, I had climbed only to what appeared on my tourist map to be the outskirts of the celebrated cone. Now I well knew that Orientals giggle in times of stress, but when I pointed to the picture of Fuji on the chart, the bus attendants went into a convulsion of merriment such as I haven't experienced since the age of fourteen. Trying to control himself, one explained with sign language that it would take nine or ten hours to get there; I could only hope to reach Lake Kawaguchi—about a third of the way.

It occurred to me when I arrived at the lake that, inasmuch as the journey had already consumed more than six hours, I probably ought to hurry home. Not a chance. I'd missed the last return motor coach. Well, I've always found that there's nothing like a resolutely optimistic attitude. "Train? Railroad?" I parried at the ticket window. "No train." "Yes, yes," I persisted. Finally, a hovering hack driver recalled a nearby hamlet named Matsuda, which, although it did not appear on the map, was indeed a railroad junction.

The three-hour bus ride over slippery mountain roads to Matsuda was enlivened by the pranks of four teen-agers and the scarcely older driver, who kept turning back to me—the only adult present—for approval of their song fest. I clapped for an exuberant repertoire of falsetto folk tunes, along with "The Volga Boatman" and "Ol' Man River" in Japanese. At length, sadly I had to say, "Sayonara." The driver said, "Take heet heasy." It was nearly 9:00 P.M. when I got back to Gora, weary but not famished, thanks to the fish skins filled with cold rice shared by my peppy companions.

The inn's entire staff was on the veranda, looking anxious. Where was the American? One kimono-clad servant peeled off my shoes; another stuffed my feet into scuffs. Two women hustled me to my quarters, where a Japanese smorgasbord was wilting on the table six inches above the floor. The first started filling the square sunken tub. With a compassionate expression, the second lifted an imaginary jigger to her lips and made a quick bottoms-up gesture: did I, after my ordeal, want a drink? *Did* I? *Hai, hai!* A nice warm sake.

We were communicating.

When communicating with you, your family and friends should try to estimate the time it takes airmail from the United States to reach various parts of the world and post their letters accord-

ingly. Mail may be addressed to you in care of the hotels at which
you know you will be stopping, marked "Please hold until arrival
(date)." If in doubt about where you will be staying, you may have
mail addressed to you in care of American Express, but check first
to be sure they have offices in all the cities on your itinerary. Or,
marked "Poste Restante" (General Delivery), letters may be sent to
you at the local post office, where they will usually be held a couple
of weeks. From my experience, collecting such correspondence is
sometimes irritatingly time-consuming.

Aerogram letter forms that fold up like envelopes are available at
post offices for eleven cents each, which can be a worth-while saving.

When leaving a hotel, give the hall porter or concierge your for-
warding address.

And, just to be on the safe side, stick airmail stamps to envelopes
and cards yourself—or watch the clerk put them on. Too many
times, friends to whom I've sent "airmail" notes have received
them months later.

After you've returned home, you will have your own transoceanic
mail to delight in. But Maggie is the maid with the most. For
several months preceding her vacation she vocalized Italian from
an antiquated set of borrowed Linguaphone records, then flew to
Castiglione della Pescaia. The only American visiting this hamlet
on the Tyrrhenian Sea, she was warmly taken up by townspeople,
who roared with affectionate laughter at her rococo language
("Not since Dante has anyone used expressions like 'Alak'!").

With Alfio she rattled in a truck every morning to Siena, where
he delivered his baskets of tomatoes, artichokes, and eggplants.
And at the Bar Temperani, the crossroads café where she met
him, she was also introduced to Ivetta, a Sophia Loren who goes to
sea daily in her sailboat, *Ivan Ilio,* to take supplies to lifers on the
island of prisoners near Elba. Like the other girls, in the evenings
Ivetta and Maggie would link arms and join the village promenade,
flirting for invitations to the dance.

Not one to slight the aristocracy, Maggie also chatted on the
beach with the *crème de la crème* of Castiglione della Pescaia—
l'Ingegnere and Signora Raspi, who, amused by the engaging
Americana, took her into the bosom of their family. Nor did she

lose time with a gentleman whom she excitedly ranked a general, he was that laden with badges and ribbons. Although Signor Franco turned out to be but a colonel, subsequently he gave her the grand tour of Piacenza in his Alfa Romeo.

Now Maggie can hardly keep up with her Italian correspondence.

9

P's and Q's in Aix

None of us likes to be thought boorish, yet as guests of foreign countries we are from time to time guilty of *faux pas* owing to ignorance of their conventions and values. To beacon the p's and q's and pitfalls in Aix, et al., I asked officials of all nations in which we are permitted to travel, "What, in terms of your own culture, are the most objectionable social blunders committed by Americans who visit your country?" Happily, most voiced no complaint. Occasional answers, however, were astonishing, citing acts that are beyond censure in the States. Others revealed shocking infractions of taste.

Although it is unlikely that women could be accused of using obscene language to waiters, attendants at public institutions, or government servants—for which the Turkish respondent criticized Americans—his injunction that "tourists in mosques should be well covered, as in a Catholic church" cannot be taken too seriously. "No low-cut garments are suitable. People should take their shoes off and talk in whispers." Whispers. Perhaps British, Australian, and South African women are reproached, as are we, for penetrating voices, for exclaiming and chatting loudly in public places, particularly museums and houses of worship. If puzzled, those not of the faith may take their cues from the guide; if they don't have one, they should be as inconspicuous as possible and not wander near an altar during a service, or converse. In a Protestant church it is courteous to rise or sit in unison with the congregation, but one need not there or elsewhere mimic any other manifestation of devotion.

For purposes of cleanliness, it is traditional to slip canvas coverings over one's shoes, or to remove shoes and occasionally stockings before entering Buddhist, Shinto, and Hindu holy places, as well as mosques and, in the Middle East, even Eastern Orthodox churches. Since, as a matter of religious taboo, few synagogues contain works of art, they are rarely on tour itineraries—in marked contrast to other houses of worship, which throughout history have been the repositories of cultural treasures. Were one, however, to go to a Yemenite synagogue in Israel to hear the pristine liturgical chants, which, like the Gregorian, have their origins in Ur of the Chaldees, she would have to sit in a section of the synagogue segregated from the men.

When traveling, it's easy to forget that exotic ceremonies and spectacles are regarded by the participants and their countrymen with reverence. "The nation, religion, and His Majesty the King are sacred to the Thai people," the Tourist Organization of Thailand emphasized in response to my questionnaire.

"Overcasualness in attitude leads to many misunderstandings," commented the French government representative. "One of the worst is the brash assumption by Americans that money buys everything, even respect. An American assumption that 'anything goes'—morally—in Paris, for instance, is very mistaken and often resented by the French."

Ireland is probably not the only country to be piqued by Americans who blatantly contrast Irish customs unfavorably with practices in the U.S., and to be annoyed by visitors who are paranoid about being overcharged. The Irish—and without doubt other nations in similar circumstances—resent being ticked off for "not effecting improvements which available resources of money and population make impossible or uneconomical." Like others with whom tourism is not a big industry, they wish Americans did not expect standards of service equal to those in resort areas.

It is shameful that even a few of us should have to be told not to drop litter—chewing gum, cigarette butts, paper—on streets and in public buildings, let alone holy places. Yet this complaint was expressed more than once by respondents to the query.

"Tactless ignoramus!" I labeled a European with whom I was having cocktails in Florence when he—as have others—remarked matter-of-factly, "Of course, there is no culture in the United States." With considerable heat I enlightened him—quite forgetting my amusement over what I regarded the hypersensitivity of an Arab who once asked me, "Did you realize before coming here that Egypt is a civilized place?" Perhaps many had made it obvious they hadn't.

"Americans usually come into Yugoslavia unprepared," reported a spokesman for that country. They have heard of its scenic beauty, he said, but generally have scant knowledge about its political, social, and cultural background. "They are surprised that Yugoslavia is as civilized as any other European nation." It's the surprise that ruffles them, as it would us.

"Brazilians," commented their consulate, "are very tolerant of anyone's mistakes—including our own. But we don't like to be patronized, and we wish Americans would try to pronounce our names correctly. It irritates us when it is assumed that we speak Spanish and that Buenos Aires is our capital. We speak Portuguese and our capital is Brasília."

"As in most countries," the Mexican Government Tourist Department stated, "Americans offend most when they are loud, boastful about their financial superiority and condescending to the 'natives.' These qualities are probably more offensive to Mexicans than to the residents of almost any other foreign country, since a violent and tragic history has made them a very proud people, and particularly since a part of that history was a war with the United States which lost for Mexico huge land areas—Texas, Arizona, New Mexico, Nevada, California, and parts of adjacent states."

Citizens of former colonial dependencies are particularly sensitive to an arrogant manner and any indication, however unintentional, of disrespect. "We are a humble people. We don't like, naturally, imposition by others." This, poignantly, from a Kenyan official, whose words would find many echoes among peoples struggling for stature as a nation.

"Do not put your hands on your waist or in your pockets when you are talking with somebody, particularly an older person," advised the Consulate of Indonesia. In that country, where dark-skinned people used to have to get off the streets to let a white man pass by—and Carlos P. Romulo was no exception when many years ago he visited there—dignity is held dear. Yet their public servants, as well as the Indians', who have been in a similar position, can be exceedingly kind. Just be careful not to summon even a busboy with "Boy!" You may, however, snap your fingers or clap your hands for attention.

"Excuse me, sir," I said nervously to the man in charge of Garuda's affairs at the airport in Djakarta, "could you tell me, please, where I might find a porter?" I was worried about leaving my suitcases unguarded at the entrance to the airport but couldn't carry them *and* a beautiful but clumsy wooden goddess I'd picked up in Bali. Much as he likely cherished the prestige of his white-collar position, he rushed out and carried in the baggage for me.

There are countries, among them the Soviet Union and Mexico, where local mores frown on women who smoke on the streets, drink copiously uncloseted, and wear creeping short skirts. But in Denmark a girl may puff on cigars in public with impunity. Danish women do.

With a few exceptions, the manners of Western Europeans closely parallel ours. Nevertheless, they do not like to be called by their first names on short acquaintance, and lay great store on being addressed by their titles, professional or scholastic. In turn they accord all unwed women of a marriageable age an honorary Mme. —in the same spirit with which females to the age of ninety are addressed in the States as "young lady."

Like Moslem males, Europeans of both sexes shake hands a great deal—much more than is customary with women in America. If the Swiss admit to being "busy handshakers," the Norwegians are "mighty handshakers." "Never forget to shake hands with the ladies, too," cautions the Norwegian National Tourist Office. "Before you leave for Norway, it might be an idea to strengthen your greeting mechanism by shaking excessively the paws of your family, office pals, creditors, debtors, and anybody else you meet." Before going anywhere, women whose clasp has the muscle of macaroni might well heed the advice.

A lady, of course, extends her hand first to the gentleman she is greeting or to whom she is being introduced. She should, however, permit the prelate of any religion to make the first move. Traditionally, if a married Eastern Orthodox priest extends his hand, she should kiss the back of it rather than his ring, as one would with a Roman Catholic bishop, and say, "Bless the Lord." But if the Orthodox priest is unmarried, the greeting is "May God assist you." Nowadays many Eastern Orthodox priests, following the custom of Catholic, Protestant and Jewish clergymen, are simply offering their hands to shake.

Europeans usually terminate an impersonal grip with a quick, downward jerk. There is, though, what Amy Vanderbilt describes in her *Complete Book of Etiquette* (Doubleday) as "the very Continental style—reserved for women—which, though not a hand kiss exactly, is cozy and overlong, ending in an intimate little squeeze." It is incorrect for a man to kiss the hand of an unmarried woman unless she is "of a certain age"—which is not precisely complimentary any way that you look at it. What she does if he touches her palm or kisses it, I do not know; it is an even worse insult and probably deserves a punch in the nose. Men sometimes take terrible advantage of a girl's hand.

In Asia many peoples greet each other by raising to their chins their palms pressed together as if in prayer, and bowing their heads. Indeed, I was told by a Thai that the gesture means, "I pray to you, I admire you so much." Japanese, however, clasp their right hand over the left at the waist and bow, the arc of the spine being governed by the prestige of the persons involved. Americans should make at least a slight bow; a nod of the head is insufficient response. However, most nationals one is likely to meet socially in those countries will have had contact with Western manners and shake hands, thereby simplifying etiquette for the self-conscious.

At times it is difficult to tell who has had contact with Westerners and who not. From force of habit, I thrust out my hand to an Indian woman to whom I was being introduced in Banaras, and she recoiled—then quickly gave me instead her prayerful greeting. "Oh," another Indian woman said, dismissing the first one's revulsion over shaking hands, "it has to do with cleanliness." Which didn't comfort me either.

Few among us would realize that in Islamic lands it is offensive to eat, give, or accept something with the left hand—let alone extend it to shake hands, as we occasionally do when the right is holding a parcel or a glass. To Moslems the left is the "unclean" hand.

Even if the reasons therefor are offensive to us—it is the hand that serves bodily functions as double-ply tissue does ours, and the one to which erotic stimulation is reserved—when visiting Moslem countries one must be mindful of their customs, this among them.

A *Pocket Guide to the Middle East* (one of the excellent series put out by the United States Government, available from the Superintendent of Documents), warns GIs that "Moslems resent being touched or handled." The reverse is not necessarily true of Islamic men vis-à-vis American females. Nevertheless, one should never pat the heads of fellahin children, since that is where their souls reside—nor express admiration for them to their parents, lest the tots thereby catch the Evil Eye. The grown-ups should cross their fingers, as we do, to ward off the jinx.

If other people have their taboos, we have ours: that against urinating in public view, for example, yet this is common practice among children and men in many lands. The initial, most shocking sight to the average American woman—let alone the sort who would avert her eyes from the little Manneken Pis fountain in Brussels—is the casual use of roadside and street for relief. In France and Italy, of course, this is discouraged by the prevalence of coiled public latrines, which shield all but a gentleman's lower legs. The "pissoir," also known as the "vespasienne," has a long history. According to the *Grand Larousse Encyclopédique*, "Vespasienne (Gallicus vulgaris: *Pissotière*) was named after Titus Vespasianus, Roman Emperor (69-76 A.D.), who was first in establishing a tax on such public establishments." In much of the rest of the world a turned back may be the extent of discretion.

My first encounter in adulthood with such spontaneity was in the Valley of the Kings at Luxor, where the site of the excavations resembles nothing so much as the Badlands of South Dakota. Up and down the stairwells to the burial chambers of Tutankhamen, Seti I, and Nefertiti, I scrambled after my guide, whose stride was uninhibited by a long, flaring, bottle-green robe. Slacks would have permitted me a good deal more leverage in this pharaonic grave-hopping; however, I had been advised that trousers on women offended the modesty of Egyptians, and wore a tweed suit. Hatshepsut, the George Sand of the eighteenth dynasty, was so given to assuming false beards that she evidently put them off all masculine garb for females.

My guide—whose credentials read: "Official Dragoman No. 7 Diploma of Higher Archaeology College. Contractor for Upper & Lower Egypt. Arrangement for Camping Out in the Desert and Sailing Dahabieh on the Nile"—had a drizzly cold, and he whistled a bit when he spoke, due to a shortage of front teeth. Nevertheless, I hung on to his words as he explained the ancient world and hereafter described in the still-vivid pictographs and hieroglyphics in the crypts of the nobles, pharaohs, and queens. Spellbound and agape at the vaulted ceiling murals, I was abruptly pulled back to matters more earthy by a trickling to the rear testifying that No. 7 also suffered a demanding bladder. And thus, my own modesty offended, I fled, cheeks flaming and indignant, from the tomb of Rameses VI—a minor pharaoh, to be sure.

Subsequent exposures to impromptu relief measures have so inured me that in Peru I scarcely raised an eye lash at a fountain display by inebriated Quechuas that can only be described as spectacular. One has to adjust to other folkways, and it may be that we make too much of such matters.

No people are as demanding about plumbing as Americans—and none are as evasive about admitting that they need it. Ladies trained in the No. 1, No. 2 school, which may have been rendered obsolete by contemporary fiction, will suffer the greatest discomfort abroad before they can bring themselves to utter the word "toilet." Particularly to a strange man. Far from emancipated myself from such subterfuge, not long ago I asked an Indian with whom I was picnicking in the Mogul Gardens if there were a ladies' room in the vicinity; it was getting quite warm, I explained, and I wanted to take off the sweater beneath my cotton tunic. To my frustration, he led me to a room that was private, but no privy. Desperation ninety minutes later made me explicit.

Ask for "the little girls' room," and in many parts of the world you would accurately enough be shown the gutter; while the nearest thing to the "johnny" or "john" is the "Wanita" in Indonesia. In numerous countries a bathroom contains a tub but no toilet, which it is only civilized to station in a separate cubicle or "water closet." Pronounced "double-you-see," w.c. is a term widely used in Europe and lands that have been under Britain, as, to a lesser extent, is "the facilities." In areas influenced by the French, "les toilettes" ("lay twa-*lett*") will get you to your goal. But few peoples have ever heard of a "rest room," "wash room," "powder room," or "the conveniences." And one could get pretty discommoded trying to find a "comfort station" or, indeed, a "commode."

Public accommodations for women are provided above and below ground in various foreign cities. However, it is not always considered imperative to separate the sexes; thus the occupant of the next compartment may be male, and the attendant either an old man or a crone. (He or she should be tipped a very small coin, usually worth less than a nickel.)

Watch for signs lettered DAMAS, DAMES, FRAUEN, SEÑORAS, SIGNORE, and SENHORAS—but in Portuguese-speaking lands, mind that in haste you don't read WOMEN for HOMEN, which means "men." Other common designations are TOILETTES, TOILETTEN, GABINETTI, PRIVÉ, even ABORTÉ. Overseas one rarely encounters anything as cute as HIS and HERS, ROMEO and JULIETTE, or the like. The merriest I've come upon was in a Palma de Majorca bar, which afforded a PIPPI PALACIO, an overrated chamber.

Nor do foreigners mince words in their constant concern for the traveler's comfort, about which they couldn't be more matter-of-fact. One does, of course, hear "Would you like to wash your hands?" and, in Morocco at least, intercity bus drivers inquire at periodic stops, "Do you wish to descend?" Although it is better to nod than to pretend one is above it, I confess to having responded ungraciously on occasion. At the Alhambra, nettled by what seemed to me the singleminded solicitude of the local guides ("*¿Quiere Ud. ir a los baños?*"), I snapped, "For heavens sake, I don't constantly have to go!"—and thereby missed seeing the sybaritic baths of the sultan's seraglio.

Typical were the parting words of a restaurateur in Casablanca. Holding my hand intimately, he murmured, "Madame, you are leaving?" "*Oui*," I whispered, lowering my lashes. "Madame," he continued softly, "*voulez-vous les toilettes?*"

The appointments one finds vary widely. The most primitive— the so-called Asian or Turkish toilet—can at worst be located in an open corridor or alcove behind a café kitchen, but usually it is in an outhouse equipped with a creaking door that doesn't quite close, thus providing at least some illumination if less than complete solitude. The fixtures, literally but two steps out of the jungle, are level with the ground. About sixteen inches apart, flanking a hole in the earth, are a pair of size 14 EEEEE shoeprints, onto which the patron places his or her feet straddling the cavern. In countries where people are accustomed to sitting on their haunches, there may not be the customary iron handle on the wall to steady those with Western sedentary habits. Such dirt accommodations never flush or have even squares of torn newspaper, which I have encountered in edifices as lofty as the Louvre.

Women planning to travel off the beaten path might well add knee-bending exercises to their morning calisthenics, for, outside hotels, occasionally in Europe and widely in Asia and North Africa, one finds similar fittings of porcelain set into the floor. Some flush —particularly in Europe, where the sluice has the force of a fire hydrant, and Japan, where they're more subdued and kept cleaner. If they don't flush, from time to time a tired attendant throws a bucket of water into the receptacle's well. In Ceylon it is not unusual to operate sit-down toilets too in this fashion, which is known as "water-flushing" and to be avoided.

There are sports in the evolution of plumbing. The airport at Srinagar in Kashmir provides a chamber pot covered with a square box and wooden seat. And at a Japanese inn in Nagoya the proprietress happily proclaimed, with a deep bow at a bench on the top of which was an Asian model slightly recessed, "Amelican toiret!"

The nicest to be near are in Hong Kong, where, at least in the Peninsula Hotel, they are flushed with a frothy, deodorizing detergent, doubtless inspired by the city's continual drought. However, Holland has the most exquisite. In a Dames room in Delft there's a toilet made, as is the wash basin, of delicate blue and white Delftware.

In general, foreign toilets don't have the suction of ours; many, though pretentiously noisy about it, will only flush properly if the handle or chain is pumped up and down. Plumbing is particularly prone to clogging in Asian airports, where the ladies' rooms (and, for all I know, the gents') are apt as not to be flooded. For this contingency it is wise either to keep plastic rubbers or rainboots at hand or to utilize the plane's lavatories before landing.

To avoid having to make an untimely getaway, one is also well advised to complete her primping before removing the plug from

tubs that disgorge the bath water into a trough alongside the wall
leading to a drain (sluggish) on the floor. Otherwise one may pre-
cipitously find herself ankle-deep in a pond.

In hotels abroad frequented by Americans, the bathrooms are
usually luxurious; however, showers are more often than not uncurtained and their spray utterly cockeyed. A sloping floor with a hole
at the base may theoretically swallow the water, but this engineer-
ing is less than dependable. First time I was in Beirut I ran down
to the hall porter and said, "Look, I want to take a shower, but the
plumber forgot to put in a drain." There was only the slightest
incline on the floor separating the uncurtained "stall" from the rest
of the room. Tossing his head, the concierge accompanied me to
my bathroom, where he triumphantly pointed to a minuscule drain
behind the bidet. That night I stood for ten minutes under the
delicious downpour, then stepped out of the resultant wading pool
onto a towel inside my bedroom, the floor of which was for good
reason somewhat higher. The next morning I had to brush my teeth
barefoot in the still-inundated bathroom.

At the Teheran Palace, too, there was no noticeable depression
under the shower and, again, no curtain to shield the toilet from
the slap-happy spout. However, a large, perforated drain in the
center of the floor was obviously designed to drink up the flow.
Lazily I was enjoying the hot water, the while steaming out wrinkles from a few garments, when cries of "Madame!" and staccato
knocking on the door interrupted my reverie. "One minute,
please!" I called out rather crossly. "I am taking a shower." A redundant explanation, since by that time the Persian carpet in the
bedroom was under an inch of water, which was rapidly irrigating
the hall. It never dawned on me that I had to extract the drain's
plug.

After four hours the bathroom floor was nearly dry. Two days
later the Oriental rug was still soggy.

In Banaras there was a giant-sized jug from which, Asian fashion, I might ladle water over my soaped body before rinsing under
the cool drip of a Spartan shower; a like tradition in Japan found
me, some years earlier, innocent of the custom. Enchanted with the
huge sunken tubs into which one descended a couple of steps, I
gaily tossed under the faucets packets of bubble bath that I might

luxuriate in Fujiyamas of perfumed foam. Little did I realize that in Nippon's eyes this constituted soaking in one's soil—than which there is no greater barbarity.

If American plumbing is supreme, there are still refinements to which we may aspire. Nevertheless, in sea or tub, others have been less inhibited than I about buff-bathing en masse, popular among the Japanese, Scandinavians, Turks, even certain Yugoslavs and French, to name but a few. An American blonde whom I met in Hvar, a tiny island off the Dalmatian coast, gathered quite a stag line during a single venture to a nearby islet where sun-worshipers got a kick out of tanning their bottoms. In Finnish saunas, flagellation with small birch twigs is said to be equally stimulating. On the upper Nile, fellahin leave off their rowing and chanting to dive naked from the feluccas into the muddy water for the evening's scrub—and the Balinese are always taking a splash unclothed in ponds near the highways.

To a puritan people accustomed to loin-draped or -leafed statuary, the abundance of classic, unclothed sculpture decorating Italy, for instance, comes as a shock. It's a question, though, which is the healthier or more pious—the organdy tea apron on a large crucifix in Cuzco or the erotic carving on many Hindu temples. The Nepalese theorize that lightning is a virgin and therefore will shy at striking an edifice adorned with carved copulations. In lands of the graven lingam like India and Nepal, the phallic monolith is frequently set squarely on an elliptical base representing a cross section of the yoni—and I wouldn't have known what that is had I not read the *Kama Sutra of Vatsyayana*, the classic Hindu treatise on love and social conduct.

Unless they tip the guide for the privilege, women are usually not admitted to certain rooms at Pompeii displaying lewd sculpture. Casually peddled in art shops in Denpasar are pitchers and other artifacts similarly depicting gentlemen in idealized states of emotions.

Standards differ widely on what constitutes immodest exposure. Although we fake more bosoms than any other people, we are the most undone by them bared. Japanese women, who think nothing of nude bathing with men, have for centuries worn thick obis when dressed to de-sex their contours. Orthodox Moslem women near the Mediterranean shroud their faces with heavy black crepe, and one still sees Afghanistan matrons clad in the chaderi, an accordion-pleated cloak that falls from an embroidered skull cap like a rippling teepee with latticework for the eyes. Beneath the hems peeps anything from trim, high-heeled pumps to masculine clodhoppers. In Iran its counterpart, the homely chador, a printed or black square the size of a tablecloth, is worn principally by maidens and crones. Draped over the head and pinned between the teeth, the chador is sometimes resorted to by housewives as well, to camouflage plastic curlers.

Europeans commonly dispense with bathing suits for the young. And in the tropics peasant tykes are nearly always undressed, at least below the waist while restraint is uncertain. However, in India, as token of their femininity, the hips of otherwise unclad little girls are often encircled with a delicate chain and pendant.

Public displays of affection, disapproved in some countries, are routine in others. Danish couples seldom stroll without their arms intertwined or crisscrossed about each other's backs. When I was in Copenhagen even the plainest girl had a beau, thanks to an edict denying bachelors apartments—which gives one food for reflection. In contrast, the petite Japanese brides with whom, when I visited there, Nippon abounded due to its having been an auspicious time for weddings (Japanese, that is) walked a respectful distance behind their proud new spouses. But sweethearts from eighteen to eighty nuzzle and kiss publicly in Paris in the spring—and the other seasons. Moreover, anyone who thinks the English are a dispassionate lot should take a walk at high noon through Green and Hyde parks.

Nevertheless, I saw a traditionally reserved British pater part on a plane from his nine-year-old son with a handshake and, "Well, cheerio. All the best!" Completely composed, the boy, who was flying alone from Hong Kong to Manchester, turned to me cheerfully and asked in a crisp treble, "Would you care to join me in a game of casino?"

In the airport at Rawalpindi I watched the emotional ovation given a portly Pakistani National Assemblyman, who was garlanded by one precinct captain after another with leis of red and white roses and ropes of Christmas tinsel until he looked as if he had just won the Kentucky Derby. Joining in Urdu whoops of "Hip, hip, hooray!" were Arabs in burnooses, flowing white robes and kaffiyehs; turbaned dignitaries in balloon trousers; constituents wearing skull caps elaborately embroidered with gold—boosters all, with beards, beards, beards. Buntings in the national colors—green and white—were inscribed with the local equivalent of "Welcome home, Ahmed," while blaring from the plane was an animated recording of "S'Wonderful!" You could see he was well liked.

Even average Pakistani men greet each other after a separation with hugs, first over the left shoulder, then the right, then again the left, along with much mutual clasping of knuckles and wrists. And, of course, we have all seen the kisses Mr. Khrushchev bestowed on the astronauts and Castro. The fact is, many practices that in the United States are considered effete, not to say deviant, are regarded as perfectly normal elsewhere.

Moslem males walk arm in arm or with their pinkies linked. Latin men are highly scented—in fact, they smell a lot better than the women—and they wear fancy watchbands and rings. Cuban heels and pointed-toed shoes are modish from time to time among foreign men, as are pointed fingernails and colored hair.

There are countries, such as Portugal, where the women use their heads to carry all the loads, while the men occupy theirs with cerebration. And in Germany and Austria it is mortifying to be forced to let even a brawny servant girl serve one as porter.

Elderly Oriental ladies don't bewig their balding; simple Berber girls, who never heard of penis envy, tattoo beards along their jawbones. Most European women couldn't care less about having hairy legs and armpits, but Turkish women reputedly depilate their whole bodies.

More sarongs than trousers are still worn by Asian men, many of whom carry their assets on their person in the form of earrings, jewels in their noses, and gems on three or four of their fingers. Sikhs never cut their locks, but braid them and their beards into intricate topknots, which they cover with turbans in a spectrum of hues both pastel and bold. They also beribbon their sons' plaited hair and blacken their eyelids seductively with kohl like their daughters'. This is said to screen the soot, avoid the Evil Eye, and promote the growth of lashes. I must get some.

Although false lashes are not widely used abroad, more foreign women than not crayon their eyes to look like sultry, mysterious shiners. Indeed, the large, filigreed silver pins worn by Sherpa women are fringed with tweezers, tooth- and ear-picks, tartar scraper, and kohl brush.

Toothpicks, discreetly palmed, are used at the table by realistic Asians and Continentals, and fresh fruit is attacked with a knife and a fork. After becoming so adept with the chopsticks that I could pick up a single grain of rice, I learned that shoveling it into the mouth from a raised bowl is better manners and that a little slurping of the soup properly indicates relish.

Americans accustomed to a national obsession with diets are apt to forget that in most countries there is no greater affront to hospitality than to turn down a snack, tea, or coffee, offered in offices and shops, as well as in homes. However, even if your nectar is thick Turkish coffee, in Islamic lands the third is the one for the road. And should your host start swinging the incense, the party is over.

Although most peoples drink to each other's health, the Norwegians wince at how a simple ceremony like saying "skoal" can be misunderstood. "What 'skoal' boils down to," they tell us, "is no less than a personal and intimate greeting, another way of saying, 'How nice to meet you.' It is applied—even enforced—at every formal and private meal in Norway when wine is served. The procedure is this: First find a victim. He must be younger than you, or he (or she) must represent a position inferior to yours. Then raise your glass, look firmly into his eyes and say, 'Skoal.' He will do likewise, and then you drink simultaneously. Finally you both lower your glass at breast level and nod your heads. Ceremony completed. Then look around for the next victim. Your superiors will be saying 'skoal' to you in due course."

No one, however, is permitted to say "skoal" to the hostess. She might get roaring drunk if everybody did, and, since everybody wants to, this is out of bounds. Just remember when you leave to say to the hosts, "*Takk for maten,*" which means "thanks for the food."

Though not customary in some countries—the Philippines, for instance—a note the next day to one's hostess is usually appreciated, as is a small gift. The hall porter in your hotel can arrange to pack and deliver it if you have not done so yourself. It may be flowers or fruit; however, people are almost invariably happy to receive a present that has been brought from the States—reproductions of modern art, picture postcards, American magazines, costume jewelry, long-playing records of the classics or the latest craze, paperback editions of best-sellers about which they may have heard. Where scarcities exist, gifts of food, cosmetics, and wearing apparel are liked. Our color-fast printed cotton or synthetic-fabric blouses are treasured in countries where the most exquisite embroidery is made and disdained. Many people welcome American cigarettes. It is an insult, however, to offer them to Sikhs, because they do not drink or smoke; nor do other orthodox Hindus.

In a Moslem home do not be surprised if after being introduced to the women they disappear, leaving you not too unhappily alone with the men. In Cairo I was invited to lunch in the apartment of an Egyptian whom I had met aboard ship. He presented me to his sisters, who prepared and served the meal, then absented themselves. During the afternoon several of the host's friends dropped by to chat. "Where are your sisters?" I asked him after a few hours. "Oh," he explained, "they do not know these men." In Islam camaraderie between young, unmarried men and women does not obtain; when a fellow wants to date a local girl he has to mean business.

There is a social gesture known as the "New York invitation": "Now, dear, I want you to come to dinner very soon. I will call you." And that's the end of it. In certain other areas an invitation to be valid has to be repeated many times. Rosalina A. Morales writes, in an article to Peace Corp volunteers, "A Filipino who wants a friend to dinner usually gives a 'strong' invitation to distinguish it from a *pabalat bunga* (literally, 'skin of the fruit,' *i.e.*, insincere, casual) invitation. A casual invitation is also described as 'coming from the nose'—*sa ilong nanggagaling* (meaning 'not from the heart')."

I got the *pabalat bunga* of my life in Mexico, and returned home livid because my last night in the country had been spoiled by being stood up. When I reported this to the friend who had arranged the introduction, he said, "But Pepe just meant to compliment you when he said he would very much like to take you to the fights."

"He *told* me he would pick me up at my hotel at nine o'clock," I said doggedly.

"That was just to emphasize how much he liked you."

I didn't grasp it—and for a time was soured on the entire nation.

In Kabul an Afghan insisted that I go with him to the buzkashi games rather than in a car provided by the government tourist department. He came to the hotel dining room to confirm the appointment while I was having breakfast. But that afternoon he stalled and stalled our departure until it was too late for his car to get past the police cordon, then archly suggested a tête-à-tête and tea. So I missed seeing polo played by desert tribesmen with the carcass of a calf, a once-a-year spectacle in honor of the king's birthday, and I was anything but a good sport about it.

Yet one cannot damn a whole people for the chicanery of a few; everyone knows that generalities about nationalities tend to be false. Far from being phlegmatic, the British I've met have had a quick and subtle sense of humor, and it is not true that they are unfriendly to strangers; quite the contrary. It is not true that Frenchwomen are invariably chic and individualistic in dress: last time I saw Paris, the female population was wearing either a beehive or Brigitte Bardot hairdo, and every other woman was in a short, tight skirt and long, baggy sweater. Finally—perhaps I'm not their pasta—I have yet to be pinched by an Italian.

10

Keepsakes in the Bargain

There are women so incorruptible they can return from abroad
with purchases well within the duty-free allowance—even women
who serenely eschew souvenirs, the treasures of their trips tucked in
their heads. And, of course, there are others who zero in on the
marts, their target acquisition. Most of us fall somewhere in between. It's exhilarating to make sensory tracks in exotic locales, but
it's also fun to take a day off now and then just to be a dame
tracking down a bargain. The world is full of them.

Machu Picchu, the Inca ruins high in the Andes, where, it is
said, the Virgins of the Sun fled after the Conquistadores had
sacked Cuzco, has a quality that is unbelievably mystic. It is
brought back to me every time I wear a coarse-fibered, red, black,
and brown striped Indian poncho purchased near there and made
fit for Park Avenue by my dressmaker, the ingenious Siran.

But, to tell the truth, I simply like to buy myself presents.
Mostly inexpensive bibelots and baubles—a carefully wrought
mother-of-pearl pendant from Kashikojima, humorous wooden
dolls from Hakone and Haifa, brass coasters intricately engraved
with the temple elephants of Ceylon. I love wearing the cutwork
blouse from Madeira, the scarlet pompon shawl from Madrid, the
stole from Granada with its curiously Aztec motif, the handknit
sweaters from London, even a straw coolie hat from Majorca and
the rebozos from Cuernavaca.

I was charged too much on the Piazza San Marco for the Vene-
tian lace collar, but it makes me feel like a portrait by Van Dyck

165

nonetheless. The appliquéd cocktail skirt from Salzburg is, after three alterations, still a lemon, and it breaks my heart that the Hungarian peasant blouses from Budapest have shrunk to a skimpy 28, but those hand-embroidered, hand-stitched linen blouses from Florence—all eight of them (I'm insatiable about exquisite needlework)—are holding up after more than a decade. And the Oriental fabrics with which I have been Ming-Toying are making me positively neurotic, backing and filling over whether to wear the yellow Thai silk or the green, the brocaded theatre coat created from a Japanese ceremonial obi, or simply American basic black glamorized with a gold-threaded stole from Mysore—or would the Kashmiri shawl be more effective?

Although few heads turned when I entered a smart restaurant in Teheran proudly crowned with the best quality karakul hat worn in Afghanistan and Iran by Pathan and Persian tradesmen, the identical chapeau was the cynosure of Manhattan's safer subways. And for me winter holds no shivers—not in the nutria I picked up at Jakes in Buenos Aires.

If I had to give away the Grecian sandals because I was too charitable in Athens about the size of my feet, the alpaca scuffs I bought in La Paz will be great if I ever get gout in the Arctic. And nothing else tones up my kitchen like those beaded, scarlet mules from Kowloon.

Moreover, it's comforting to know that the whole apartment is protected against bad magic by my Thai spirit house, an abode for the proprietary ghost of the premises, the Chao Ti—who needs but be propitiated each day with offerings of sweets, fruit, candles, incense sticks, and flowers, specimens of which are apt to be found on the floor. Only thing worrying me is that if the Chao Ti *chez moi* is that boozy spook who preceded me in 3-B, a can of beer might better mollify her spirit.

There are books devoted wholly to shopping abroad. Guides to individual countries also list the merchandise most popular with tourists, as do brochures and booklets available from government tourist organizations and, among other major airlines, TWA, Air France, Pan American, Finnair, Sabena, and JAL. Indeed, from Japan Air Lines one may secure a "bonus book" containing coupons that entitle the shoppers to special service, small gifts, and even discounts from the Tokyo stores listed.

The "Facts on Travel" series issued by the Institute for International Youth Affairs has suggestions for purchases in Iron Curtain countries and tips for bargains, *vide:* "An interesting place to look for souvenirs is in the Soviet 'Commission Shop'—i.e., pawnshop. Soviet citizens looking for a little extra money to make ends meet bring a fascinating variety of household objects to these Commission Shops. . . . The Commission Shops on occasion may yield interesting souvenirs from pre-Soviet days."

Most hotels also supply brochures designed to help the traveler spend her money. To pacify any bad conscience about these sprees, purchase at the same time the gifts for others that will be needed the rest of the year.

Overseas visitors do not have to pay the purchase tax in Britain, levied on many luxury and nonluxury items, if they are delivered directly to the ship or plane on which the customer will depart, or if they are mailed to an address outside the country. In Parisian stores, ask for a *carnet d'achats*, which will entitle you to discounts on merchandise paid for with traveler's or even personal checks. When purchases are sent to a ship, plane, or foreign address, the reduction may be increased.

By presenting your passport in Japan you will be exempted from the commodity taxes imposed on cameras, binoculars, pearls (above a certain price), lacquer and cloisonné ware, ivory, and wood-block prints. Price tags on articles include the tariff, so ask what the cost is without the tax.

Increasingly, international airports are setting up duty-free shops. In some, such as Shannon, bargains abound; in others the selections are limited. But all usually have good buys in liquor and French perfume—considerably better than can be secured by purchasing through the various mail-order organizations handling such products. Because the latter must ship to the States, the cost of postage considerably increases the price.

The last time I was in Hong Kong, I ordered through a purchasing agent the five fifths of liquor one could then bring back duty-free. (Now it's a quart.) As usual, I selected brandy and liqueurs—the savings on them can be as high as 66⅔ per cent—and enclosed a personal check with the mail-order form (which is available through Perera, travel agents, and in some hotel lobbies and airports). When I was leaving the airport at Tel Aviv, I saw on display for $10.50 the identical brands that had cost me $8 more.

In other than duty-free shops, the merchandise at airports is almost invariably overpriced and below the quality obtainable in town. The traveler is foolish, therefore, to acquire any unless she wants to unload one or two dollars' worth of the local money she has left over.

Bundles containing merchandise purchased at a foreign airport immediately before departure are not weighed in with one's luggage and usually can be taken into the plane's cabin—though why it is safer to fly with overloaded passengers returning to the United States than going abroad I don't know. Request that other parcels with you be shipped air freight if their weight would run up high excess-baggage charges.

Before going to a country with definite purchases in view it is wise to note down the prices prevailing at home. Be sure also to window-shop wherever you are before buying. Check how much articles cost in the boutiques of luxury hotels to inform yourself on the finest available, then watch for cut-rate counterparts in neighborhood stores. Shipping charges can sometimes double the outlay for an article—and be worth it. In Isfahan I paid $13.30 for a big brass lantern skillfully scissored into a mass of arabesqued lace. It cost another $13.30 to mail it, but the lamp would command a couple of hundred dollars in America. I just wish I had room for it in my apartment.

Department stores the world over have fixed prices. But proprietors of smaller firms are often quick to suggest a "discount" to a sluggish buyer—particularly if she is torn between two items or hesitating about purchasing several. In fact, after pricing the merchandise, always ask a shopkeeper if there is a reduction for buying in quantity. And, of course, in bazaars you haggle. Preferably accompanied by a citizen of the country who knows his way around rather than a guide, whose cut is customarily included in the cost.

Parlaying a shipboard acquaintance, I wound up being squired through the souks of the Khan el Khalili Bazaar in Cairo by five Egyptian men, all named Moustafa. They knew the alleys where you can secure the best buys in everything from carnival kewpie dolls to Mohammedan "worry beads." Also they were adept in the fine art of bargaining, so, after drinking six demitasses of syrupy coffee at as many establishments, I was able to get my Nefertiti necklace "with genuine beads from the tombs of the kings" knocked down from two pounds to ninety piasters, a saving of three dollars.

Dismiss overseas any distaste for dickering. The farther east the country, the more it is expected by shopkeepers themselves, who feel disappointed if deprived of the sport of pitting their wits against yours. Our own federal government advises the serviceman "to become a ham actor. Learn to register surprise, amazement, regret, and disinterest.

"Prices marked on merchandise in the bazaar will be at least a third too high. Don't appear too interested and don't hurry. You will be expected to browse around in a leisurely fashion. Many merchants will offer you coffee or tea and a cigarette on the house.

"When you begin your haggling, offer a third of the asking price. The merchant will appear shocked at your ridiculously low offer. You then act as though you aren't really interested and tell him you want to look around in other shops. This often brings the price down. With patience, it's possible to make your purchase at a fair price."

Although it is not a government-approved practice (here or abroad), hardened bargainers in areas with money controls further slice the price, after it has been measurably lowered, by inquiring softly—if it has not already been suggested—whether there is a discount for paying with traveler's checks or "the green." Undeclared traveler's checks bring a bigger reduction than the declared, large denominations more than small, while "the green" usually tops all. Before venturing into bazaars, where pickpockets always thrive, women have been known to tuck into a money belt or bra fifty or a hundred dollars in cash just in case they encounter a bonanza.

Purely in the interests of international market research, I pinned a few twenty-dollar bills to an undergarment in Fez. By the time I reached there, I was an authority on the cost and craftsmanship of hand-brocaded caftans in Casablanca, Meknès, and Marrakesh; hence it was with some assurance that I allowed myself to be steered by a guide into a shop in the Andalusian bazaar. The proprietor displayed the brass trays, the leather hassocks, the jewelry.

"Do you have any brocaded fabric?" I asked him. He showed me a caftan that surpassed any I'd seen. Completely hand-embroidered with twenty-two-karat gold thread, it was, however, the size of an Arab tent. The asking price was $75. "It's much too large," I said indifferently, hoping the shopkeeper hadn't spotted the glitter in my eye. "Try it on," he urged me. "It will fit you." Even my bulky wool suit was lost in the caftan. The vendor lowered the price $15 to cover the charge for alteration. "How do you clean it?" I hedged. "*Avec du pain*," he replied matter-of-factly. What else would one use to clean a solid-gold frock but some bread?

"Look," I said abruptly, "I'll give you $35 in the green for it." It was a deal.

Now that Siran has cut the caftan down to size, it could pass for a $750 garment. Which would be swell for any woman with occasion to wear such a treasure. All I can say is, if the President ever gets down to me on his invitation list, I'm ready. I might better simply take it to a taxidermist and have it stuffed.

In the meantime I'm getting more use out of the knitted fezes I purchased at Djemaa el Fna, the huge Marrakesh square, where I was wandering about taking pictures of the late afternoon's activity —the snake charmer, the acrobats, the Saharan dancers, the story-tellers—when a woman, veiled to the eyeballs, dangled before me a handful of tasseled caps with chic geometric designs. My heart turned over. They were pure boutique—well anyway, hat bar. "*Deux dirhams*," she said, holding up two fingers. "I'll take this one and this one," I said, handing her the equivalent of eighty cents. Suddenly I was box-office—surrounded by hordes of craning Arabs and Berbers, not to say multitudes of other importuning vendors. They had deserted the readers of the Koran, the tumblers, the fortunetellers, even the snake charmer, for word had spread through them like brush fire: "Hey, Mahmud, get a load of this American sucker shelling out two dirhams for caps any child could haggle down to one!"

The ideal time for good buys is during the off-season, late in the day, when merchants are eager to take in at least a little cash. Next best is to arrive at the shop early in the morning so that you may be the auspicious first customer, about whom many proprietors are superstitious.

A woman's savvy about quality is her shield against getting stung —e.g., I don't much like to talk about the Mogul brass coffeepot I snapped up in Agra for three dollars less than those in Calcutta because it didn't occur to me that its price might be linked to its leakage.

The European capitals—London, Paris, Brussels, Rome, Milan, Vienna, Copenhagen, and Madrid—are filled with fascinating shops, as are Buenos Aires, Rio (particularly for jewelry), Trinidad, Bermuda, Singapore, Tokyo, and—most dizzying of all—Hong Kong.

Not that I would undersell the Vale of Kashmir. To hear some impressionable types go on, you'd think all that Kashmir has to offer is paradise: beneath the misty Himalayas, lagoons carpeted with fluted shrubs and voluptuous lotus blossoms; a vale where, reclining like an odalisque on "full-spring" harem cushions, a lady can relax on shikaras paddled by grizzled gondoliers with pale blue eyes, who chant, in wry echo of bygone GIs, "Whiskey! Soda! Cigarettes! Pop!" You'd think the big deal in Kashmir was the fish and wild game, the golf course at Gulmarg, the hikes from Pahlgam to the glaciers, the six-to-ten-dollars-a-day de luxe houseboats at Srinagar.

"Serene-a-gar," they pronounce it, and serenity I expected as I crossed Dal Lake to the private marsh where the H.B. *Cutty Sark* was moored. A houseboat "special class" with black-bordered white awnings, she has an upper-deck terrace, a dining room, parlor, and two bedrooms, each with a bathroom featuring "modern sanitary fittings" (and when you get the hang of just how to yank the chain, they work fine). The beefy arms of her settee and chairs are late-thirties ultra-modern Kashmiri Grand Rapids. She has turquoise lace curtains, red Oriental carpets, and plenty of brass bric-a-brac and Air France ashtrays to make her real homey.

As I stepped gingerly from the unsteady water taxi onto her veranda, for I am no athlete, Gulam Rasool, "Barber, Ledies and Gents Hair Dresser and Massager," parked his shikara parallel with mine. "Salaam, memsahib!" he greeted me heartily. "You need a

haircut? A shampoo?" "No. No, thank you," I said, trying to visualize my head. "Please, I give you fine massage. Very good for the
nerves." "*I* can give you massage," interposed my manservant, Abdul. "That's swell," I said, "but what's for lunch?" Abdul consulted the cook in the tiny kitchen boat to the rear. "Lamb cut-
lets," he reported. "Well," I said, "all right for now, but let's have
Kashmiri food in the future."

"May I come in?" inquired a swarthy gentleman in a dark business suit and brown karakul hat, coming in. "You are interesting in
a cashmere coat?" he asked, handing me a card reading, "West
End Tailors and Cloth Merchants." "I'm sorry," I said, "I already
have one." "Please, you would like a nice suit? I make for you very
cheap." "Say," I asked, "can you run me up a Punjabi?" For years I
had been dying for a Punjabi, the harem-trousered costume with
thigh-length tunic and gauzy stole worn by Pakistani and neighbor-
ing Indian women. "Yes, yes," he said—I thought a bit impatiently
—"I will make for you the Punjabi. This afternoon I will bring you
swatches." "Come this evening," I suggested. "This afternoon I
am going to see the Shalimar!"

We were gliding by the floating gardens on the *A-One Enterprise,* my very own shikara, when Abdullah the capmaker (not to
be confused with Abdul the houseboy and camera-bearer) came
abreast in his boat. "Salaam. Memsahib, you like to buy beautiful
Kashmir hats?" Well, ever since I took up elementary anthropol-
ogy I've been intense about native artifacts and adornments, especially those that might enhance my apartment and wardrobe, so I
said, sure, I'd look at them. Opening a large, dingy cloth bundle,
Abdullah, who was wearing one of his own beanies, pulled out a
kaleidoscopic array of Juliet caps intricately embroidered with gold
and silver thread, paillettes, pearls, and bright beads. I popped a
couple onto my head, but they were for women with a larger ce-
phalic index. "Please, tonight I bring you better ones," he said.

Just then Osmana & Son, the gunmakers, drew up to my left.
"Good afternoon, madam. You like to buy knives? A nice dagger?"
"No, thank you," I said, "I hardly ever need one." "Please, a sword
stick? A shooting stick?" "No." "A catapult?" "No. No, thank you."
"Madam, you are interesting perhaps to buy a nutcracker?"

Abdul shooed away the munitions dynasty, and for a few minutes all was silence save for the sucking of the oars in silt. In some of the channels the vegetation is so lush you feel as if you were rowing in a thick minestrone. We passed embankments where Kashmiri peasants stood calf-deep in the tortoise-shell water slapping the hell out of the week's wash against the rocks, while brown, naked children splashing alongside them screamed at me across the lake, "Meeeem-meeeem, salaam!"—the local equivalent for "Hello, Dolly!" to which the correct response is a salute. From time to time a drab river woman, crouched like a frog on the prow of her unpainted punt, poled rapidly toward us, her head averted from the evil spirit in my single-lens reflex.

The brief tranquillity was rent by the appearance of A. R. Chakru, "excellent art manufacturer in wood carving and plain furniture," who held up a black and silver Tibetan rice bowl and was about to display from the recesses of his shikara other Asian vessels, when I stalled him. "Later, later," I plead. "You are kindly invited to come to my showroom in Srinagar," he said. "I will send my shikara for you tonight." I nodded absent-mindedly. First of all, the Shalimar.

Ignorantly, I had always taken it for granted the Shalimar was some sort of limpid pool, though why it should seem better grammar to be loving pale hands beside a pond, which it isn't, than a large, formal garden, which it is, I don't know. Anyway, Emperor Jahangir, that sentimental Mogul, designed this "Abode of Love" for his inamorata, Nur Jahan, some four hundred years ago. They say that until the couple could get their union legalized—she was a commoner—Nur used to brew and peddle perfume.

The Shalimar was parched and seedy, its principal attraction the mosaic tree-of-life motif on its marble columns. The chinar leaves inlaid there are ubiquitous in Kashmiri folk art, as indeed are those nightingales the bulbuls—who, for my part, can have the Shalimar.

On our return to the *A-One Enterprise* we passed a languid young Sikh sitting under a tree embroidering a doily. Thirty to forty thousand Kashmiri, I'm told, are engaged in fancy needlework, most, if not all, of them men.

As we approached the stoop of the *Cutty Sark*, a white-turbaned caliph from an old Persian miniature greeted me from the shadows of his shikara with a soft-voiced salaam. "I am *Butterfly!*" he announced like one of the Magi bearing gifts. "Butterfly has the most beautiful shawls in all of Kashmir. You will not find their like anywhere." Butterfly, "by appointment to H.E. the Marchioness of Linlithgow, H.E. Sir Reginald Dorman-Smith, Governor of Burma, not to say H.E. General Sir Claude Auchinleck, the C-in-C in India," stretched out a truly lovely cashmere stole with a crocheted pattern that had first captivated me the previous year in Calcutta. "Butterfly, it's heavenly, but I have just arrived, and I want to shop around. To see," I said pointedly, "where I can get the best prices." "I have embroidered shifts," he said. "You like Baby Doll pajamas? Tea cosies . . ."

Out of the dusk materialized the West End tailor. He stepped down into the parlor, took off his shoes, and sitting cross-legged on the floor with his karakul hat on, opened a square cloth-wrapped parcel full of the softest, most subtly hued wool. A powder-blue caught my eye. Powder-blue always catches my eye. "What would you charge for a coat in this?" I toyed, caressing its ribs. "For you, madam, only fifty dollars." "It would be crazy. I haven't anything to wear it with." "I will make you a matching skirt. Altogether, sixty-five dollars." Having just entered the portals, Mr. Aziz, who with his brother, Mr. Sultan, owns a flock of these houseboats, remarked that I might as well get a jacket, too, and told the couturier to throw one in for another ten bucks. "I can't afford it," I protested. "I just ordered two suits in Hong Kong." "Madam, I beg you, do not lose this opportunity!" I could see he was getting emotional. "Can you," I asked, suddenly recalling a page that I'd ripped out of Pan Am's copy of *Vogue*, "duplicate a coat by Balenciaga?" "Madam, it is simple," he said, reaching for the tape measure. "But where," I hedged, "is the Punjabi material?" "Please, I bring that tomorrow." Clearly, Punjabis didn't much interest the West End tailor.

"Memsahib," came Butterfly's thin, patient voice, "now may I show you my shawls? I have been waiting for you for two hours." "Tomorrow, Butterfly. I am tired and hungry."

With his frail gentility Butterfly tugged at my heartstrings, but Deen, his stocky competitor next in the queue, unknotted my purse strings. "I am a *poor* man," he told me, his eyes bloodshot with sincerity as he ribboned the carpet with shawls. "I do all of my own embroidery. Deen will give you the best prices." "Like how much for this stole?" I inquired. Deen suggested the going rate. "No, no. Too much. I am a poor woman." "Make me an offer," he challenged—so I sportingly halved his quotation. "Madam," he cried, "it is impossible!" I shrugged; others were courting my commerce. However, to still his sighs I said I'd take four. So, tearfully, Deen agreed to the bargain.

If I had forgotten our tryst, the milliner hadn't. In the dim light I tried on two dozen caps, selected a red one and a gray, ordered four more at three dollars each, which he said would take his aged father three days to embroider from an old family design. Mr. Aziz exchanged glances with Abdul. "You will pay him ten dollars for the six," asserted my solicitous landlord. They were getting six dollars apiece for the identical chapeaus in New Delhi.

A half hour later the $25-a-month cook capped a ground lamb *gushtaba* with a gossamer soufflé, after which in the front room Abdul served anised coffee. Palming a jawbreaker yawn, I asked Mr. Aziz what one did about bolting the doors for the night. "Oh," he said, "it is not necessary to lock the doors. Abdul will sleep here." I glanced at Abdul's stubbled chin with misgivings. Razor burn is rare in Kashmir.

The next morning was gloriously sunny, and I was reflecting that we needed fresh flowers when the florist appeared under my pantry window. "They're beautiful," he proclaimed, holding aloft a large mixed bouquet. "They're bea-*u*-tiful," piped his small, ferret-faced grandson. "They're mag-*ni*-ficent. They're stu-*pen*-dous." I handed a bunch to the sleepy-eyed Abdul as the floating drugstore took over. "Madam, you wish to buy cigarettes? Shampoo? Chocolate bars?" I noted in his showcase Surf, Halo, Colgate's toothpaste, and Delsey's double-ply tissue. The last, he responded to a not entirely idle question, cost four rupees a roll—about eighty-four cents if you don't play around with the black market.

Hot on his stern was the postcard merchant, which was sheer telepathy, for I had wakened with an urge to communicate with my cronies. Not such a sensitive was the furrier, who simultaneously appeared at the threshold waving a string of chinchilla. "Those," I said, "are above my station," and sat down to some cornflakes.

I was just hazarding an after-breakfast smoke when M. A. Ramzana, showing up with the gems, piled at my feet sparkling rubies, emeralds, topazes, and garnets, along with some rather dull jade. Just like Tiffany's. While I was wondering whether I'd be committed for buying those amethyst earrings—I calculated that the settings alone would cost me more in New York—Mr. Aziz arrived to squire me on a tour of the town. Our first stop was the Indo-Kashmir Carpet Factory. Employed there, and paid as a unit working on individual rugs, were dozens of families, whose youngest members, squatting knees to chin before the great looms, were but six or seven years of age. To tie knots with the speed of hummingbirds' wings, fingers have to be trained early. What baffles me is how anyone learns to translate into patterns the arithmetic code above them. Although for years I have ascetically insisted I *like* bare polished floors, a brief fondling of carpets that looked like silk, carpets that were silk and so pliable they could be draped like a toga, left me lusting for even a four-by-six Shalimar runner. What finally undid me was the crewel-embroidered fabric—tree-of-life pattern—for one-seventh the tag in the States. I left a deposit of twenty dollars, the balance to come later when I'd measured how many yards I needed for draperies.

Utterly spent, I was hoisted by Mr. Aziz into a horse-drawn tonga for the short trot to Sunshine Alley, an establishment whose specialty is "paper machie." The proprietor lacked Deen's nice sense of trade, but his lamp bases and boxes were so refined I quite forgot those Cheap John had been pushing in the morning and laid in an ample supply. Then, for diversion, we had a look in the basement at a mound of antique rugs—priceless carpets from Tibet, Bokhara, Shiraz, Kerman, and Meshed, going for a song that was out of my range.

As I sipped the comforting tea that the oarsmen had made on a charcoal brazier in the rear of my shikara, I observed that many of the houseboats we passed on our return to the *Cutty Sark* were far from de luxe—hovels with doors four feet high. Through them women, with flamboyant bandannas and bared ears circled with heavily fringed silver crescents, crawled onto tiny porches.

Poor Butterfly was on mine when we landed. "You mean you will not buy anything from Butterfly?" he asked, his long fingers nervously plucking a threaded needle from his turban. "Butterfly has embroidered linen dresses for little girls. You will not find their like anywhere." Wearily, I ordered one for each of my nieces.

Gulam Rasool was making his last rounds. "Memsahib," he called out as I was opening the door, "you are interesting in a massage?"

The little girls' dresses from Butterfly were received shortly after I returned home, but the other merchants had to be prodded many months later by the Handicrafts and Handlooms Exports Corporation of India to get on with the shipments. When I learned that the infrequent repetition of that tree-of-life pattern in the drapery material would necessitate several yards' waste, the dealer refused to apply the deposit against anything else, so I have twenty dollars rotting away in Kashmir. Most unhappily, the suit that I ultimately received from Abdul Gani, of the West End Tailors, was neither the size nor the style that I tried on, let alone anything resembling Balenciaga. Thanks again to the cooperative Handicrafts and Handlooms Export Corporation, Mr. Gani was persuaded to remake the suit. To be safe one should always take along garments to be duplicated or patterns for clothes to be tailored, which are beautifully executed and a steal in many lands. Hong Kong tailors are wizards at copying pictures; speaking from my limited experience, I would judge that others are not so talented.

Moral: even if vendors protest that they have been blacklisted for political reasons, order only from those recommended by the government tourist organizations. Otherwise take your purchases with you and have large ones shipped by your airline office via air freight or send them by registered mail. Retain the receipts so that, if necessary, parcels can be traced through the local post office or shipping agent. It's worth a tip to the hall porter to have him take care of wrapping and mailing them for you.

Fortunately, goods are seldom not shipped as promised. It's important to the vendors to be able to display letters from satisfied customers, and the tomes of them exhibited are often imposing.

If they have been out of the country for at least forty-eight hours, residents of the United States are permitted every thirty-one days to bring back without payment of duty $100 worth of foreign purchases (as of this writing, the President is being urged to raise the limit). At present the total is computed at the full retail price of individual articles, for which sales slips may be demanded by customs officials. To encourage business, small merchants will often volunteer to falsify bills of sale, and there's no question a number of these get by even the knowledgeable customs inspectors—probably because the charges shown are reasonable for the items acquired. Such finagling can, however, subject the tourist to delay and penalties.

Confiscation will be the fate of articles purchased abroad that originated, or may be presumed to have originated, in Communist China, North Korea, or Cuba. Certificates of origin, appropriate for Foreign Assets Control purposes, testifying that commodities traditionally of mainland Chinese manufacture were actually made elsewhere, must be obtained with every such purchase in Hong Kong. The price for each is about a dollar, and a single one may be used for several articles bought in the same store at one time. Valid certificates of origin are not available in Singapore, the assertions of some shopkeepers there to the contrary. Many items prized by women travelers are among those for which certificates of origin cannot be issued even in Hong Kong: beautifully embroidered linens and silks, including wearing apparel and household goods, jade jewelry and figurines, old scrolls and antiques. A full list is obtainable from the Federal Reserve Bank of New York, the Office of Foreign Assets Control, Treasury Department, Washington, D.C., or United States consulates abroad.

Eager vendors will frequently urge customers to let them mail *verboten* goods to the U.S., posted from countries outside Hong Kong or Malaya. Periodic inspections are said to have caught a number of these contraband parcels.

Perfumes, cameras, watches, musical instruments, and other articles bearing foreign trademarks recorded in the Treasury Department may not be imported into the States without the consent of the American trademark owner. However, this consent is often waived in the case of commodities obtained for personal use, and the restriction does not apply at all when the trademark has been removed. The pamphlet *Tourists Trademark Information*, available at any customs office, lists the brand-name articles involved. They're really no problem.

Check your state laws with respect to the importation of liquor; some won't permit it. Although there is no limit on the number of cigarettes that may be brought into the United States for one's personal use, they must be declared and the state tax paid. It took New York about four years of sleuthing and heaven knows how many clerical hours to uncover an oversight of this sort concerning two cartons of cigarettes I had ordered along with a gallon of duty-free liquor. Including the penalty, the bill came to $2.47.

If they predate 1830, genuine antiques may be imported without payment of duty. But for free entry the antiquity of furniture must be verified by official examiners, who are stationed in Baltimore, Boston, Chicago, Honolulu, Los Angeles, New Orleans, New York, Philadelphia, San Francisco, and Seattle. Original art is free of duty, as are such objects as brassware and wood carvings that bear the name of the artisan and qualify as works of art.

To prevent the introduction into the United States of various diseases and insect pests, most food products are out of bounds for the average traveler, as are certain fruits, vegetables, plants, and plant products. Which bars the Swiss liqueur-filled chocolates, Polish ham, and kosher salami. One may, however, return with dressed poultry if it has been drawn and the heads and feet removed.

If they pass the health test, it's okay to import pets—say, a baby elephant or pair of cuddling cockatoos from Chop Jin Seng's in Singapore or a Siamese cat from Madame Rajamaitri's in Bangkok. The regulations and duty imposed are delineated in the pamphlet *So You Want to Import a Pet*, available from customs field offices or the Bureau of Customs.

Some concession will be made for wear, but all clothing purchased abroad must be declared at its full retail price; the same is true of other personal effects bought overseas and used. Belongings that were taken abroad, including worn clothing, may be mailed home and receive free entry if accompanied by a statement explaining that the items were brought with the traveler out of the United States as personal effects and are being returned without alteration or repairs having been made during the trip. One is also asked to declare such ministrations as replaced mainsprings and zippers. I have never heard of anyone who did. Should you be charged duty for a parcel of used clothing, do as Louise did and complain to the Collector of Customs until you get a refund.

A package may be sent to anyone in the United States without being declared or requiring payment of duty if it is a bona fide present and the total value of gift shipments received by an individual in one day does not exceed ten dollars. U.S. Customs says articles may not be sent duty free from abroad to the purchaser whether intended for herself or as a subsequent gift; the ruling is winked at a good deal. Perfumes valued at more than one dollar, alcoholic beverages, and tobacco are exempt from the privilege entirely.

No narcotics, lottery tickets, or obscene literature may be brought into the States. I once hesitated over declaring some fifty postcards I'd purchased at the Louvre Museum, then listed them. The customs inspector, who had glanced with utter boredom at the balance of my declaration, suddenly perked up. "Oh, ho," he said, "let's have a look at those cards." "You're going to be awfully disappointed," I told him. He riffled through the art reproductions with revulsion. "Ah, for God's sake—just long-hair stuff!"

If your purchases don't exceed the $100 duty-free allowance, you may make an oral declaration to the customs inspector. Otherwise, first list items that carry a high duty, leaving for the overflow articles on which the percentage is low. *Customs Hints for Returning U.S. Residents* gives the tariff on the most popular tourist items. The pamphlet is available at passport offices and the Bureau of Customs, in Washington, D.C., which can also supply more specific information. Intended as an advisory guide only, *Customs Hints* is nevertheless more reliable than the information offered by importunate merchants. Customs officials, however, are always glad to total declarations to the traveler's advantage. Under any circumstances, all shipments to you that are not "gifts" valued under ten dollars are now subject to duty.

To expedite the inspection, tourists are advised to keep purchases together in one suitcase. More than once, though, that was the bag I was not asked to open. I have gone through customs when the practice was to make spot inspections of luggage, but it varies, and anyone suspected of misrepresentation can be given a rough time.

One year a friend, taking the word of a clerk in a Hong Kong store that she did not need a certificate of origin, bought a linen blouse that was lavishly embroidered. To her consternation, she subsequently learned that testimony to its genealogy would be demanded. The alternatives to tossing it into the wastebasket, and she is on the tight side, were to keep her shirt on under a wool jacket in the hot, humid Honolulu Airport—or hope that it would pass as a Florentine blouse unnoticed in her suitcase. Deciding on the last, she nervously packed and repacked: would the garment be least conspicuous at the bottom of the bag, the middle, towards the top? Would it look suspicious inside out or wrinkled from being laundered? All the way to Hawaii she worried and worried. When she was paged at the airport she blanched. Clairvoyance was the one police tool she hadn't envisaged. Nor did she recover her color when the summons proved friendly. "Aw, you look like an honest type," the customs inspector said, scribbling a chalk mark on her unopened suitcase. With wet palms she exited from the airport, smiling weakly. Never again. It just wasn't worth it. Besides, the blouse didn't go with a thing in her wardrobe.

11

Snapping Memories

Nothing can conjure the magic of a trip as vividly as your personal photos. Aware of this, most travelers carry cameras, if only to take snapshots of each other blinking at the sun on exotic locations. A few are more reflective. There's Nelly, who took six months off to see the world and returned with color prints par excellence: of Nelly, dressed in black lace, crossing the square of St. Peter's for an audience with the Pope; Nelly, wearing a veil dashingly draped Bedouin-style, at the Pyramids; Nelly, reclining in a sari before what appears to be her very own Taj; Nelly paying obeisance to Japanese emperors at a Shinto shrine; Nelly in Hong Kong surrounded by enthralled Chinese as she lights incense to the Buddha. . . . Nelly, who is both imaginative and photogenic, is never at a loss for a co-operative camera buff.

Unfortunately, many travelers confine themselves to saying "cheese" for one another in front of historic landmarks, thereby not beginning to reap the excitement in photography. Yet almost any woman can experience the thrill of creating pictures over which friends will exclaim, "Why, that looks just like a painting!" Don't protest that you have no artistic ability; if you appreciate beauty, you can capture it in your lens. And anyone who can drive a car has a mind mechanical enough to operate a camera.

The kind of camera that an amateur uses is unimportant as long as she finds it comfortable to handle and responsive to her aims; the way a subject is treated is vastly more important than the instrument employed. Superb pictures may be achieved with box cameras and such bantams as the Kodak Instamatic. And certainly for photograph albums a simple camera is adequate. To adjust the nonautomatic 35 mm. or twin-lens reflex cameras to different lighting conditions and subjects in motion requires concentration, perhaps more than the carefree traveler wishes to expend. Or needs to, since automatic 35 mm. cameras with excellent lenses are available in a wide range of prices. However, if the 35 mm. cameras are wonderfully flexible for candid or artistic photography, their minuscule transparencies are not nearly so dramatic projected on a screen as the much larger ones of the less versatile twin-lens reflex.

Consult a knowledgeable dealer about the right camera for your eyesight, temperament, and purposes; then, before leaving home, practice with the one you have bought. In this I have twice been remiss.

The pictures I had taken with a Kodak box camera on my first two trips abroad were so often just short of what I wanted that, frustrated with its limitations, I bought a moderately priced twin-lens reflex—a Minolta Autocord. Three days later it was thumping against my diaphragm as I happily trailed a castle functionary atop the ancient walls surrounding the Portuguese hamlet of Obidos. Twelve times we stopped while I painstakingly photographed as many aspects of its countryside. But when I tried to reload the camera, its advance lever locked. Breathing deeply, I reread the instructions, verifying the placement of the spindles. The film still wouldn't wind, and I became frantic. Joachim's efforts were equally fumbling. Embarrassed, he suggested in Spanish that we go to a camera store for repairs the next morning.

The film vendor proved ignorant of Minoltas. "No, no! You'll break it!" I cried when he attempted to force the camera's awkwardly distended arm. Joachim said he would take me to someone accomplished in such matters. Disconsolately, I lumbered with him through the lanes of the whitewashed village to a miniature bakery, whose proprietor, I was assured, not only knew cameras but had taught himself to speak English.

A little white-haired gnome, the baker tenderly examined the Minolta, commenting unintelligibly the while, for he applied Portuguese values to English consonants and vowels—and even a Spaniard can't understand those. At length, sighing, he printed on a piece of wrapping paper that we would have to go to Caldas da Rainhas, the next town. I bobbed my head in agreement.

He cranked up the wall telephone to summon a taxi, took off his floury apron, and locked up the bakeshop.

Caldas da Rainhas is a fair-sized metropolis, and the store that we entered was well supplied with photographic equipment. The clerk took one look at the Minolta, clicked its shutter, and started turning the no-longer recalcitrant lever.

All the way back to Obidos I racked my brain wondering how I could best express my appreciation to the little baker, for one could not insult a dignified Portuguese with a tip. When we left the taxi I said that I hoped he would accept, as gratitude for his kindness, a small contribution to be distributed among the poor people of his country—who at the time were all too sadly in evidence.

"For me, no." He paused and glanced at the money in my hand, the equivalent in escudos of a few dollars. "For the poor people— yes." And he thanked me profusely while I fought back the tears that were making mud of my mascara.

I always tend to choke up when confronted with my own generosity.

The second time I blithely walked off inadequately instructed about a new camera was at Haneda Airport in Tokyo. Still enamored of the Minolta, I wanted a camera with which I could take rapid candids. So, a few minutes before take-off, I purchased a fast, single-lens reflex—a Nikkorex F with an $f/1.4$ lens, which is really too fine for the likes of my photography, since the considerably less expensive $f/3.5$ is up to the needs of most amateurs.

"That looks like a dandy little instrument—if you can figure out how to run it," remarked my seatmate on the JAL flight to Djakarta. I flushed because he had caught me lip-reading the diagram of the camera's components against their counterparts in my lap.

The experience with the Nikkorex was shattering. Sometimes the button that is depressed when rewinding the exposed cartridge remained sunken; on other occasions it rose unobserved to its normal position, thereby shredding the film. I lost yards of never-to-be-duplicated pictures. To have avoided this, I should have kept my fingernail on the button throughout the rewinding. It is uncommon, however, for a Nikkorex—a superb camera—to behave so badly. Too hastily purchased, mine during its debut appeared possessed by all the evil spirits in Bali.

When reloading—especially after such a mishap—search the components of the camera's back for particles of paper or snippets of film that may interfere with its operation.

But first one must decide the kind of film to buy. Tonal values in color prints tend to alter and fade—as, much more slowly, do they in transparencies. Long-lived and inexpensive, black-and-white pictures allow a generous margin for error in composition and exposure, for, within limits, both can be corrected in the darkroom. A skilled operator can brighten drab shots somewhat. By "burning in" he can also darken patches of glaring white, or by "dodging" lighten black shadows, thereby bringing out detail.

The suffixes "color" and "chrome" added to the brand name identify the film as, respectively, color negatives or transparencies. Color negatives may be converted into transparencies and vice versa, and either can be printed enlarged or made into black-and-white pictures, at a price. A first-rate color laboratory charges about $20 to make an 11 × 14 inch enlargement of a single transparency printed by the Colorstat process, which is similar to a photostat in quality. A color negative enlarged to the same size by the Type C Ektacolor process, used in professional work, costs $25, while the price for making the necessary color negative from a transparency is an additional $10. An 11 × 14 inch enlargement of a black-and-white negative printed on sturdy semigloss paper costs $2, but the price for converting a color transparency into the black-and-white negative is $3. Small wonder that most gifted amateur photographers prefer to work with black-and-white film.

Arresting black-and-white prints are more dependent on composition than are photographs in color. For this reason, and because, without considerable practice, few can translate the colors they see into the chiaroscuro that will appear in a black-and-white print, the average amateur generally finds color film an infinitely easier medium in which to produce brilliant pictures. Their flaws, however, are harder to correct.

For various reasons, no color pictures reproduce hues with absolute accuracy. Kodak seems to come closer than most, but, carefully exposed, any color film can provide gratifying results. From time to time photography magazines run articles on new color film with illustrations showing the differences in rendition of various types: some may be rosier, greener, bluer, whatever. If you have the time and inclination to shop in this fashion for film, write to the periodical, ask for the latest issue in which they had such a feature, and select the film that is most pleasing to you.

It's a temptation to buy the speediest film available. If one is only going to take so-called "record shots" and has an adjustable camera it liberates the photographer from dependence upon good light. Nevertheless, just as fast film obviates any need for the novice to buy an expensive camera with extremely low $f/$ stops, so possessing such an instrument makes the highest-speed film redundant.

For a fixed-focus camera with no exposure meter, one should purchase Kodak Plus X black-and-white film or a medium-speed color film, such as Kodachrome X-64, and only photograph subjects in the sun or brightly lit open shade. With an adjustable camera and exposure meter, either coupled or separate, Tri X and other fast black-and-white film may advantageously be used in normal as well as dim light. Anticipating average weather conditions, the amateur owning an adjustable camera might well take mostly medium-speed film in color, along with a few rolls of fast black-and-white for picture-taking in subdued light or on gloomy days, when it's wasteful for the nonexpert to attempt color. One authority advises buying twenty-exposure rolls and trying to shoot them all in the same light, which, though extravagant with film, results, he says, in improved processing.

Whatever you do, take more than enough film. It's maddening to run short abroad and be forced to buy American brands at exorbitant prices or find that you cannot get foreign film processed in the States. Try to arrange with your camera dealer to return unused film for refund or credit. If that is impossible, the expiration date of unexposed film can be extended by placing the unopened rolls in the refrigerator or deep freeze. To be on the safe side, just before departing on your next trip, shoot a thawed roll and have it developed.

Although to forestall your profitable resale of film most countries ostensibly limit the duty-free importation to a certain number of rolls or "a reasonable amount," I have never been questioned by customs officials about it, and I usually have enough to total three hundred exposures. If you are taking a prolonged journey and have a great deal of film with you, you may if challenged request that the amount exceeding that permitted in duty-free be placed in bond, to be retrieved for a small fee when you leave. Or you may be allowed to list for customs the number of rolls of various types that you have, which will be checked against their record upon your departure—a practice that one follows in certain countries (India, for instance) when carrying more than one camera. It is also possible that you may be required to pay a deposit against duty, retrievable if demonstrably no sale has been made. Either of the latter two alternatives presupposes that you will not mail home film to be processed.

Some travelers break the seal of all film and mark the packages "For personal use only." That, I think, is unwise: first, because where film is at a premium mutilated wrappings would not inhibit its black-market sale; second, because it is unlikely that you would subsequently be able to return excess rolls to your dealer for refund or credit.

Since exposed film should be processed as quickly as possible, particularly color in the tropics, you may wish to consult with your dealer on the advisability of mailing it back to him, a processing laboratory, or the manufacturer for development. Or you may prefer to mail it home addressed to yourself. In none of these cases would duty be charged by American customs on film manufactured in the United States if the packages are marked "Undeveloped photographic film of U.S. manufacture. Examine with care. Not for any commercial purpose whatsoever." The United States Post Office, however, may impose a small handling charge on packages of film arriving from abroad, which, according to international postal regulations, must be at least $2\frac{3}{4} \times 4$ inches in size if not packaged in a prepaid processing mailer.

I have never found that exposed color film deteriorated on a journey of up to two months' duration, regardless of climate. On the other hand, considering the delays occasionally experienced with postcards and letters, I would not count on packets not being

sent by slow steamer via the Cape of Good Hope, the airmail postage on them notwithstanding.

Thanks to the latitude for exposure error in black-and-white film,
the instruction charts that are packed with the rolls, suggesting the
settings for various lighting conditions, may be relied upon. With
somewhat less assurance the printed charts for color film may also
be followed when photographing subjects of average brightness.
However, for those darker than normal, increase the light that they
get by opening the lens diaphragm one-half to one full *f/* stop
wider than indicated; for subjects lighter than average, do exactly
the opposite.

Because minor mistakes in under- and overexposure so readily
distort color rendition, most authorities advise the use of a photo-
electric exposure meter. They are an integral part of many cameras.
If yours is not an "electric-eye" camera or does not have a coupled
exposure meter, purchase one and consult it frequently for color
film. Light can be exceedingly deceptive; moreover, the strength of
the sun changes at different times of the day—particularly in open
shade—as well as in various altitudes and climates. A reliable meter
need not be complicated nor expensive (mine isn't), but no gadget
is more vital to the perfection of your pictures.

With black-and-white film, take a reading from the darker,
though not darkest, sections of the subject; with color film, the
lighter though not lightest.

Even with an exposure meter, professionals insure perfection by
"bracketing" their most interesting shots: they take the first picture at the *f/* stop indicated by the meter, one with the diaphragm
opened one-half stop wider, one with it a half stop smaller—all at
the same shutter speed. This is especially important as a safeguard
against the extra light that white walls, clothes, even clouds in a
sunny sky reflect into the meter, thereby causing it to give a distorted reading. Sand and snow and whitewashed buildings can also
play tricks with the light.

What do you do with two out of the three pictures? If they are
color slides, throw away the overexposed one unless its soft tones
particularly please you. Keep the underexposed one if its color satu-
ration is intense but not muddy; if you decide to have it made into
a color print, it will turn out less bleached than would the perfectly

exposed shot, since conversion always diminishes to a degree the brilliance of a transparency.

Extremely dramatic pictures may be taken by "shooting into the sun," not really into the glare, but with the subject backlighted; try a few of land- and seascapes, then note how the sun dances on the foliage and water. For such shots—indeed, for all photography—a lens shade is a must; it not only protects the picture against streaks of light on the outer edges but shields the lens against damage as well.

Filters come in a variety of colors and density to achieve different effects; the amateur really needs only a Kodak yellow K-2 for black-and-white film to darken a sickly sky, reveal clouds on a clear day, and increase contrast; and a Kodak Skylight 1A filter for color film to cut ultraviolet rays, which cause bluish tones. Neither the K-2 nor the 1A will penetrate mist or fog. The K-2 requires an increase in exposure of one $f/$ stop; the 1A needs no adjustment and may to advantage be left on the lens outdoors all the time. If you plan to shoot exceedingly fast black-and-white film, to counteract overexposure in sunlight use a neutral density filter to reduce the film speed to a figure compatible with the limitations of your camera. Your dealer can advise what strength density to purchase.

The camera's lens should be kept clean. For this some advocate a camel's hair brush that unscrews from a lipsticklike container; others favor a tiny ear syringe, which blows off the dust. To remove fingerprints from a lens, special tissue is necessary; even so, it must be used with the utmost gentleness in order not to scratch the surprisingly soft surface.

Ever try to read an exposure meter or set a camera in a dim light? Take a penlight for that contingency.

A great many travelers carry flash attachments to photograph indoor dance and theatrical performances and to lighten shadows in close-ups of people. If you do, be sure the batteries are fresh and that you have plenty of bulbs. A flash attachment is, unfortunately, worthless outdoors for subjects beyond about fifteen feet.

Although it is awkward to tote, some sort of reflector is useful for illuminating the shadows of a face in back or side lighting. It may be as simple as a large white dish towel or a section of newspaper.

On a trip a white umbrella would be perfect since, apart from its pluvial function, it would serve to distract the subject from staring at the camera. Whatever the means, it must be held or stationed opposite the dark side of the subject while you take the picture. However, anything white will reflect light—a wall near the subject, his own shirt or turban. I once got an appealing shot of a throng of Balinese children whose shadowed features were clarified by the shining blond hair of a little Dutch girl whom they had adoringly surrounded. The picture would have satisfied me more had I subsequently protected the transparency in plastic "sleeves" against scratches.

Some travelers take miniature tripods or camera-holding devices that can be clamped onto benches or chairs when shutter speeds slower than $\frac{1}{25}$ of a second are needed and holding the camera by hand would create blur. The number of times the average amateur would use one would not, I think, justify their weight.

Exposed film trapped in a jammed camera may be removed in a changing bag and thus salvaged. Spiratone has one with a zippered pocket, into which the ribboned film may be slipped without exposure to light. An emptied flight bag will serve just as well.

However much a burden it may seem, keep your camera and all breakable accessories on you when in transit; baggage attendants are frequently brutal with suitcases, and there is tremendous vibration in the luggage compartments of motor coaches and cars. Never place a camera or film in an automobile glove compartment or trunk, which can become much too hot for their health, as can a vehicle parked in the sun. Protect film exposed to unusual heat in insulated frozen-food bags or between clothing in a suitcase.

All these accessories and precautions are secondary to the subject and how the photographer treats it. She may be content with snapshots of the people of the country, its monuments and landscape, taken, without concern for composition, simply to record "this is the way they look." Record shots are invaluable mementoes of places seen.

The tendency on one's first trip abroad is to be undiscriminating with respect to film subject, but after a while it becomes apparent that scenically anything short of the spectacular could be located in a comparable climatic zone. So with such views it is more interesting to focus on—or at least include—distinguishing details that identify the locale with the particular land: a windmill or a mosque, a vicuña or a camel. More earnestly, one may watch for significant aspects that tell a story: a score of schoolgirls in caftans and veils riding bicycles in Fez says more about Morocco than all the palm trees in Marrakesh.

Trying to embrace too broad a horizon in a picture (long shots of sea- and landscapes, and those panoramas that guides are always pestering one to take) usually results in meaningless strips of sky and terrain, unless you come equipped with a wide-angle lens. Instead, select the facet of a view that to you pinpoints its fascination, then "close in on it": get as near as possible without—in the case of something live (six to ten feet is perfect)—alerting it to your camera, or, when photographing subjects seen from above (again, desirable), tumbling into a ravine.

Unless the clouds are extraordinary, a little sky goes a long way. Indeed, pictures—particularly of architecture—that eliminate it and concentrate on a lower portion of the structure often give one a sharper sense of being right there than do photos crowned with a conventional ribbon of blue.

One can create exciting geometrical designs by shooting up at columns, domes, and spires, but it is virtually impossible, without a specially constructed camera, to get a realistic rendition of an entire building from ground level, except at considerable distance, since perspective causes the highest lines to converge. For such pictures one might better buy postcards or professional color slides. Taken under ideal light and at advantageous stance, often inaccessible to the traveler, historic architecture and monuments may be shown with a clarity and lack of distortion exceedingly difficult for the hurried tourist to achieve. Because official permission must frequently be secured to photograph the interiors of museums and houses of worship, postcards could also be the solution for these.

If they lack imagination and the uniqueness of being exclusively one's own, ready-made pictures are economical and manifestly represent no hazard with respect to results. Many travelers purchase a selection as a backstop against the chance that some of theirs will be failures. Nevertheless, with a little care, you can bank on a high measure of success.

Peer critically into the view framed in your lens. Move the camera to the right, to the left, up, down. Change your position. Suddenly your heart will quicken; you have noted a splash of orange, turquoise, red that recurs in a garment, a window shutter, a piece of pottery—or you have observed that it is possible at a certain angle to create a picture subtly composed entirely of, say, sienna, gold, and silvery gray. Perhaps the elements of the view constitute geometric blocks or complementary lines, angles, or curves that, abstractly regarded, are arresting, or produce a feeling of rhythm. Factors like these add to a picture's quality and enrich the traveler's vision. She should not, however, let any blindness to them inhibit her photography; like rules of composition, they may be ignored. Pictures should be taken with joy, not worry.

In general, however, they are more pleasing if the masses encompassed—sky, sea, and shore, for example—are not equally sliced and if the focus of interest—a group of fishermen, a ship, perhaps—is neither centered in the photo's frame nor teetering too close to its edge. Pictures are weakened by distracting elements and extraneous clutter; the simpler the composition the stronger it is. Although they may more truthfully report an exotic scene, the intrusion of telephone poles, cars, and the like diminishes its charm; unless twentieth-century appurtenances provide a genuinely amusing contrast (a "Snack Bar du Forum" is funny), cut them—and other tourists—out of the lens's scope. Try to take time to see your picture as a whole; ask yourself, does that wheelbarrow, that broom, that pile of rubbish enhance the impact of the design and the statement that you hope the photo will make, or detract from it?

Particularly when photographing people, watch out for objects right behind and above them that in the picture will appear to be growing out of their limbs or heads. The best background for people is a wall, a doorway, or (now's the time for it, if you can shoot up at the subject) a deep blue sky.

Framing a picture with foliage, a doorway, or an arch can be effective; too frequent recourse to such gimmicks results in monotony.

Lower the camera to reduce excessive sky; add interest and the illusion of perspective by including in the foreground nearby animals, shrubs, houses, or people, being careful to maintain the entire picture in focus. If you wish to dramatize objects that are close, blur the background by shortening the depth of field. This is done by opening the lens diaphragm as wide as distance to subject permits and adjusting the shutter speed accordingly. To convey the vastness of a scene, photograph at a distance something familiar that looks tiny.

Long shots of monuments tend to be insipid; more powerful are close-ups of details, the texture through side lighting sharply defined, which is well within the range of the most average camera.

Align the horizon or a horizontal line in the foreground with the horizontal of your viewfinder. It is easy to correct an askew black-and-white; not so a transparency.

Steadiness is *the* most important factor in getting a sharp picture. Whenever possible brace your camera on a stationary object. Even infinitesimally jarring the instrument by less than gentle pressure on the shutter causes some "softness." A firm balance may be obtained by standing with one foot a fair-sized but comfortable step ahead of the other. With an eye-level viewfinder it also helps to press your elbows against your ribs and the camera against your forehead, nose, or cheek. Steady a waist-level camera by pulling it down tautly a bit away from your body. Finally, your pictures will be more breathtaking if you hold yours while pressing the shutter.

Sometimes muted hues produce a mystical effect. Conversely, especially in black-and-white shots, strength is achieved by photographing a light subject against a dark background and vice versa.

One's shadow bent over a camera seldom enhances the foreground; if possible, avoid that by trying a different angle. Indeed, always note where shadows fall; it is all too easy to wind up with anything from gray to black silhouettes of subjects with their backs to a hidden sun.

In general, avoid taking pictures at midday, when harsh shadows blacken people's features and architectural details. The best times for color slides are a few hours after sunrise and before sunset. Because of the warmer afternoon light, I prefer the latter.

Don't photograph people who are squinting at the sun; on a bright day open shade or side lighting is infinitely more flattering and requires less technical skill than coping with the shadows created by back lighting.

When entering an area where you hope to get candids, preset your camera for a distance of ten to twelve feet from the subject and a speed at least as fast as $\frac{1}{100}$ of a second. Throughout the world people agreeable to being photographed will stiffen before the camera; therefore, always try to take them absorbed in activity characteristic of their calling or country. To forestall unnatural postures and expressions ignore the ones you wish to photograph while adjusting your exposure to a subject similarly lighted. If the former insist upon grimacing for the camera, a companion may be able to distract them, particularly if he speaks the local language. By the same means unwilling subjects can sometimes be disarmed with a complimentary observation: "She says you are very charming."

Women are quickly won over by the praise of their children implicit in a smile. The only trouble is, being mothers, they invariably summon the rest of their brood, and you're stuck with a dull family portrait.

Children usually regard one as either an ogress or Pied Piper. Nothing is more endearing than pictures of beguiling foreign tots; little is more difficult than not to frighten them or to pry from their sides swarms of mugging bigger kids. If the last won't be bribed or shooed away, come as close to your pets as their trust will permit, thus eliminating the children flanking them from your lens. Or try to blur those in the background by shortening to the utmost the camera's depth of field.

Antics will at times divert fearful children into spontaneous laughter, and their attention is more easily directed than that of adults to a bogus subject upon which the photographer pretends to be focusing before swinging around to capture them relaxed.

In popular tourist locales there are often professionally picturesque characters who make a living of sorts by posing for snapshots; some stick out their palms for a tip the moment a traveler with camera enters the vicinity. They are seldom worth the price they demand.

Many proud peoples, however, resent pictures of their poverty, as well as being considered picturesque. In La Paz a Bolivian turned on me in rage for photographing the Indian market. "¿Muy cómica, no?" he asked bitterly, chasing away a bowler-hatted woman upon whom I had focused. "No, señor! She is *not* comical.

She is typical of the country," I was laboriously explaining in Spanish when the driver yanked me into the car, "and because of this is very *simpática* . . ." Obviously, the Indian couldn't understand my Castilian, let alone appreciate American good will.

To assist those who wish to film indigenous costumes and customs, including native dances, Eastman Kodak has arranged shows in various places. They are set up in Hawaii, Thailand, Singapore, Panama, and Bermuda and, as of this writing, are in the offing for Mexico, the Bahamas, Jamaica, Barbados, Puerto Rico, Peru, East Africa, Portugal, Greece, Lebanon, Israel, Hong Kong, Okinawa, and the Philippines.

Sometimes, with a guide serving as entrepreneur, a number of travelers can split the cost of a private performance of traditional dances by a local troupe. One may also stumble on an ethnic celebration, which is more exciting by virtue of not having been staged for tourists. The intrusion of cameras may or may not be regarded as bad magic.

Glimpsing masked Indians in weird costumes on a plain near Cuzco, I said to my companions in the car, "Oh, let's stop for a look at the *féria!*" It was the Day of the Assumption, and pagan-Christian festivals had been in progress all week. The one that we were approaching appeared to resemble the symbolic contest between Good and Evil that takes place in Oruro the Saturday preceding Ash Wednesday: there was a man disguised as a bear and one as a vulture of the high Andes, the condor. I couldn't tell whether St. Michael and Lucifer were also represented among the masqueraders, but I rushed to the crowd surrounding the participants.

Though not a woman lavish with a *propina*, I could see that this was no time to be tightfisted about tips. Handing a member of the Indian audience a half-dollar's worth of soles, I pointed to a ringside position. He elbowed our way to the inner rim of the circle and stood alongside me while I hastily unsnapped the camera case and held aloft my exposure meter in the direction of the drama.

The Indian in the bear mask, who was cracking a bull whip over the condor, halted, looked around, and gestured to me, "Get lost." I smiled to show that my intentions were friendly. He resumed his role in the charade, and I quickly snapped a couple of memories.

Again the players paused. I took another light reading and double-checked the exposure I'd set. Suddenly, the bear quit the performers and, growling something menacing in Quechua, strode toward me purposefully, whip raised. An angry rumble swept the crowd, and it began closing in.

I turned in terror to my well-tipped protector. He had vanished —as had my fellow tourists.

Sensing that the Indians might get carried away with their animal roles if they realized my fright, I forced a thin smile, said as brightly as I could, "Well . . . *buenas tardes*"— and walked woodenly away.

With watery knees, who can run?

I wish I could report that, anyway, the pictures were great. But I had forgotten to increase the exposure for the back-lighted subjects, and their masked faces were blacked out by the shadows.

The ubiquity of their sovereigns' images on stamps, coins, and public walls notwithstanding, many Moslems, as well as primitive peoples, are as superstitious about having their pictures taken as we are about not knocking wood. In North Africa a policeman caught me, camera-to-eye, "stealing a soul," and in rebuke demanded to see my passport. I knew from a questionnaire I had submitted to national tourist offices that photographing unwilling subjects is often regarded as the most objectionable conduct of American tourists. Yet there was I once again succumbing to an overpowering desire to capture on film the charm of a foreign scene so that through the years I might relive it on the home screen.

Like professionals, many advanced amateurs click away, taking hundreds of candids; then, after the pictures are processed, they discard all but the best or those in which the composition can be corrected. This technique frequently results in a vitality that may be lost in the calculated study that includes people. It is, however, exceedingly wasteful if photos are taken purely for pleasure. To my mind, the excellent quality obtained through initial care in exposing and composing a picture more than repays one for the shots lost at times due to deliberation.

Don't jeopardize your rolls by taking them for processing to a drugstore. Go to a camera store and ask that they be "developed by inspection." It saves money to have black-and-whites made into contact-sheet prints, from which one selects the best for enlargement.

Improvements may be made in the picture's composition by blocking out peripheral portions with strips cut from an opaque tape used by professional photographers, or from "masks," which are then Scotch-taped to the cardboard mount, or over the transparency onto glass underneath it. Stores selling Kodak and Leitz equipment will have cover glass and masks for half-frame, 35 mm., and super slides. If unavailable locally, cover glass and masks 2¾ inches square may be ordered from the firms listed in the Appendix, as may mounts in assorted sizes and shapes.

The heat of the projector, even a so-called "cool" one, may eventually dry out the moisture in the gelatin of transparencies, causing them to buckle and pop. Protect your most precious color slides against this as well as humidity, chemicals in the air, fungus, scratches, and fingerprints by mounting them between glass. Should yours be one of the few otherwise excellent projectors that will not accept slides that have been glass-mounted or cropped, you may take them to a Kodak representative to be Vacuumated or laminated, a more costly process.

When in doubt where to crop a black-and-white print for enlargement or a color slide for the most effective projection, study the original upside down, which will reveal its design in abstract masses and lines. Cut two L-shaped strips from light cardboard and shift them around as different potential frames until the composition is most pleasing to you. It is quite possible if the picture was carefully shot that it will need no improvement. Consult others if you wish, but don't become enslaved to their opinion should you disagree.

Quite apart from the esthetic and nostalgic satisfaction they give one, really good pictures can win amateur photo competitions. Among the many is *Saturday Review*'s annual World Travel Contest, the prizes in which range from fifty dollars to a trip abroad—in some years, around the world. Other competitions are announced in newspapers and photography magazines. Note, however, the conditions of the contest with respect to surrendering your rights to the picture submitted; you may lose them for any subsequent commercial or competitive purposes.

Sometimes amateurs can sell especially beautiful or unusual photographs through picture agencies, which is a bonanza because then they can deduct from their income tax at least a portion of the cost of the film and its processing. Black-and-whites bring a lower price but have a readier market than color transparencies, which usually must be 2¼ inches square or larger.

Agencies and their general requirements are listed periodically in such magazines as *Popular Photography*, from which I have gotten many other useful hints. Before departing ask a few agencies what subjects they are short of in the countries you will visit and watch for opportunities to snap them as you travel.

One's photographic skill can be improved and social life expanded by joining a camera club. The membership, sharing a passion for picture-taking, cuts across American society. Enthusiasts of the one I belonged to ranged from a celebrated male ballet dancer to the maintenance man of an office building, the club's most talented exponent and, to all, the Maestro. Don't, however, let any commitment by the camera club to "ashcan," European salon, or any other arbitrary standards destroy your pleasure in your own pictures.

Your photographs express you—and your trip. It would be incomplete without them.

12

Covered with Old Glory

In the years past newspapers have headlined anti-American demonstrations in Tokyo, Lima, La Paz, Djakarta, Pnompenh; Algerian riots in Paris; fighting by Greeks and Turks over Cyprus; border raids between Syrians and Israelis. "Was it foolhardy of me," I once asked Ambassador John Allison, "to have at such times visited Japan, Peru, Bolivia, Cambodia, France, Greece, and the Holy Land? Even though I sensed no malice toward me as an individual tourist, let alone evidence of turmoil?"

"I see no reason," he said, "why a single girl should not travel in Asia or the Middle East or areas other than the more stable ones in Europe, providing she uses her head and doesn't try to be a smart aleck.

"If she is wise, she will find out where the nearest American embassy or consulate is and call there as one of her first actions in the strange country. If she is in the capital of the country, she should go to the embassy and ask for the consular section. Embassies are only found in the capitals, as the ambassador is the personal representative of the President of the United States to the chief of state of the country in which he is located. Consular officers are scattered around the country and deal with the local officials. As such, they are the officers of the American Foreign Service who most frequently come into contact with American citizens abroad.

"I suggest," continued the Ambassador, "that the young lady ask the consular officer if she can make a temporary registration. This should cost nothing but a little time. The consular officer will make

199

a note of the number and date of her passport, where she is staying and what her plans are during her visit in the country. Should she thereafter get into any sort of trouble, or lose her passport, the consular officer will have on record that she is an American citizen, and he will be able officially to go to her aid. In most cases this first visit to a consulate will also be the last.

"In the more unstable or newer nations it can happen that an American tourist may quite innocently fall into the hands of the local police as the result of doing something that would be perfectly normal at home but is offensive abroad. In such an event she should yell and scream until she is allowed to see an American consul or vice-consul. If he is good—and most of them are—he will probably be on friendly enough terms with the local officials to get her off. Unless she has really done something bad. However, even then he can help, so she shouldn't hesitate to appeal to him.

"And whatever happens, she should keep smiling. She may not be on *Candid Camera*, but it sure helps."

As do discretion and tact. The Indonesian consulate's advice that American visitors in their country should refrain from publicly criticizing the political leaders or government officials applies to many other nations that have suffered a bad press in the U.S. There is wider application, too, in the suggestion by the Governmental Affairs Institute pamphlet *Soviet Russia: A Guidebook for Tourists:* "We who are accustomed to throwing candid remarks back and forth with perhaps too little thought must be careful lest we inadvertently jar . . . sensitivities. . . . Americans are well advised to be cautious about making direct and invidious comparisons between American and Soviet conditions." It's the most companionable thing in the world for Americans meeting as strangers in buses, trains, and planes to compare notes and laugh about experiences they have had traveling in various countries—little realizing that such comments may irritate nearby foreigners who understand English.

Americans who would not dream of bragging about their personal standard of living to a less affluent neighbor sometimes forget how gauche it is to do so on a national scale, especially when they are guests in another country. And it takes great restraint not to retaliate when challenged about unfavorable aspects of the United

States—an equally tasteless practice on the part of citizens of a host nation.

Peoples in impoverished lands frequently ask American travelers personal questions about their income, rent, or the cost of their clothes. One must realize, though, that this is motivated by an overwhelming curiosity concerning everything in the States, particularly in those countries where news of America is scanty. The interrogator will as readily tell you how much he makes a week, gives the landlord, and has to pay for shoes. It's an exchange of comparative statistics, and interesting when you come to think of it.

When I was in Budapest, I got into a conversation with a woman sitting next to me in a restaurant. Her English was quite good, so I seized the opportunity to quiz her about conditions in Hungary. She spoke of them proudly, noting that under Communist rule there was no unemployment and the government had a retirement plan in which everybody participated. People could quit working at the age of fifty-five and get a pension from the state. She told me about new housing developments, the expansion in education. Then abruptly she blurted out, "Could you tell me, please, what is your salary?" In rapid succession I answered a number of similar questions, trying at the same time to give her a picture of the average situation when mine deviated from it. "Oh," she conceded, "Americans have much more than we." "But," I reminded her, "you have that government retirement plan." "Isn't it the same as your Social Security?" she asked me. "The pension that pays is exceedingly low," I said. "Nobody can live very well on it." "People can't live on ours either," she confessed. "Children have to help their retired parents."

After that she no longer tried to propagandize me. Avid for news of America, she asked if I had brought any magazines. She particularly wanted to see those that pictured household appliances. I look longingly at them myself. Nevertheless, I was sorry that I did not have one of our women's consumer magazines; there's a tremendous interest in them, and they speak loudly in defense of a free economy.

I also regretted not having with me a book of facts and figures with which to answer other of her questions. The Governmental

Affairs Institute suggests taking a copy of the *World Almanac* (Doubleday) or some other reference publication, as well as copies of the Help Wanted section of Sunday newspapers and the real estate ads. All can be useful to counter distorted impressions of the U.S.

The most important things, though, that any woman can take with her abroad are an open mind and restraint.

Astonishing as it may seem to us, a considerable portion of the world—and not only the Communist-oriented—regards America as an imperialist power. I first encountered such an attitude in Cairo, where I was invited to meet the number-four man of all Islam, the Vice-Rector of El Azhar University. Housed in a mosque built in 972 A.D., it is one of the oldest universities in the world. To it come Moslem students from all over. Several of them were attending every word of the Vice-Rector when I was brought into the large bare reception room for the audience. With his cadaverous cheeks and hooded eyes, tarboosh and flowing robe, the Vice-Rector seemed the epitome of spirituality and scholarship. Through my interpreter, Mohammed, he asked if I cared for a cup of coffee, which I, as it turned out, not so politely declined; for, smiling obsequiously at him the while, Mohammed—or Moe, as he had been dubbed in the States—muttered to me that it would be an insult to my host if I did not take it. So I sipped my fifth coffee of that morning while the Vice-Rector addressed me vigorously about American foreign policy, a topic on which I was all too uninformed.

Why, he demanded, was the United States in league with the imperialist powers England and France? Why were we helping the nations in Europe at the expense of Egypt and others in the Middle East? Why were we supporting Israel against the Arab countries? It was a large responsibility for a political vacuum like myself to attempt to cope patriotically and intelligently with such a fusillade, mindful as I was of the dignity of my adversary. He climaxed a forty-five-minute tirade by warning me that unless we quit being imperialists Egypt might go communistic.

"Would you please ask the Vice-Rector," I timidly instructed Moe, "whether a devout Moslem *can* accept Communism?" At least I had learned enough about Islam to know that one of its tenets is respect for private property, and another the acceptance, as Allah's will, of inequalities in wealth.

A couple of days later I was invited to have cocktails at the home of one of the Moustafas, a Nordic-looking young man who occupied a seven-room duplex with as many Great Danes. The other four Moustafas ranged in complexion from sepia to black. I was pleasantly surprised that the cocktails did not turn out to be tea, for until then I'd seen the men drink nothing stronger than Coca-Cola. This, however, was a farewell party for me and a bit of fling for them, unaccustomed as they were to American-style entertainment.

What, it flickered across my mind during the third Scotch and soda, shall I do if these gentlemen's senses become inflamed—alone, as I am, with five of them? I needn't have worried; their interest in me was a pure and political thing. Even after he had clapped his hands for the servants to bring on the feast of roasted pigeons, the blond Moustafa continued to pelt me with questions about the United States, as did his fellows. It was just before the 1954 Supreme Court decision on desegregation, and its outcome was uppermost in their minds.

"Now, Moustafa here," said the blond one, placing his hands affectionately on the shoulders of the black man, "in America, would he be treated as a Negro?"

Reluctantly, I answered, "Probably."

"But he is an Egyptian," insisted the towhead. "We don't like Negroes."

"Who," I asked him in amazement, "do you regard as Negroes?" For until then I had not considered that there are many dark-skinned peoples—Indians, for instance—who are not Negroid. And, unfortunately, some of them, too, have their biases.

In Madurai, a city in the state of Madras, I was meandering about the small temple in the center of the Teppakulam tank when a blue-black, fine-featured Tamil started to chat with me about the comical, brightly garbed and walrus-mustached statues leaning against the columns. He had been to America and, like all Asians I encountered that autumn of 1963, was deeply shocked by the murder of President Kennedy.

"Of course," he remarked on the return sailing across the artificial lake, "there was an anti-integration plot behind the assassination." I said, no, I didn't think so—and immediately was challenged by first one then another of the boat's excited occupants about the condition of Negroes in the States. I tried to answer as truthfully and objectively as I could.

There has been a considerable improvement in their lot, I said, but they still have a long, long way to go before achieving economic equality with white Americans. Nevertheless, it is the policy of the United States government to raise the Negroes' status. I wished I could cite the number of Negroes prominent in public life. Lamely, I concluded that even the poorest Negro in the States lived better than the average low-caste Indian.

In its manual for Americans confronted with this question in the Soviet Union, the Governmental Affairs Institute notes that many travelers "have tried to point out that the forward progress of the Negro in America has been tremendous in the past generation and that, in fact, the prominence of the Negro question in the news in recent years has been due primarily to judicial and governmental action intended to further this progress.

"Some Americans have pointed out that, in part, the headline-making developments in several Southern states have resulted from a conflict between civil rights guaranteed by the Constitution and our equally important and Constitutionally guaranteed rights of local self-government. Other visitors have emphasized American efforts to find widely acceptable solutions to the vital human and social problems related to the racial question in many sections of the country. Some visitors have found it useful to point out, in connection with the school segregation issue, that thirty-three out of the fifty states have always had integrated schools and that public education is now desegregated to some extent in the other seventeen states. Any substantial discussion of race relations in the United States should include some reference to the Civil Rights Act of 1964, which is accelerating public school desegregation and also provides for the elimination of racial barriers in employment and most places of public accommodation."

In a recent editorial the New York *Times* notes that "hotels, motels, restaurants, lunch counters, theatres and other public ac-

commodations have been quietly desegregated in hundreds of cities
where 'whites only' was once the rule."

However, with the best intentions in the world, an American
woman traveling among predominantly colored, former colonial,
or just impoverished populations sometimes faces a perplexing situation.

How, for instance, should a hard-working, self-made career girl
respond to the many beggars she meets? Ours—the world's best-
dressed—are easy to deny. Not so the human bundles of wretched-
ness and rags, the piteously diseased urchins who stretch out their
hands. To how many is their role the inevitable result of depriva-
tion? To how many a cynical means of livelihood? And what about
alms to the intinerant holy men to whose religion begging is an
integral? At every intercity bus depot in Morocco mendicants enter
the vehicle and, raising their right hand, first and second fingers
pointed to heaven, beseech passengers, in the name of Allah, to dig
into their pockets. Are they less to be honored than our own clerical fund-raisers?

Pathetic waifs are the hardest to refuse, a fact that has not es-
caped their parents. In Spain, where beggars must at least sell lottery tickets, I determinedly ignored the pleading of a naked little
boy until I caught him surreptitiously twisting back his eyelid that
he might appear deformed. Touched by the sadness of the trick, I
emotionally gave him a half-dollar—and probably the next time a
bus stopped, he distorted both his eyes. For such children are usually intelligent.

"Why is it necessary that I give you a *propina*?" I asked a small
Peruvian girl, thinking to teach her a lesson. "What service have
you performed for me?" Frightened speechless by a totally new
concept, she ran away.

In the West Indies, Mexico, various parts of Asia, indeed recently in New York, enterprising children seeking tips have caught
on to the service angle, voluntarily "guarding" cars, flagging down
taxis, opening doors, scurrying underfoot to polish one's shoes.

Wherever one goes off the beaten path, there are beguiling little
boys who ask to be your guide. Although at Angkor "cigarettes for
me papa" were sufficient reward for a nine-year-old Cambodian
acting as impromptu scout, others like him, shrewdly aware that

youthful enterprise appeals to Americans, are sometimes banditti when it comes time to pay them.

"You are English, memsahib?" asked a Nepalese boy who was politely following me on a shiny new bicycle in Katmandu. "No, American." "I like very much the Americans," he said. "I am studying at the American school."

Completely charmed by him and the throngs of tots who squealed, " 'Allo! Bye-bye!" as he led me in and out of ancient temple courtyards, I was in a benign mood when the lad remarked, "I like very much to have a book, memsahib." "What sort of book?" I asked. "I like very much a Nepalese-English dictionary." As we parted I gave him five rupees (about seventy cents) as a contribution to his scholarship. "No, no, I like the big one," he said, pointing to a ten-rupee note in my hand. "Don't be a little pig," I told him. The next day three other small scholars—these in tatters—also expressed a desire for a Nepalese-English dictionary.

In an article reprinted in *Atlas* magazine, the Italian novelist Alberto Moravia viewed as menacingly American a request by a young Nepalese bicyclist for twenty rupees to buy "a book about all books": "A book about all books. In this extraordinary invention are expressed both the Asiatics' hope of possessing at one stroke, as though by the touch of a magic wand, all of European culture and also the modern, rather American idea of the extracted, the digested—in short, the industrial product that saves time and money."

Mr. Moravia also pointed out that there are no book vendors in Nepal.

Again in Madras I heard, from a chamber man, or room bearer, the melting refrain: "I like very much the Americans." And, expressing his sorrow over John F. Kennedy's death, he added that he wished he had a picture of the President. Later he wrote me:

Dearest Madam/Sir, I must really thank you for the lovely book of Mr. Kennedy and family which my family enjoys very much. I will always keep it and pray and thank you'll each time we see it. My daughter Mary Elizabeth liked the book very much and kisses the picture of Mr. Kennedy each time she sees it.

I hope you are keeping in the pink of health which we always pray for.

By the way I hope I am not asking for to much. You promised me an old wrist watch [I did not]. If you are coming to Madras, please do not forget my humble request. . . .

With our united love and kisses, I thank you.

Yours obediently,

—— ——

P.S.

Dearest Madam/Sir, This will be a real surprise to you but let me introduce myself to you. I am the Room Service Steward. My name is —— ——, and ——, my bearer, showed me the lovely book you sent him, which I will also like to have. By the way, sir, I was recently married, and I would like to know if you could get me a ladies wrist watch. . . .

He, too, very much likes the Americans.

We are so much better off than they; is it mean to withhold baksheesh and presents? Or does American foreign aid discharge any further obligation? I don't know the answer.

I did, however, learn in Ceylon how a democratic attitude can be misunderstood.

I should not like to give the impression that in the course of my travels I have not had some idyllic encounters. That with Pedro dos Santos was not among them. Pedro is descended from one of Vasco da Gama's sailors who were shipwrecked in the fifteenth century off the coast of India. His forebears during the course of generations acquired a dark pigmentation, although their faith remained Roman Catholic.

Reared in Calcutta, Pedro emigrated to Ceylon, where he became a gentleman guide. That he was capable of the most conscientious and courtly deportment (he was, indeed, referred to in the precincts of Colombo as "the duke") was attested to by a friend. The quintessence of the radiantly healthy American girl, she had experienced no difficulty with him. But, of course, Debbie did not have my maturity, and no doubt he regarded her paternally. Her only caution was that he was rather more than commonly fond of liquor. So, sensibly, she had pretended to be a teetotaler.

While I was clearing the exhaustive customs at Colombo, an attendant informed me that Mr. dos Santos was waiting for me in the lounge. I thanked him and continued my responses to the cross-examination. "Yes, sir, the listing is correct; the only gold I have with me are one ring, one wrist watch, one bracelet, and a pair of earrings. No, I have no gifts for Ceylonese that I have purchased abroad."

The eager courier returned with a large bouquet of flowers with the compliments of Mr. dos Santos. The only time I don't appreciate floral tributes is when I'm coping with two suitcases, a capacious shoulder bag, two cameras, and a large plastic string pouch bulging with Balinese masks and wood carvings, Geisha dolls, Thai temple rubbings, tourist pamphlets, and guidebooks.

A tall, equine man with concave cheeks and deep-set, light hazel eyes, Pedro was casually dressed in unpressed slacks and an open-necked sports shirt, which bared a crepey neck and large Adam's apple. When he talked, his tongue poked through the cavity where two lower front teeth had been extracted, somewhat blurring his speech. He handed me a business card that identified him as a travel agent with offices in Colombo and Galle, and we shook hands. He was exceedingly deferential as he drove me to the hotel, checked my accommodations, and dealt with the porters. Though I am cool to caged game, I agreed that it would be interesting to go to the Dehiwala Zoological Gardens and watch the elephants' afternoon dance.

En route we discussed the next five days' itinerary. Weather permitting, we would drive to the great Buddhist antiquities at Anuradhapura, Polonnaruwa, and Sigiriya, thence to Kandy, Nuwara Eliya, and Galle, before returning to Colombo. And he would make every effort to acquaint me with all aspects of Ceylonese life.

"I want you to meet some typical Singhalese," Pedro told me, as we drove back from the zoo. "We shall take tea with a very nice gentleman and his wife. They have entertained your friend." We were cordially received in their garden, but, although I smiled and smiled, I couldn't think of any more to say to them than I usually can to people whom I have just met. I am not what you would call dynamic with the small talk.

After I checked out of my hotel the next morning, we went to a jeweler, where Pedro suggested I look at the sapphires, topazes, and moonstones while he was out on some errands. He added that the jeweler, who was one of his dearest friends, would give me a good discount in the event I wished to make any purchases. While I was modeling the brooches and rings, the proprietor, a handsome, black-skinned Singhalese with dazzling square teeth, asked if he might take me to an "exclusive night club" that evening. He commented that his rumba had won many prizes in Colombo. When I reported the invitation to Pedro, he appeared angry. "That man," he snorted, "is the worst crook in Ceylon."

As we approached the car, Pedro asked if I preferred to sit in the front or back seat. "Why," I hesitated, "actually, I prefer the front. You get a better view there." And, at last, about eleven A.M., we were getting under way. We passed miles of terraced rice fields and huge coconut palms, whose manifold products Pedro enumerated. "You shall have wild boar for luncheon," he triumphantly announced a couple of hours later. I remarked that at the moment I'd rather have a cold beer. Even in mid-December central Ceylon is torrid, and along the shore it is moreover uncomfortably humid. Hospitably, I insisted that Pedro join me in a bottle as we sat on the restaurant's veranda, watching the naked black fishermen bring in their catch. "Have you ever tried arrack?" he inquired, explaining that it was made of fermented coconut "water." "You shall have some tonight before your dinner."

The wild boar looked and tasted like well-done roast beef, and I inhaled the fragrance of Pedro's curry with longing. "But, Miss . . . ," he said, "you are to have only the best."

Along the highway he abruptly stepped on the brakes to purchase from a roadside vendor half a dozen lobsters, which cost about fifty cents. Tossing them onto the floor behind us, he said he would have the cook prepare them Ceylonese fashion for my dinner. It would be a great treat.

Ever solicitous about my comfort, about once every hour he would solemnly inquire, "Miss . . . , do you want—to go to—the toilet?" Nobody had put it quite so bluntly since the days they called me "missy." After each of his own absences he grew increasingly voluble, and it gradually dawned on me that Mr. dos Santos had been nipping. It also became apparent that he had total recall of colloquies with former clients. I wasn't sorry when we arrived at the government resthouse.

"I cannot have dinner with you here," he informed me after returning from a conference with the cook. "I have to eat in the kitchen." "In the *kitchen?*" I repeated. What did they *mean*, he couldn't "sit at the lunch counter"? He was commencing to be a bore, but I wasn't countenancing any discrimination. "I will sit with you," he said, "so that you will not be lonely, but it is less expensive for me if I have my own meal in the kitchen."

Pulling out a flask, he poured a hooker of arrack into my glass and his. Arrack did not prove to be a beverage to which I was likely to become addicted. Pedro clapped his hands smartly, impatiently summoning a waiter, whom he upbraided about the tardiness of the lobster. In a few minutes the latter ran back with a steaming platter.

"Call the manager," Pedro demanded. "This is curried lobster. I asked that it be broiled." The manager protested that Pedro had specified curried lobster. A tedious exchange then took place. "It's all right, Mr. dos Santos," I said. "I love curried lobster." "No, no, this is too highly spiced for you. Take it away! Bring the lady some venison." I looked wistfully at the retreating lobster.

I was climbing the staircase to my bedroom when the manager approached me. "Miss," he said, "I am sorry about the lobster, but the driver did order it curried. Every time that fellow arrives here with a foreigner he creates trouble. He is drunk."

"Mr. dos Santos comes to me highly recommended," I said coolly. "I have no reason to doubt him in any way."

About midmorning the next day we stopped at a guesthouse for coffee. A man whom I took to be the proprietor started to chat. He asked the usual questions. Where was I from? How long would I be in Ceylon? How did I like the island? I responded equally tritely. Pedro broke in. "I do not believe," he said, "that I have had the pleasure of your acquaintance." The man drifted off. Pedro snuffed. "He would never have dared talk with you if you had been with a white man! They are all envious of me because I am with you." "Mr. dos Santos," I said, "you are scarcely *with* me." But I was immediately sorry; he yearned so for human dignity.

Nevertheless, subsequently I spoke with him only when absolutely necessary. It made for a self-conscious silence—a quiet that was at dusk broken by a then-well-mellowed Pedro, who would lov-

ingly detail his dialogues with quondam clients. No comment was
necessary; Mr. dos Santos was a marathon talker.

It was my lot to see most of Ceylon, an island of great scenic
variety and unsurpassed beauty, in a downpour. This curtailed both
our mileage and sightseeing, for we no sooner detoured to inspect
a historic dagoba or the shards of an obsolete kingdom when the
heavens spilled over. Appalled that I should get my legs splattered,
Pedro would dive for my calves to mop up the mud with his hand-
kerchief. I tried to stop him. "For heaven's sake, Mr. dos Santos, if
I were to worry about every spot I got traveling!"

The sun, however, was shining as we neared Sigiriya, a monas-
tery fortress atop a rock four hundred feet high, dating back to the
fifth century A.D. "Miss . . . ," Pedro said with another of those
hesitations that begged permission to add a first name, "it is always
very windy on the climb to the top. You must put on slacks." "I
don't," I said crankily, "have any slacks with me." "Then,
Miss . . . ," he said, "be sure to wear bloomers." Too outraged to
respond, I sulked. Whatever the circumstances, I stormed, I am
quite capable of keeping my skirts down—but I cannot contend
with that much concern. "Heights make me dizzy," I said, passing
up the antiquity. I take it on faith that the frescoes it contains of
big-breasted dancing girls with eighteen-inch waists are extraordinary.

We went instead to the rock temples at Dambulla, where a Buddhist monk with a flickering candle led me barefoot through the
caves' murky labyrinths while Pedro waited outside. The minute I
emerged, before I could put my shoes on, he grabbed first one foot,
then the other, and thrust them into a basin of water. "I can do
that myself!" I cried, but Pedro, with an iron grip on my ankles
and breathing heavily, was already energetically drying my feet.
"You can get diseases," he said, "from the dirt in that place."

The next day we arrived in Kandy, where through a friend in
New York I was to meet a prominent Burgher doctor and his wife,
the descendants of Dutch settlers and Singhalese women. It was just
before Christmas, and the small, almost empty guesthouse where I
was staying was decorated with little withered balloons and tired
tinsel. By that time I was frantically trying to avoid Pedro's company at meals, for his garrulity was stupefying. However, while I

was sitting in the tiny Victorian lounge he joined me. Far gone in his cups he nevertheless sensed my displeasure. "Please, Miss . . . ," he said, "I *beg* you . . . do not dismiss me tomorrow when you meet the doctor. I am your servant—your slave!" "Mr. dos Santos," I snapped, "we don't talk like that in the States! Nobody is my slave." "Command me," he insisted hoarsely, "I am your slave." Aw, the poor fellow, I thought, not without distaste, I must not be unkind; his values are different from ours.

The following noon he drove me to a large hotel, where I was to have lunch with the doctor and his wife. "I beseech you, sir," Pedro said as we parted, "return her to me by three o'clock. We are spending the night at Nuwara Eliya." The crease between the doctor's eyes deepened. We were entering the lobby when Pedro ran back to me. "Forgive me, doctor," he interrupted, "would you excuse us a minute? I want to introduce the lady to my friend Professor Johnson. We shall be back directly." After a brief exchange with the professor, one of Pedro's erstwhile clients, I rejoined my hosts. "Dos Santos!" the doctor shouted after the retreating Pedro. "What time did you say you had to be off?" His arrogance gave me a perspective on Pedro's behavior.

"Where did you get that fellow?" the doctor asked at the table. I explained, indicating that I wasn't entirely happy with the arrangement. He made no comment, and my hopes that I would be persuaded to remain in Kandy collapsed.

At two-thirty a waiter approached with a message from Pedro. "The driver said to remind you that you must be off at three." "Would you tell Mr. dos Santos," I said, "that I am quite aware of the time." And miserable about it. At three o'clock I ignored as long as I could Pedro's beckonings outside the restaurant door. "Mr. dos Santos seems to be a bit confused about who has hired whom," I remarked to the doctor. He suggested no out, and I was diffident about asking him to help me to secure another guide.

As Pedro held the door for me to enter the front of the car, I caught the look of horror on the doctor's face.

It didn't soothe my temper to be trapped by Pedro into paying two dollars for a five-minute rehearsal by students of the Kandyan dance in a village en route to Nuwara Eliya. "My wife," he comforted me, "is arranging a performance for you of the complete

Ceylonese ballet when we get into Galle. She and the children are very eager to meet you." "And how much," I asked acidly, "will that cost me?" "Twenty dollars." "Oh, no," I said, "I'm not paying anything like that. We'll skip the culture." "You must see it," Pedro persisted. "*I* will pay half." "Nope. I'm not even going to pay ten. You guys think we Americans are made of money." I stared sullenly out the window.

"Miss . . . ," he said timidly, "I want very much for you to see the Ceylonese dance. Perhaps it can be arranged less expensively. But you must promise to wear the finest clothes that you have with you. I want to be proud of you. I took a Frenchwoman to it last year, and she wore shoes with very high heels and pointed toes," he added, glancing at my canvas wedgies, which had long since lost their daintiness. "It is of no consequence," I said, "whether you are proud of me or not. This is not a social engagement."

I asked him to stop a couple of times on the fifty-mile drive so that I could photograph workers in the tea bushes. Pedro himself paused periodically to present me with wild orchids growing along the roadside or to buy cigarettes, gasoline, and at length, frankly, arrack. "The guesthouse does not permit drinking," he commented, "but we can have some in the car—or your room." "I can do without it," I said.

It had begun to teem, and the spiral, sharply ascending road was so foggy one could scarcely see ten feet ahead. For hours, as he expertly inched the car round the treacherous curves, Pedro sentimentalized bygone conversations. Ultimately we arrived at the guesthouse. I was exhausted, chilled from the abrupt change in altitude, and hungry. But unable to stand one more minute of Pedro, I said, "You go ahead and have your dinner. I am going to rest for an hour or so." "Oh, I will wait for you," he said. "I know you don't like to eat alone."

As the Singhalese manager was showing me to my room, he remarked that they had an excellent cocktail lounge in the guesthouse—a fully stocked American bar. Could he perhaps treat me to a drink there? "No, thank you," I said, closing the door. Then I hurriedly freshened up and went into the dining room. With luck, I might finish a meal without Pedro. I got as far as dessert when he showed up, lugubriously contrite. "I *told* them to let me know

when you came in, that you always wanted me to eat with you." I
said nothing. "Miss . . . , have you ever had—cream de mint?"
He clapped his hands, and the crème de menthe was served. Sighing
deeply, I drank it.

"Miss . . . , be sure to bolt your door this evening. No matter
who knocks, don't answer it!" "Don't worry. I always bolt my
door." "But tonight, especially, don't open it for anyone." "Okay,
okay," I said. "Good night."

Ten minutes later there was a knock on my door. I ignored it.
Louder knocks followed. I called out, "Who's there?" "The manager." I opened the door a crack. "Miss, would you care to join me
in a cognac?" Utterly beat, I replied, "I'm sorry. I have just had a
drink with the chauffeur."

It was Christmas Eve when we arrived in Galle, Pedro's home
town, and he was so ebullient that I just couldn't be mean. Besides,
I was winding up the tour the next day. And he would surely have
to have dinner with his family. While we were waiting on the hotel's porch for my suite to be readied by an elderly male servant
with hair wound into a tidy chignon and wearing a sarong ("The
lady must have nothing but the best," Pedro had insisted), he told
me that he had ordered for my dinner something I had surely
never had.

"And now, Miss . . . , you must accept this. I want you to
wear them this evening," he said, handing me a jewelry box. "But
you shouldn't!" I protested. "It is a Christmas present," he said
quietly, "and it makes me very happy to give it to you. Please open
it." I feigned delight over an ensemble of inferior moonstones: a
ring, bracelet, necklace, and a pair of chandelier earrings. In his
way, I told myself, he is trying to be kind.

"My wife and children will sit with you at dinner," he said. Eating alone Christmas Eve wasn't the most gala function I could envi-
sion, yet I preferred it to the alternative. "Oh surely," I said, "they
will want to eat with you. Why don't you have them visit me this
evening? I should like to have guests in that elegant suite. I'll order
cake and wine."

The solitary occupant of a candlelit dining room, festooned with
red and green crepe paper, I had barely finished my soup when
Pedro, in a gray Palm Beach suit and oatmeal-colored shoes, re-

turned with his wife and seven children. She was a shabbily dressed, fragile-looking woman with tired, tragic eyes, but the off-spring were husky: a seventeen-year-old daughter and six shiny-cheeked boys ranging from four to sixteen. They smiled at me brightly, and I invited them to sit down. As they were taking their seats, the dining room darkened, and a waiter strode in, holding aloft a flaming omelet on a silver platter, which he ceremoniously placed before me. "There," exulted Pedro, "have you ever seen anything like it?"

Bidding us good-bye, he hissed at me *sotto voce*, "Why didn't you wear the necklace?" The clasp had broken while I was putting it on, but I pretended not to hear. "Do you open your presents this evening or Christmas morning?" I asked Mrs. dos Santos. "Oh," she said, "we do not have any gifts. Except for the little fellow," indicating the youngest boy. They all smiled at him affectionately.

In my bedroom that evening I brooded. How outrageous that Pedro should have bought me this to-him elaborate jewelry—even if it was included in his fee—and provided nothing for his family. He might at least have gotten that wistful little wife a trinket. By God, she was going to have a present—if only I could think of something to give her. Taking mental inventory of my suitcases, I remembered a new nylon slip. I'll bet she'd love to have some nice, lacy lingerie. I sprang from my bed, removed a gift I'd been given in Thailand from its festive wrapping, and inserted the slip. One of my printed cotton blouses would have to do for the daughter. And I'd give the little fellow a few foreign coins. Pleased with myself, I sank sweetly into slumber.

In the morning Pedro, still in the natty gray suit but needing a shave, arrived with his daughter and four of the sons to take me to their home. He whispered that he had been gambling all night and felt a bit poorly. "Serves you right," I muttered. "That's no way to celebrate Christmas Eve." From his wife's tortured eyes, it was evi-dent she thought he had spent it with me, and she accepted the unopened gift lackadaisically. The daughter, however, was keen for the blouse; she admired my red straw shoes and told me she also very much wanted to have a pin with a picture of Elvis Presley. In turn, they pressed on me one of their treasures—a small speckled seashell. There were two wooden chairs, a frail desk, and a three-quarters bed for the parents in the flat's two tiny rooms. The children slept on the dirt floors.

Fulfilling his promise that he would show me all levels of society in Ceylon, Pedro took me on a tour of a variety of homes. I protested that we just couldn't visit people unannounced, but he maintained that I must see the Ceylonese "in their normal state." We went first to the "typically American" mansion of a millionaire Moslem, whose women were in purdah; then to the hut of the very poorest Tamils, who, flustered by our entrance, rushed about with brooms, nervously sweeping out the rubbish. Ashamed of having shamed them, I was reluctant to continue, but Pedro assured me that the next family—middle-class Buddhists—were great friends of his and would not be discomfited by unexpected guests. They were graciously serene even when Pedro, after wishing them a very merry Christmas, derided a lapse in their knowledge of the royal succession in ancient Lanka. Again mortified, I begged off any more holiday calls. A final one, he urged me; I must meet a family of Hindus. With them he was quarrelsome about local political corruption.

"Now," he said, glowing with satisfaction, "you have seen all sides of Ceylon."

I was so glad to be returning to Colombo that I chatted with him amiably on the road. And at sundown, when I got a couple of good snapshots of fishermen on stilts in the Indian Ocean, my spirits really soared. Pedro, however, was depressed.

"Miss . . . ," he said to me, "I shall miss you very, very much. . . . It is always like this for me when a foreigner leaves. For a month or two I cannot think of anything else."

"Oh, you'll get over it," I said briskly.

"No, I won't!" He was silent for a few minutes. "You have forgotten, but—I washed your feet! I have never before washed anyone's feet, but I washed your feet, and I got great satisfaction out of it. I have never," he emphasized, "even washed my wife's feet."

"Well," I said, "you should."

Pedro made a grab for my hand. "Please, please—just for a moment." I jerked it away. "Will you stop it!" I shouted. "I have tried not to hurt your feelings, yet you force me to. As I have indicated to you before, this is not a social engagement. But you've kept intruding yourself, and," I wailed, "you've absolutely ruined this lovely, lovely island for me!"

His Adam's apple bobbed. "Miss . . . , I am sorry," he said, "if I have offended you."

Well, I don't know what went wrong with Ceylon. Probably Pedro was not ready for democracy. Manifestly, I was not ready for a chauffeur.

13

Globes of New Friends

Ghil, a vivacious French girl now living in the States, was considering a trip to Asia. "But aren't you," she asked me, "ever scared traveling so far by yourself? Of course, if a fellow pinches your bottom in Paris it's all right, but in the Orient. . . ." "All *right?*" I interrupted. Well, she explained, you simply take a swing at the guy with your purse. One time, though, she did get into a tangle thereby: the chain of her pocketbook got hooked onto the Casanova's zipper and, what with his yells and her screams as she tried to yank it away, they drew quite a crowd on the Champs-Elysées. Evidently she hadn't aimed for his head.

Accustomed to wearing a shoulder bag overseas, I have always relied on the fact that, thanks to the American cinema, "Scram!" is universally understood—and respected, evoking as it does visions of a landing by the U. S. armed forces. Jeanne, who is prettier, finds it fatal to acknowledge overtures with so much as a syllable. However, with her ear for exotic riposte, Mary, an otherwise gentle blonde, rejects sidewalk suitors with idiomatic rebuff; she has, for example, deflated many an aspirant Latin lover with the Spanish *coup de grâce*, "Go marry your mother!"—or verbs to that effect.

Blondes may indeed look the most fun, but it has been my observation that the run-of-the-mall masher is indiscriminately optimistic, albeit his wooing may range from an old-boyish wink in Dublin to hisses in Lisbon or tailing in Beirut, where on my first visit it was worth at least one's composure to walk a few blocks to the jewelers paced by Cadillacs filled with glad-eyed petroleum princes given to such lovelorn honking of horns as I never did hear.

If Copenhagen was quieter, the Danes also were importunate. Having landed at dusk with energy unabated, I decided to take a turn about the city before dining. While aware that strolling alone after dark invites sportive attention, I carelessly equated the Nordics with their climate, and was dreamily redecorating my apartment with the stunning housewares displayed when I suddenly perceived, in front of Georg Jensen's, that the same man had paused alongside me before a succession of stores. Retreating, ostensibly for another look at competitive silver, I met him head-on, waiting stonily at the opposite corner. I pretended not to notice, crossed the street, and continued, now self-consciously, to size up the crystal. For by this time I was rather distracted, though, since the area was well lighted, unalarmed. When I quit the Royal Copenhagen crockery, the lout, who, I rejoiced, had abandoned the pursuit, emerged from a doorway and approached me with the inevitable unintelligible mutters that mean goodness knows what; I'm no linguist.

The next morning, in the kaleidoscope that is the Tivoli gardens, I was again shadowed—at one point simultaneously—by a brace of big Danes, and I wasn't even guilty of the come-on that I later learned is symbolized by window-shopping. At night even stopping outside a restaurant to read a posted menu can attract buyers. This I discovered to my astonishment in London, which I had credited with no carnality since Hogarth. Unfamiliar with the signals of the doxy, a girl can make many innocent blunders, but, as a rule, if she takes it easy with the cheesecake and acts like a lady, she will be treated like one. In what seems like a really tight spot she should be absolutely regal. I say "seems like" because being away from home tends to balloon the imagination.

Vide the time I went nightclubbing with Yusouf, an ex-pasha who had an imperious way of banging his cane for service. There were few women in the oasis, which was vibrant and jammed with young men. Doubly excited by the serpentine grinds of sleek identical-twin Salomes, the stags leapt to the tables with shouts of the Arabic for the warmest approval. Even Yusouf, who was on the elderly side, caught the spirit of the dance and suggested, some-

what thickly, that we "elope in the desert." Observing that the
Scotch, to which I was conditioned, had gotten him crocked, I
suggested we call it a night. He nodded, bleary-eyed, and we returned to his black limousine, where he mumbled something gut-
teral to the chauffeur.

". . . 'lope . . . in the desert," he said to his chest, his fez listing
at my lap. "Where are we *go-ing?*" I squeaked in ruptured voice.
" 'lopin . . ." He swallowed. "In the deser'." And he steadied his
chin against the cane that had seemed so debonair on earlier acquaintance.

Since most sheiks look like Saudi Arabia's Faisal (not unnatu-
rally, considering the hundreds of sons the king's grandpa begat),
the potential of this type of camping was alarming. A terrified
glance at the black, empty road and I realized my folly—our formal
introduction notwithstanding—in drinking with a stranger whose
culture denied such good fellowship to its virtuous women.

Well, I know a lot of swell ways to quench ardor. Stiffening like
Queen Victoria on my favorite gin label, I went into a torrent of
praise for his nation's agrarian reforms and expressed my heartfelt
wishes for its success in desert reclamation. When Yusouf was
clearly snoring, I whispered to the driver, "The Semiramis. Hurry!"
He maintained his funereal pace along the silent, stygian highway,
and I was all but catatonic when at length we drew up to the hotel's stately portals. To my drowsy, bewildered host I bade a hasty
good night, then raced to the elevators—for all the world like a
Sabine woman fleeing rape.

The fright was real—how justifiable is a moot point.

Hardly any girl who has survived the rigorous courting of our
coeducational system needs any social instruction. However, for
those who have been more sheltered, I can recommend various
means of curbing advances short of screaming for the cops or
throwing the gent in judo. To forestall crises, try complaining a
good deal; it keeps one from looking too seductive and makes almost any man yearn to be elsewhere. Simple calling cards, which
abroad are exchanged nearly as frequently as handshakes, are a
must; those identifying you as a woman of achievement are invaluable for inspiring special touristic attention from assorted officials

—and they are virtually infallible for depressing a swain. You have just an ordinary job? Prattle about it; fill him in on the minutiae. Burble about your nieces and nephews; any adorable little children he doesn't know will distract him from romantic ideas, implying as they do a desire to settle down. Or abort all his sentences; finish them, explain what he is trying to say; keep a stranglehold on the conversation. This, as a matter of fact, is an excellent way to get rid of everybody.

Perhaps you're wondering how you get acquainted in the first place. Unlike summer camps or ships, foreign lands are not equipped with social directors. Nearest thing to that setup is the packaged group tour, on which a large percentage of the passengers will likely be other women or couples, many of them elderly. Nevertheless, it is better to join one than to stay home in dread of loneliness, because the people aboard are almost invariably friendly, and the tour guide will tell enough jokes and lead enough communal singing to stave off melancholia—assuming old chestnuts and choruses of "Frère Jacques" don't in themselves bring on the vapors.

Furthermore, any fairly large gathering will usually afford at least one kindred spirit. Of the group tour that she took, Helen, an attractive divorcée, typically reports: "The people were mainly old, including several in their eighties and two in their nineties—but they didn't hold back in any of the activities. The couples stuck together. The single women were for the most part older than I, and even the younger ones didn't have any bounce. So that just left George, who was my seatmate, but only about thirty years old. We hit it off very well in spite of our age difference, and had some fun for ourselves. He would have been pretty much alone otherwise, too. If tours could be arranged so there wouldn't be such disparity in ages and temperaments, they could be fun, because you are relieved of mundane worries and only have to enjoy yourself."

To my mind, for goals other than connubial, disparity in age is unimportant among people who share the same bents. And luckily, for those who would like to focus on specific facets of travel with reasonably congenial companions, there are abundant possibilities.

Special Interest Tours Information lists journeys, varying in price and duration, that concentrate on archaeology, art, bicycling,

bird-watching, castles, contract bridge, culinary arts, drama, eth-
nology, fishing, gardens, golf, horses, hunting, music, philately,
photography, railroads, skiing, viniculture. There are tours for
students of all kinds—tours for votaries of Zen and more Western
persuasions, tours conducted by scientists and professors, announcements of which appear from time to time in the Personals
columns of *Saturday Review*.

Indeed, sponsors seem to be increasingly imaginative. The
French Book Guild recently offered a Literary and Artistic Journey,
during which passengers would pay homage to landmarks in
France identified with Molière, Péguy, Proust, Lamartine, Balzac,
and George Sand, among others. Another operator offered a Desert
Journey in the "footsteps of Lawrence of Arabia," which featured a
safari from El Jafr to Wadi-Ramm astride dromedaries in a caravan
escorted by troopers from the Arab Legion's camel corps and Bedouin guides.

There are also tours—exceedingly costly ones—for the handicapped. That, however, is not an adjective one would apply to
Peggy, a photography critic, who doesn't permit two crutches to
inhibit her gadding abroad by herself. "Thanks to them," she says,
"wherever I go I'm sure to meet the nicest and most interesting
people." For instance, during a visit to the Vatican, Pope John,
seeing Peggy pause to rest, invited her to sit with him in his garden.

Whatever the mode of travel, a foreign vacation is infinitely
more memorable for the acquaintances made with people of other
lands. The simplest exchange can be an adventure. Were I going
on a special-interest tour, which, like any conducted trip, might
limit spontaneous meetings, I should wish to be assured that the
other passengers would be drawn from a variety of countries.

Young people between the ages of sixteen and thirty who seriously wish to participate in the ways of other cultures may do so by
applying to Experiment in International Living. Founded in 1932
as a private, nonprofit, educational organization to foster world
peace through international exchange programs centered in family
living, the Experiment now has representatives in more than thirty
countries in Europe, Latin America, Africa, and Asia. An average
home stay lasts about a month. At the conclusion the traveler
spends two or three weeks exploring the country by bike, foot, bus,

or train in a binational group. In semitropical countries like Spain, Italy, or Mexico, transportation is generally by rail or motor coach; in Denmark—doing as the Danes do—bicycling prevails, while hiking and mountain-climbing are, of course, *de rigueur* in Norway. "Whatever the means of locomotion," says the Experiment's *Handbook*, "the aim is to see the country as its own people see it, rather than out of the pages of a Baedeker. Those who hurry from one important monument to the next, staying only at the best hotels, completely miss the most revealing side of travel."

The United States National Student Association, which has a similar purpose, would agree. USNSA's special interest travel and study programs include orientation, student parties, visits, and sometimes home stays, with foreign families.

Just as some travelers like to plunge into a milieu as different as possible from that at home, others are more comfortable with their counterparts abroad. For them there are the foreign branches of the fraternal, religious, and professional groups with which they are affiliated in America. It is best to write to them in advance, following up the initial letter with a note immediately preceding or upon arrival at your hotel. If unavailable locally, their addresses may be secured from the government tourist offices or consulates.

When traveling in the United Kingdom, Australia, New Zealand, Bermuda, Canada, Malta, India, and Pakistan, members of the English-Speaking Union of the United States may enjoy the welcome extended to them by the seventy-five affiliates of the sister organization, the English-Speaking Union of the Commonwealth. In England, Scotland, and Wales alone there are more than forty branches. Although completely autonomous, the two E-SUs have identical aims: "to draw together in the bonds of comradeship the English-speaking peoples of the world, and particularly to foster between the people of the United States and the peoples of the Commonwealth mutual understanding, trust, and friendship." Nonpartisan, nonpolitical, and nongovernmental, the English-Speaking Union of the United States has over 31,000 members in its seventy-eight branches, which in turn extend courtesies to visitors from abroad. Each year E-SU's Pen Friends Division acts as liaison between some 40,000 Americans and their contemporaries in other English-speaking lands. For further information, write to the national headquarters of the English-Speaking Union of the United States.

The American Friends of the Middle East maintains offices in Jordan, Syria, Egypt, Iran, Iraq, Morocco, and Tunisia, where a hand is extended to travelers from the U.S. Formed as a people-to-people program, the AFME tries to counteract the influence of Communism in those countries by strengthening American–Middle Eastern rapport. The AFME is opposed to "'expansionist Zionism' either in our own country or in the Middle East"; however, they assert, "we are equally explicit in discouraging any idea among the Arabs that we advocate the forcible liquidation of a normal Israel." The last is defined as "an Israel integrated into the Middle East, living in the spirit of the universalities of the Judaic tradition," but physically shrunk to the boundaries of the 1947 United Nations Partition Plan and agreeable to, among other issues, the repatriation of Palestinian refugees.

When in Israel, a traveler may telephone or visit one of the Hadassah Tourist Clubs, which will recommend types of tours, suggest what to see, including Hadassah projects and points of general interest. The tourist need not be a member of Hadassah to avail herself of the organization's services.

The Pan American Women's Association is happy to facilitate the visits of its members to countries in the Southern Hemisphere, where PAWA has close relations with women leaders and organizations. Services include introductions to key individuals and assurance of entry into homes and centers seldom available to the average traveler. A nonpolitical educational and cultural organization, PAWA wants to see the doctrines of human rights adopted and realized among the peoples of the Americas.

Some American consulates have visitors' bureaus which can be helpful in introducing women travelers to people in their own professions. And numerous nations have programs enabling those traveling independently to meet English-speaking citizens with similar interests. Either in this country or theirs the respective government tourist organizations will arrange introductions in Britain, Ireland, Switzerland, the Scandinavian countries, Belgium, Germany, Austria, Spain, Yugoslavia, Bulgaria, the Soviet Union, Turkey, Israel, Jordan, Iran, Pakistan, the United Arab Republic,

Tunisia, Indonesia, New Zealand, South Africa, Venezuela, the Philippines, Jamaica, Barbados, and Brazil. Most volunteer hosts serve coffee, tea, or a meal, but provide no overnight lodging.

Some travelers, however, break the ice as paying guests with families screened by the government tourist offices. Others avail themselves of central tourist bureaus set up in many large European cities near or inside the main railroad station, where, with no advance reservation, they may secure accommodations with private families—at exceedingly low rates. In the New York *Times* travel section of April 19, 1965, Thomas F. Mofford reported experiences he and his wife have had as impromptu paying guests in Belgium, the Netherlands, Germany, Denmark, and Italy.

Within minutes after their arrival in Brussels, he writes, "we pulled a velvet cord that rang the bell of a huge stone house. A maid in a lace cap led us through a marbled hallway of glittering chandeliers and to where our hostess was waiting for us to join her at the dinner table. Later, we bathed in a deep tiled tub, and slept under a canopy. The next morning the maid brought us breakfast in bed. Madame presented us with a four-inch house key and good advice for getting around to museums and shops.

"This special treatment cost $3.50 a day, including two meals. More important, we made a Belgian friend. Madame still sends us embroidered Christmas cards. . . ."

The Moffords found they could best see a foreign country by observing and taking part in the daily life of the family with whom they lodged.

"The service always was gracious because we were treated as personal guests. We usually ate with the family and were frequently guided through the city by a young son or daughter. Yet we never felt obligated to them or felt that we had lost our independence to explore. . . .

"The best part of this type of traveling was the conversations with 'our' families. We stormed them with questions about everything from folk legends to contemporary politics. However, it was when they began to ask us questions that we really began to understand them."

No reason a woman traveling alone couldn't follow in the footsteps of the Moffords.

Britain's Tourist Hospitality Service has enrolled families in all walks of life throughout England, Scotland, and Wales who entertain overseas guests one to three days, during which visitors reside with them, meet their friends, and join in their everyday activities. Though not part of the arrangement, sometimes sightseeing may be added. A succession of home visits may be planned through the Tourist Hospitality Service, to which payment is made—as of this writing, including all meals—$9.80 for one day and night, $15.60 for two days and nights, $19.60 for three.

To free mothers wishing to travel for extended periods alone, the Danish National Tourist Office reports that Denmark has an abundance of competent English-speaking baby sitters. Women may also park their children, aged eleven to twenty-four (that's right), with English, French, German, and Swiss families enrolled by Britain's Junior Tourism organization. Some offer only board and lodgings; others add outings and sports—tennis, riding, swimming, and sailing. It is possible for the children, who are accepted as part of the host family, to attend nearby schools or receive tuition at home. Depending on what was provided, prices recently ranged from $19.60 to $33.60 a week.

Letters of introduction to friends of friends may be fruitful, and so much the better if you can deliver a small gift. Certainly, if you have a chum who corresponds with a Thai prince, twist her arm before going to Bangkok. Through well-connected sidekicks and colleagues I have met similar élite—among them a gentleman in Athens whom Henry Miller described in *The Colossus of Maroussi:* "For Katsimbalis is not the type of soulless and isolated erudite, but a powerful personality of vivacity and dynamism, of sharp and delicate literary taste, a keen and lively spirit of inspiration and creative enthusiasm; a volcano of life and energy, of nobleness and initiative." He also knew a nifty seafood place on the old harbor of Piraeus.

But there was that awfully sweet family in Buenos Aires whose hospitality was also engendered by a friend. For hours on end I smiled in their parlor and admired the children, rather less than engaged with their progress in school. So, if you have no letters of introduction, don't worry about it; they can also result in a frightful waste of time.

Usually the mutual friend will give you the name, address, and scuttlebutt about the incipient hosts, then write them about you. Because it's often as easy to establish communication with one of the nearer planets as to reach someone by telephone overseas, shortly before or immediately after arrival in their country drop your contacts a friendly note expressing your eagerness to meet them. Mention the name of your hotel, along with the dates you will be there, and extend an invitation to luncheon or tea—this to spare them inconvenience in having you to their home. Probably there will be a message from them awaiting you at your hotel, and nine times out of ten they will wish to entertain you. But if after a couple of days they haven't responded, it may be better to forget it—for I must confess to a couple of snubs.

In the event you are the hostess, it forestalls awkwardness to arrange in advance with the captain in the cocktail lounge or restaurant of your hotel to bring you the check to sign. I shall never forget the tug-of-war over a bill I had in Tokyo with a witty Japanese woman journalist who, like me, had become aggressively hospitable under the influence of Suntories and soda. She proved the more muscular, and to this day I regret the lavishness with which I assumed I was treating her.

Oftener than not, in places where I have had no connections I've had the best time—perhaps because happenstance acquaintance is spared the polite gush characteristic of contrived get-togethers.

Young girls will everywhere find male companionship among the multitude of students traveling about; in fact, youths given to beards, sackcloth, and sandals—and I don't believe they're monastic—abound in the East, as do retired elderly widowers on round-the-globe flings.

According to Pan American Airways, island life is fun. "In Bermuda, the Bahamas and Caribbean you may choose a guesthouse or smaller hotel where you'll meet every guest. These places usually have a 'community' cocktail hour; small and informal dining rooms where your host will seat you with other guests. Larger hotels often welcome new guests at a party." This is not the practice elsewhere, although in remote areas, and smaller hotels generally, fellow Americans tend to be clubby, particularly if they have no choice but demi- or full pension.

"Do participate in sports—even as a spectator," advises Pan Am wisely. "You'll find a tennis court or swimming pool an excellent place to meet new friends."

However, if exercise and sun are anathema, avoid most resorts. Swarming with honeymooners and clannish bourgeois families, the non-Bohemian playlands lure few free-wheeling, sufficiently mature males with whom even to flirt. Spot an attractive man on butte or beach and, like as not, he'll appear at dinner in the grip of that frump whom he married; large dowries are the only apparent explanation for some of those Continental mismatings. Or in the event there's a cheering leer from someone seemingly unshackled, chances are he's one of the sharks at the casino.

While obviously it's more invigorating to dine with three men, new people, regardless of sex, can be stimulating, and an evening with another woman or a couple is not to be scorned. In the latter case, it's thoughtful to offer to pay your share of the meal. Even if you are refused the first time, do it more insistently when next invited. Should this appear to embarrass the husband, don't make an issue of it; he and his wife may be persuaded to have cocktails or tea on you at your hotel. Again, see to it in advance that you get the check.

Unaccompanied, though not necessarily unmarried, men on business and government missions show up a good deal in the world's capitals. The entrepreneurs, by grace of expense accounts and tax credits, hole up at the luxury hotels; the government men, with more Spartan allowances, at the less costly. Nightclubs and bars are no place for a lady to make their acquaintance. Nor, as a rule, is the hotel cocktail lounge one to inspire a proper invitation, if any, although there are exceptions. I can cite one in Seville—but then, from my perspiring face and disheveled hair it was obvious that after a long outing in the midday sun all I wanted really was a cold beer. Thus disarmed, a couple of American engineers invited me to dine and dance on the roof. Never worry about looking a mess; lots of men feel more relaxed with women who do. One sees evidence of this constantly.

While some girls bank on bosoms, any curve—convex or concave —will serve overseas: trim ankles, of course, but, especially in areas where by custom nobody wears belts, a slim waist. Plumpness, conversely, is prized in lands with a subsistence economy—Egypt, Turkey, and Ceylon among them, though none go so far as medieval Ghana's tributary city, Aoudaghast, an erstwhile culinary paradise some 180 miles northwest of Timbuktu. There, reports Eleanor Hoffmann in *Realm of the Evening Star*, a fascinating history of Morocco, "One hundred pieces of gold could buy a Negress expert in such regional specialties as macaroni with honey, nut cakes, and snakes in absinthe. With such a diet it is not surprising to learn that magnificent buttocks, too decorative to be sat on, were the greatest asset of the women in the city. They always either lay on their sides or stood supported."

Most girls have been refining their wiles from the age of four months, when they began cooing at daddy. For those lacking coquetry, there are supplemental sources that recommend a kitty of tricks, including such stratagems as blocking the aisles with outsized chapeaus or dragging yourself down to the dining room for breakfast. This may be a great idea if you arise from bed dewy as a Botticelli Venus; until noon I look like a boiled owl—as these days do my masculine contemporaries.

Although sometimes men don't seem very bright, they tend to detect the phony; on the other hand, a purely functional gesture like searching for a match is regarded by most as a dropped hanky updated. The fact is, one never knows what may prove provocative. Because it was so arduously won, I most treasure the overture of an American in the airport at Hong Kong: "Say, you sure can handle those chopsticks! I was watching you last night at the Princess."

There are conversation pieces more easily come by. American consumer slicks arouse interest, mostly female, whereas among young people of both sexes there's nothing like the fan magazines for making the world one. A cultural lag may have some sites still doting on Elvis Presley long after the Beatles are passé, but the Hollywood stars—particularly of Westerns—are always good for an exchange.

Should you wish to communicate on a loftier level, carry paperback editions of American writers well known overseas: Walt Whitman, Mark Twain, Herman Melville, Jack London, Sinclair Lewis, John Steinbeck, William Faulkner, Pearl Buck, J. D. Salinger, Saul Bellow, Mary McCarthy, Arthur Miller, and, above all, Ernest Hemingway.

For several months in advance of your trip, watch the book re-

view sections of the large newspapers and literary magazines for
mention of works that have been hotly discussed overseas. Originals or English translations of controversial foreign authors—Moravia, Sartre, Pasternak, Kazantzakis, Günter Grass, Jakov Lind, Uwe
Johnson, Françoise Sagan, Nathalie Sarraute, Friedrich Dürren-
matt, Jean Genet, Robbe-Grillet, to name but a few—provide cul-
tured citizens of other lands with a respectable pretext for conversation, as do books concerning their country. And, fortunately,
women need not be too brainy about them: people are flattered to
be asked for the score, irritated when given it by an alien.

I've gotten considerable mileage out of a battered Meridian edi-
tion of *The Glorious Koran* that Jay gave me more than a decade
ago. Most recently in the airport at Kabul, where, once again, I was
distracted from ever comprehending it by an invitation from a 250-
pound vizier to join his party of Pakistanis at tea. White-robed in
the manner of hadjis who have made the pilgrimage to Mecca,
he turned out to be the ambassador to Afghanistan from Saudi
Arabia—thereby substantiating my contention that one meets
tonier types in eccentric purlieus.

Rare, moreover, is any plane trip during which pleasantries are
not exchanged; the real pitfall is being seated alongside too garrulous a companion. Overnight flights, especially, break down reserves,
thanks to the morning lineup for the lavatories with other tousled
passengers—not to say that subtle sense of intimacy engendered
among people with whom one has, however discreetly, been sleeping. Thus, although you may opt against seeing Tokyo with a
Levi salesman from Seattle, in the air such opportunities arise.

Train rides, too, inspire cordiality, particularly in dining cars,
where one of necessity shares a table. In her *Complete Book of
Etiquette*, Amy Vanderbilt cautions: "Certainly a woman never
accepts the hospitality of a strange man by allowing him to pay for
refreshments or a meal en route or by accepting an invitation to
lunch or dinner when both reach a common destination. . . . A
man may easily leap to conclusions if his invitation to a woman to
whom he has not really been properly introduced is unquestion-
ingly accepted."

Excellent advice for very young women; hence perhaps it's no
credit to my person that I have from time to time enjoyed, without

inspiring objectionable advances, the hospitality of male dinner companions from Aswan to La Paz.

Actually, a strong case could be made for maturity as a social asset. An elderly woman in Copenhagen vowed that the older she got the more she enjoyed traveling, since now she could without suspicion strike up a conversation with any man she elected. Or take Fannie, a retired librarian. Not long ago she had the heady experience (if that is the word) of being simultaneously cuddled by a trio of big Sikhs. But then she does have enormous vitality.

Small-town people are neighborly the world over. No matter how reserved you normally are about greeting strangers, when moseying about their villages smile to all passers-by and say "Good day" in the local language if you've learned how to (and you should), or nod your head if you haven't.

City-dwellers tend to be stand-offish, but a good way to meet other travelers is on the locally-contracted-for daytime group tours; not only do they provide an economical once-over of the highlights in and around town, they attract single men. If you're solo, there's a fair chance you'll be seated next to one; even if you aren't, during a sightseeing stop an unaccompanied man will generally begin a conversation, and these often blossom into dates. At the very least, you will meet other girls, and those who, like you, are alone will by their very spirit of adventure tend to be entertaining companions.

So if you hate being by yourself, stick to the areas that for long have been popular with and catering to tourists: Mexico, the Caribbean, Western Europe, and the Holy Land. The farther you diverge from them, the fewer opportunities for new friendships arise.

First time I went to Rome I arrived too late in the day to join an afternoon tour, but even after a couple of hours' stroll about the city, I still had a lot of life in me, the January freeze notwithstanding. At a loss for evening activity—I'm not much for opera, and you can go to the movies at home—I asked the concierge to book me on the gala Rome by Night tour, hoping that it wouldn't be composed entirely of dames.

It wasn't. About 9:00 P.M. the tour conductor collected me at my hotel, and I entered an unheated Greyhound—empty save for

him and the driver. Shivering, I shrouded my head and shoulders
in a Mexican rebozo and took a seat in the center of the bus. We
paused to pick up other revelers at the Flora and Excelsior, the
Hassler and de la Ville, the Savoie, the Grand, the Plaza, the Atlantic, the Continentale, the Mediterraneo, the San Giorgio. Nobody got on. By that time even another girl would have been welcome. Finally, emerging from a side-street *albergo*, a gentleman
joined the party. To my surprise, he was the same tall, lean man
who that morning in Athens, thinking I was short of Greek coin,
had offered me his residual fifty thousand drachmas to settle a ten-
dollar hotel bill I was disputing at the King George.

Now, doubtless having tagged me a troublesome personality (few
women are alluring in altercation), he grunted a perfunctory hello
and, slouching in a nearby seat, turned up the collar of his trench
coat—a dashing enough garment, but not insulated against icy
drafts.

"*Allora*," proclaimed the tubby, five-foot conductor. "We now
begin the romantic Rome by Night tour. Observe, please, to your
left, the beautiful Fontana del Tritone created by the great Baroque sculptor—Bare-*knee*-knee." The Bernini statuary looked
bleak, and the fountains were dry. "Please," said the guide, "we go
first to a typical Roman *trattoria*. There you will kindly drink wine
and listen to typical Italian love songs. Observe, please, to your
right—the beautiful Fountains of the Four Rivers designed by the
great Baroque sculptor—Bare-*knee*-knee." I peered through the
frosted windows at the allegorical figures representing the Danube,
the Nile, the Ganges, and the Río de la Plata. The man in the
trench coat, who was slapping some heat into his shoulders,
grunted.

The bus drew up to a café in Trastevere. We entered and ordered a Cinzano. Not exactly firewater, but it inspired a few routine questions. We discovered we both lived in New York and
were, broadly speaking, engaged in the same calling.

The tour conductor, who was tactfully sitting by himself at a
table to our rear, came over and said we might ask the strolling
accordionist to play our favorite Italian serenades. All my con-
gealed brain could come up with was "Santa Lucia," which seemed
too square to suggest. My companion appeared equally unmusical.

"We go next to la Biblioteca," said the guide. "You may *dance* with the lady there." I began to perk up. The gentleman grunted.

If our being the only two people on a romantic Rome by Night bus tour left him cold, the trench coat thawed somewhat in amusement over the guide's pride in the recurrent Berninis—on the Sant' Angelo Bridge, in the Piazza del Popolo, the Piazza della Minerva, the Piazza San Pietro. He seemed in fairly good spirits when we arrived at the Biblioteca, the walls of which are lined with wine bottles to simulate a library. "Imbiblioteca is rather more like it," I quipped none too cleverly. The man in the trench coat sneezed. We had a Campari and soda, which is a marvelous tonic.

"You may dance with the lady here," the guide reminded him, nodding towards the floor, on which there were a few couples. Looking bland, I surreptitiously flexed the icicles in my ankles. My escort blew his nose and became talkative about his travels. We were soon conversing with animation because I, too, had some opinions to offer about the people and places that *I'd* seen.

Our bitters finished, the social director hustled us back to the bus; we still had the grand finale of the evening before us: champagne at what, according to the brochure, was the smartest nightclub in Roma. I wouldn't be surprised if there were others more stylish; however, we drank deeply of the wine. It, at least, was warm. "You can dance with the lady here," the guide remarked pointedly. Now quite garrulous, my companion ignored the observation. Perhaps, I reflected, he has an artificial limb.

The guide brooded awhile in his corner, then returned. "If *you* don't care to dance with the lady," he said, "there's a gentleman over there who would like to very much." My bus mate sighed and pushed back his chair. "I suppose," he said, "that I shall have to. Come on."

Once you got him on the floor, we could have danced all night. He tipped the guide and dismissed him; we'd carry on alone. The cicerone looked troubled. "You don't have to stay with this man. I will escort you back to your hotel," he whispered while my dancing partner was ordering another bottle of champagne. "It'll be okay," I said. There was nothing to be afraid of with another American.

Especially this one, who, it was all too apparent, would be going to bed with an upper respiratory infection.

One's own hotel may have a supper club where it is possible to dine alone while watching, say, the ten o'clock floor show. There are also nightclubs—and I don't mean the lesbian variety—where a couple of distaff travelers who have joined forces may from a discreet table watch the entertainment while having a drink or a bite to eat, without being treated like call girls. Ask the hall porter's advice. Of course, the music will likely be nostalgic of your mother's junior prom, and the dancing either equally dated or a frenetic stab at the latest spasms in the States.

In London there is a respectable professional escort service for women who wish to take in the night spots accompanied by a man. Paid escorts are obtainable elsewhere. Particularly in Continental hotels, handsome waiters, all too sanguine about the mobility of American society, may, while serving you a cocktail, invite you to the *Kursaal* or to have a cognac with them later. Not that anybody's a snob. Just remember it's within their own social structure to expect you to foot the bill.

Hot-eyed adolescent bellhops also keep a lady feeling like a dish. They're less laggard about leaving your bedroom if, after a tiring journey, you stash the restorative in the chandelier until they've brought you the setup and departed.

It's quite proper for a woman alone to pause for a late-afternoon refreshment at a sidewalk café. Some European cities also have outdoor tea or beer gardens in which during the day one may quietly enjoy a soft drink or ice cream. On a September afternoon I stumbled on to one in Munich. After powdering, I decided I might as well sit down for a while since the clusters of girls and young men at the tables were mostly unpaired. Moreover the garden, which was quite pretty, had a festive air.

When the music stopped, two fräuleins in their Sunday frills were politely returned by their partners to my table, which I had thought to be free; but immediately a relay invited them to waltz. I was commencing to feel wistful, when a black-haired Bavarian asked me in heavily accented English if he might have the honor, which I readily enough granted, the caverns between his teeth notwithstanding.

After a turn or two about the floor he inquired if he might take me that evening to the famous old opera house, which, he said, was constructed in 1589. Although I could have done with a more prepossessing squire, as usual I went limp at the idea of a structure so aged.

"I'd love to," I said, then hesitated. "But I don't have evening clothes with me." "Nobody dresses up," Otto assured me. "Where are you staying? I'll drop by at nine in my Mercedes." Viewing him more kindly, I gave the name of the small, renovated hotel near the railway station to which a porter had trundled my suitcases from the Romantic Road terminus that morning. This was a year that I was traveling with no reservations. "Oh," Otto commented, "that used to be the red-light district. They're trying to clean it up."

I put on the nearest thing I had to a frock, and promptly at nine Otto arrived. He handed me into a little Ford truck, and we chugged on to what was truly a celebrated landmark—not "the old opera house," but the old Hofbrauhaus, an enormous Bavarian beer hall. The ground floor was packed with happy proletariat, but the middle-class story we elected was just as crowded and merry. On the dais were Fat Boy musicians in Tyrolean hats and lederhosen oompahing it up with *"Ach du lieber Augustin," "In München steht ein Hofbrauhaus"* and like German tunes, in which the jolly burghers, elbows linked and seesawing like caterpillars alongside the outsized tables, joined in singing.

Otto ordered a liter apiece of lager, which arrived in steins big enough to soak your head. *"Prosit!"* cheered our fellows at the table, lifting to us their equally large tankards. A few gulps and I was one with the carnival, laughing and singing, for once deaf to my melancholy monotone. *"Ein prosit der Gemütlichkeit!"* we bellowed with joy—and then abruptly I sobered.

"How," I asked Otto, "could *these* people have been Nazis? They're such fun!" He had never, he had already told me, been one, although, like all children in his boyhood, he had to belong to the Hitler *Jugend*. "If I were to come in here alone," he said, "within fifteen minutes somebody at the table would say to me, 'Heil Hitler!' " "It's incredible," I said. Otto made no comment.

Three-quarters through the beer and I was ready to say *Onkel*. Otto called for the check, then casually asked me if I had a few marks. I said sure. We returned to the flivver, and he suggested we go to a typical Munich cabaret. I recollect that it was very dark, nobody recited any poems, and he was again short of change.

At four A.M. I was roused from my sleep by a man shouting in the next room. "Why don't you get out? Just get *out!*" A woman laughed lewdly. "Jesus!" he cried hoarsely. "What a *terrible* way to make a living!"

Completely awake now, I relived the evening's entertainment. It suddenly dawned on me that Otto had never paid me back.

Yugoslavia also has al fresco casinos, but for two nights I shied at those along the waterfront in Hvar, which drew a lively patronage each evening. " 'Island paradise,' indeed!" I snorted on my third day in the tiny Renaissance town. "It may have been founded by the Greeks in the fourth century B.C., but this is Boresville if ever I saw it." The charm of sipping a ten-cent slivovitz on the hotel terrace overlooking the Adriatic was palling, as were the "Missouri Waltz" and "Jambalaya" blaring from the piped campanile. I'd already seen Djenet Makdanold and Nelsan Edi in *Naughty Marietta*. One couldn't even read: the twenty-five-watt lights were shut off at 10:00 P.M. due to acute power shortage. A sign above my minuscule lavabo, penciled in three languages, cautioned in English, "DONT SQVANDER WATER!"—which, considering the single spigot's lukewarm, drop-by-drop trickle, would have taken some patience.

I was beginning to get stir crazy when, during my last dinner, a sunny American blonde was seated at my table. "Have you been dancing at the sidewalk cafés?" she inquired. "No," I said, "I don't like to go alone." "But it's great fun," she said. "Come along with me tonight—at least to sample the *prošek*," which, pronounced "proshek" or sometimes "prosheko," is an immensely popular Yugoslav wine, drunk like beer on busts in Montana.

So we walked down to the harbor (Hvar is so small they don't need any taxis) and entered one of the open-air taverns. There an astonishing number of people were drinking or dancing and, immediately we were seated, a great hunk of gridiron material swaggered over. I glanced at my girl friend as I rose to dance. "You have to be *blonde?*" In a minute she, too, was on the floor—with a rather more polished partner. Mine, clearly an underachiever in the classroom, lurched to the music enraptured. Desperately I clung to his neck, hoping that in one of his wilder sporadic whirls I wouldn't through sheer velocity be hurtled into space.

"Iss goot," he said, beaming as we returned to the table. He sat down with us. The orchestra struck up a folk dance, in which the Yugoslav couples, forming a ring with their hands on each other's shoulders, circled the floor in small, intricate steps. Then another jitterbug number. Buster Brawn pulled me to my feet. "*Nein, nein,*" I protested. "*Ya, ya.* Ve tanz. Iss goot." The band repaired to the seventeenth-century Arsenal.

"You-me, bar," urged my Serbian Tarzan. "Ruck 'n' roll. Iss goot." I looked in anguish, not to say envy, at the blonde; by this time she had acquired three thoroughly clean-cut admirers. "I don't see any way out," I said, "but to cut loose and go pack."

There's something to be said for not being too eager to be seen on the floor.

The next morning I took an ordinary Adriatic steamer to Split, where, in the Diocletian Palace area, history is bared in cross section. During the reign of the Roman emperor, the fourth-century palace housed some one thousand people. Many of the Corinthian columns and arches he constructed are intact, but subsequent peoples—the Avars, Venetians, Turks, Croats—also left their mark, most evident in the anachronistic windows hacked out of Diocletian's awesome chambers. Today the palace site bustles with throngs going about their business, many of whom live in the hundreds of hovels that honeycomb the narrow, narrow streets between the still-magnificent Roman remains.

An architectural monstrosity, it is utterly fascinating—as I remarked to the retired English schoolmaster with whom I dined the two days I spent in Split. Slouching in the baggiest tweed suit I have ever encountered, he discoursed over a whisky on Greek- and Latin-root words and cautioned me not to go to Opatija. "You might as well," he said, "be in Brighton." It appeared to be the Styx, or sticks—I wasn't sure which.

At 8:00 A.M. the following morning I boarded a ferry at Tito Wharf for a thirteen-and-a-half-hour sail along the Dalmatian coast to Rijeka, the country's northernmost port. Shortly after the British don said "Well—cheerio" at Zadar, I sauntered into the lounge for some coffee. The moment it was brought to the table that three husky farmers had invited me to share, one whipped out a flask and poured a dollop of slivovitz into my cup. "Iss goot," he said, rubbing his belly: nothing like a shot in the morning to tone up the gut. Vass goot.

Lunch, served family style at a big table below deck, comprised huge platters of meat and potatoes. A roly-poly Slav to my left, inquiring in German if I cared to share his wine, filled my glass. His own seemed bottomless, and afterwards, when the tosspot tried to link his deck chair with mine, that he might more cozily snooze on my shoulder, I realized that I should have rejected the juice. An attentive police officer shooed him away.

It had been a glorious, crystal-clear day, and I had taken many pictures of the islets garlanding this particularly lovely portion of the Adriatic. As sunset approached I determined to immortalize it with my lens.

"For what wait you?" a gentleman asked me in German—not unreasonably since I had been standing at the rail staring into the viewfinder, index finger poised on the shutter, for a good fifteen minutes. Looking up, I saw a bemused Mephistopheles in a navy pin-striped suit and blunt-toed, mustard-colored shoes. He had nice square teeth, of which two incisors were glistening gold.

My German was largely limited to "Where is . . . ?" "I wish a . . ." "I don't understand," and "I don't want to." Luckily, I could comprehend a bit more, for his English consisted of "Sank you vairy much." It made him seem rather stupid.

Pointing to the rocky isle alongside us and the one just ahead, I indicated that I hoped to include both in my composition. Thus encouraged, he asked if I were going to Rijeka or, like him, to Opatija. I shrugged; there were still a good two hours in which to decide. He told me that his name was Ivo, that he was a Croat and lived in Krk. He asked my name, where I was from, and how much money I made. Always entertained by the unabashed manner in which this question is put by people in depressed economies, I wrote on a slip of paper what was a modest enough sum. *"Ein Monat?"* he asked. *"Nein, ein Woche."* A week! He was astonished. Smiling wryly, he reported he made one-seventh as much.

How much rent do you pay? What did your camera cost? Your shoes? Your purse? Do you own an automobile? To these and similar questions I replied patiently until he came up with one I'd rather not discuss: "How much money have you in bank?" "In America," I said testily in plodding German, "it is not nice to ask, 'How much money have you in bank.'" He meant no harm, he assured me; it was just that he was so interested in the United States. But, gracefully changing the subject, he repeated, "Are you going to Opatija or Rijeka?"

Well, I reflected, noting the harbor lights in the distance, perhaps I'd better go to Opatija; then this gentleman can help me with my baggage, which will surely be a problem if there aren't any porters. "I go to Opatija," I announced.

Ivo grabbed my twenty-nine-inch suitcase and his and told me to carry the smaller pieces—my flight bag and the five-liter keg of *prošek* he had brought along from Krk, since everybody knew the quality was inferior in Opatija. As I stumbled down the gangplank, weighed starboard by his cask, he asked if I had ever gone "*prošek trinken.*" Lying, I said no. He said we'd fill that lacuna the next day.

It was dark when, after a twenty-minute ride, we dismounted the bus on the outskirts of Opatija to deposit his wine and valise at an inn where he was staying. I waited outside for him to register, but when he started to take in my luggage, too, I perceived that he had gotten an erroneous impression. "*Nein, nein!*" I protested. "I go to Kvarner"—the only hotel name in the vicinity I could remember. "It is very costly," he cautioned me. And, sighing, he picked up my two bags.

We walked about a half-mile before we arrived at the Kvarner, a large, faded beauty whose elegance in the heyday of the Hapsburgs was reflected in her crystal chandeliers and the fine molding beneath her cracked paint. In high-pitched Serbo-Croatian, Ivo dickered with the reception clerk over the price of my room. It was, Ivo reminded him, September 16th, and off-season rates were now in effect. At the official exchange, the spacious twin-bedded room with adjoining bath came to about $2.50. An outrageous price, Ivo remarked; his room cost him fifty cents. And what a waste to leave unused that extra bed.

Nevertheless, it was for him the beginning of an idyl, since he had the singular experience in my company of being able to do 90 per cent of the talking.

For me he exemplified, in a social way, the piquancy and pitfalls of traveling alone.

The next morning we went *spaziering* along the coastline and through the woods, pausing now and then under grape arbors for a glass of the local *prošek*. Soon it took little to make us laugh, and I found myself glancing contentedly at his gilded front teeth.

For luncheon he suggested a small outdoor café, where at last, after all that wiener schnitzel, I got some genuine Yugoslav food. My initiation was *ražnjići*, but during successive meals Ivo introduced me to *ćevapčići* as well. Both are made of pork—respectively, chunks *en brochette* and sausages grilled on a pungent charcoal stove. With them came mounds of chopped, raw, white onions. A few days on that diet and I was as spare as Ivo.

My vocabulary was too impoverished to explain to him in *Deutsch* that I wanted to go dutch, and when he paid the check for our first lunch I felt like a thief.

By midafternoon I was also feeling tense. Noting my troubled expression, Ivo asked, *"Was ist los?"* Several days earlier, when I had approached a Starigrad waiter with the phrase-book Serbo-Croatian for "Where are the facilities?" I was directed, with a slightly surprised look, to an uncloseted room appointed with urinals. While I was desperately trying to figure out by what gymnastics I could employ one, a gentleman barged in. I fled, praying I wouldn't become a disgrace to my country. Evidently *Gde je nužnik?* means "Where's the toilet [masc.]?"

"Ich will ein Badezimmer," I told Ivo, unable to recall the German for what was not an American circumlocution. *"Was wilst du machen in Badezimmer?"* he asked, baffled. *"Wilst baden?"* ("What dost thou wish to do in the bathroom? Wishest thou to bathe?") In nothing flat he'd latched on to the chummy second person.

"Nein! Nein!" I said, looking madly about. Never, I flared, have I seen a country like this for lack of comfort stations; Science should do some basic research on the secret of the Yugoslav bladder. As I trudged grimly along, Ivo glanced at me worriedly from

time to time. Suddenly I caught sight of a hotel. "We go," I said, "to Slavija." Ivo's eyes lit up. If he had had a mustache he'd have twirled it.

"Wait here," I told him, and, squaring my jaw, ploughed through the corridors. There was a powder room at the Kvarner, surely also at the Slavija. A bellhop inquired what I wished. "A ladies' room," I replied. He vanished without comment. Frustrated, I joined the confused Ivo on the veranda. We were about to descend the stairs when the manager stopped us. "Permit me to introduce myself," he said briskly in English, extending his hand. "My name is George Zimmer. I understand that you would like a little room for a short time." "No, no!" I wailed. "All I want is to use the ladies' room. The *toilette*. The toilet!" I sighed. Mr. Zimmer looked frosty. "I am sorry," he said. "The syndicate will not allow it."

An hour later we came upon a public rest room with conveniences for ladies.

Towards the end of the afternoon Ivo asked if I needed to change any money. I said yes, that I must soon go to the bank. He offered to convert a few dollars for me; he would, he said, be glad to give me the same rate as the bank. Only lack of fluency kept me from snapping, "Big deal! I can get twice that from any waiter if I want to mess around in the black market." But I was only momentarily cross, for here was a graceful solution to a dilemma. American women are always being charged with emasculating men, but if there is one way I am loath to unman one it is by reaching for the tab—as I just had after a wine break, to indicate we'd take turns. If I let Ivo give me dinars for dollars, he would profit sufficiently to play host without strain. Carried away with generosity, I even sold him at cost plus tax six pairs of locally scarce nylons, which I had hoped to sell or barter at triple the price.

Since he seemed to enjoy simply caressing it, I permitted Ivo to shoulder my purse as I accompanied him to his room to execute the transaction. Straightway he brought out his keg of *prošek*, cautioning me as he poured that it was a powerful aphrodisiac. Certainly it had a high sugar content, which may or may not stoke an amorous appetite.

Warmed by the wine and his pot-bellied stove, he went into

another of his soliloquies, rephrasing when I didn't understand. He told me that living was *schwer* in Yugoslavia. Salaries were low, rent, food, and clothing high, while luxury items like radios, television, and cars were totally out of reach unless one was an active Communist, with a consequently more lucrative and imposing position. A thirty-five-hour work week obtained, but anyone wishing to augment his income could put in but two hours' overtime. In Ivo's opinion, it was the cynical purpose of the government to keep the 90 per cent of the people who were not Communists on a subsistence level—not starving, but constantly worried about being heavily in debt, with insufficient spirit left for opposition activity. You can imagine with what concern I commiserated, "Ach, so!"

Then he asked cheerfully if I'd like to see his clothes. He showed me his brown suit, his lovely beige slacks and sports jacket, his bare-backed bikini, his dancing pumps. Before long, though, it became apparent that he was buying that propaganda about the *prošek*.

I reminded him that we were there to exchange dollars. Instantly distracted, he reached for his suitcase at the top of a closet, feverishly unlocked it, and, shaking with sudden ague, extracted a packet of currency from neat layers of dinars. He was sweating profusely when he hastily gulped a Yugoslav Miltown.

I was so delighted to secure this grass-roots view of informal banking that it took a while to comprehend why the crusty old concierge gave him such billingsgate as we departed. Obviously she had misunderstood the nature of our commerce.

When I emerged from my bathroom at the Kvarner in garb more suitable for the evening than a sweater and skirt, I noted that Ivo appeared disappointed I hadn't put on anything frothier than basic black and some pearls. I also noted that the position of my purse—which I just couldn't insult him by taking with me when I left to dress—was altered on the bed, where I had pretended carelessly to toss it. There are times my lack of trust rather disgusts me—as it did after a surreptitious check of my wallet evidenced that he had simply been curious about its contents.

In high spirits I accompanied him to the casino at the Kvarner, for, with his hair freshly oiled and those dazzling gold teeth, Ivo looked divinely Balkan. And when, to the strains of some Strauss, we got onto the dance floor, I was overjoyed at my good luck in having met up with the Fred Astaire of Krk. Oh, how we *tanzed!* My head was in such a spin I didn't get peeved till the next morning that he hadn't given me change for the equivalent of five dollars I advanced him for the two twenty-cent banana liqueurs that carried us through the evening.

Since he was so contagiously effervescent, it took several repetitions before my feelings about Ivo became truly mixed. With each encore of his *"Komm mit mir zu Krk; bleib bei mir in Krk,"* I was less inclined to tease him, "I think it would be great fun to *go* with you to Krk—but nix on the bleibing." And when he suggested a permanent, legal association ("After only one year you can take me to America!"), I caught myself trying to visualize him with nice porcelain caps on those gold incisors.

Depressed that he had turned out to be a fortune-hunter, I shut him out of my life for a full afternoon. Nor did I unfreeze when he called for me later with a handful of field flowers. After dinner I looked the other way, deaf to his whispers concerning the check. He had been relying heavily on my admiration for his awning-striped tie, and this crushed him. Perversely, I brightened. I didn't care if the bill amounted to only eighty cents; a convention was involved.

Ivo sighed and sighed as he led me in a limp foxtrot. And when I ordered a thirty-five-cent cognac, he looked utterly wretched, because he was correct in anticipating that I would again duck the check. I had blown so cold on him that I wouldn't even permit him to come to Kvarner at six the next morning to take me to the bus depot, where I would leave for Trieste en route to Rome.

Which was a mistake, because my hotel bill was inflated. *"Der Rechnung ist zu gross!"* I protested to the desk. I tried to explain that I was on the off-season rate; moreover, every time I ran the tub they charged me another fifty cents, whereas Ivo had arranged that bathing was on the house. Suddenly they didn't understand German.

Dispirited, I followed the porter to the station, where I settled on a lonely wooden bench and began a glum ninety-minute wait for a motor coach that never came. Other passengers were clamoring at the ticket window as I approached it, hoping to find out what was *los.* The one who spoke English explained that the driver had unaccountably bypassed Opatija. The next bus was due in six hours.

How to occupy myself in the meantime? I had severed relations with both Ivo and Kvarner. Checking my bags in the cloakroom, I quit the depot, morose. Well, the immediate problem, I told myself briskly, was to find a restaurant serving breakfast. So engrossed was I in the search that I did a double-take when, at a distance, I spotted the aquiline features of my erstwhile beau.

"Ivo!" I shrieked, racing to him, camera and purse flapping. Townfolk who had caught our Daphnis and Chloe routine had told him of my aborted departure. After he ordered the *Frühstück*, I handed him my hotel bill. "*Der Rechnung,*" I said tersely, "*von Kvarner.*" " '*Die*' *Rechnung,*" he said, studying it.

During Ivo's stormy exchange with the management at the Kvarner, I caught the word *Polizei*. They refunded three dollars. "With this," I said, "we're having scampi for lunch." It seemed an especially memorable way to blow the reimbursement since he had never eaten shrimp. They were too dear, he explained. The scampi arrived unshelled and shriveled—with a scant half-inch of flesh on each. Ivo looked at the small portions in consternation, then burst into wild laughter. "*This,*" he asked me, wiping his eyes, "is the wonderful scampi? For what these cost, my family eats a whole week!"

I felt like a worm.

As we walked slowly back to the bus station, Ivo sadly repeated his refrain: "*Komm mit mir—bitte—zu Krk. Bleib bei mir in Krk. Immer.*"

But, of course, I couldn't because I had a rendezvous in Roma with the gentleman in 2-D. I shall never forget Ivo. Nevertheless, there's nothing like meeting old buddies abroad.

Alfredo's was glittering with expensively-clad diners, a number of whom were enjoying large platters of fully matured scampi. 2-D, who is so patrician he traces his own ancestry back to the shrimps, generally finds sustenance in New York a floor below me munching a matzo spread with Kraft's American. This night, however, he ordered the *spécialité de la maison* and a bottle of well-chilled Orvieto. Further to celebrate our reunion, he asked the accordionist to play his favorite airs.

A bus boy wheeled over the pasta, but the captain himself buttered and cheesed the fettucini, tossing it with the celebrated solid-gold fork and spoon like ticker tape in a bull market. The sommelier sniffed the cork, poured my host a sip of wine, and anxiously awaited his verdict. More actor than tippler, 2-D rolled it on his tongue, studied the chandeliers, then pronounced it *bellissima.*

"You know," I said, "my brain is now so blockaded with German I can't remember a single word of Living Language Italian."

"Oh?" he said, reflectively. Not one to pass up an opportunity to grab the floor, 2-D addressed me the balance of the evening in his newly acquired tongue.

Well, anyway—he picked up the check.

As may be inferred from these memoirs, although the traveler can count on globes of new friends, the odds are poor on Miss Rollingstone's landing Mr. Right. However, to conclude with some upbeat advice, should you hit the jackpot, have any marriage you contract overseas either witnessed by an officer of the American consulate or registered there as soon as possible thereafter. According to international law, the wedding would be recognized in the United States if the nuptials complied with the law of the land where the ceremony took place. Nevertheless, without a consular record our courts might take the position, in the event of litigation, that you simply had had a particularly diverting Maiden Voyage.

Sources of Information

Antigua Tourist Information
   Center
549 Pleasantville Road
Briarcliff Manor, N.Y.

The Argentine Consulate
   General
12 W. 56th Street
New York, N.Y. 10019

Australian National Travel Association
636 Fifth Avenue
New York, N.Y. 10020

350 Post Street
San Francisco, Calif.

Austrian State Tourist
   Department
444 Madison Avenue
New York, N.Y. 10022

323 S. Michigan Avenue
Chicago, Ill. 60604

195 S. Beverly Drive
Beverly Hills, Calif.

2433 N.W. Lovejoy Street
Portland, Ore. 97210

Bahamas Ministry of Tourism
620 Fifth Avenue
New York, N.Y. 10020

Barbados Tourist Board
355 Lexington Avenue
New York, N.Y. 10017

Official Belgian Tourist Bureau
589 Fifth Avenue
New York, N.Y. 10017

Bermuda Government Official
   Information Office
610 Fifth Avenue
New York, N.Y. 10020

6 N. Michigan Avenue
Chicago 2, Ill.

Consulate General of Brazil
630 Fifth Avenue
New York, N.Y. 10020

British Travel Association
680 Fifth Avenue
New York, N.Y. 10019

39 S. LaSalle Street
Chicago, Ill. 60603

612 S. Flower Street
Los Angeles, Calif. 90017

Bulgarian Tourist Office
50 E. 42nd Street
New York, N.Y. 10017

Caribbean Tourist Association
20 E. 46th Street
New York, N.Y. 10017

Colombia National Tourist
Board
140 E. 57th Street
New York, N.Y. 10022

Curaçao Information Center
604 Fifth Avenue
New York, N.Y. 10020

Czechoslovakia: Institute for International Youth Affairs
211 E. 43rd Street
New York, N.Y. 10017

Denmark: See Scandinavian
National Travel Offices

Dominican Republic Tourist
Office
630 Fifth Avenue
New York, N.Y. 10020

Finnish National Travel Office
10 E. 40th Street
New York, N.Y. 10016

French Government Tourist
Office
610 Fifth Avenue
New York, N.Y. 10020
18 S. Michigan Avenue
Chicago, Ill. 60603
9418 Wilshire Boulevard
Los Angeles, Calif. 90036
323 Geary Street
San Francisco, Calif. 94102

German Tourist Information
Office
500 Fifth Avenue
New York, N.Y. 10036
11 LaSalle Street
Chicago, Ill. 60603
323 Geary Street
San Francisco, Calif. 94102

Greek Press and Information
Service
69 E. 79th Street
New York, N.Y. 10020

Haiti Government Tourist
Bureau
30 Rockefeller Plaza
New York, N.Y. 10020

Hong Kong Tourist Association
501 Madison Avenue
New York, N.Y. 10022
291 Geary Street
San Francisco, Calif. 94102
55 E. Washington Street
Chicago, Ill. 60602
617 S. Olive Street
Los Angeles, Calif. 90014
535 Boylston Street
Boston, Mass. 02116
211 N. Ervay Street
Dallas, Tex. 75201

Hungary: KLM Royal Dutch
Airlines (See MAJOR
AIRLINES)
609 Fifth Avenue
New York, N.Y. 10017

India Government Tourist
Office
19 E. 49th Street
New York, N.Y. 10017

201 N. Michigan Avenue
Chicago, Ill.

685 Market Street
San Francisco, Calif. 94105

Consulate General of Indonesia
5 E. 68th Street
New York, N.Y. 10021

Iranian Consulate General
630 Fifth Avenue
New York, N.Y. 10020

Irish Tourist Board
33 E. 50th Street
New York, N.Y. 10022

135 S. LaSalle Street
Chicago, Ill. 60603

681 Market Street
San Francisco, Calif. 94105

Israel Government Tourist
Office
574 Fifth Avenue
New York, N.Y. 10036

5 S. Wabash Avenue
Chicago, Ill. 60603

615 S. Flower Street
Los Angeles, Calif.

805 Peachtree Street N.E.
Atlanta, Ga.

Italian State Tourist Office
(ENIT)
626 Fifth Avenue
New York, N.Y. 10020

203 N. Michigan Avenue
Chicago, Ill.

St. Francis Hotel
San Francisco, Calif.

Embassy of the Ivory Coast
2424 Massachusetts Avenue
Washington, D.C. 20008

Jamaica Tourist Board
200 Park Avenue
New York, N.Y. 10017

37 S. Wabash Avenue
Chicago, Ill. 60603

3440 Wilshire Boulevard
Los Angeles, Calif.

S.E. Second Street and Biscayne Boulevard
Miami, Fla. 33131

278 Post Street
San Francisco, Calif. 94108

1214 Joseph Vance Building
Seattle, Wash. 98101

Japan National Tourist
Organization
45 Rockefeller Plaza
New York, N.Y. 10020

333 N. Michigan Avenue
Chicago, Ill. 60601

651 Market Street
San Francisco, Calif. 94105

109 Kaiulani Avenue
Honolulu, Hawaii 96815

1420 Commerce Street
Dallas, Tex. 75201

Jordan: Needham, Harper &
Steers, Inc.
530 Fifth Avenue
New York, N.Y. 10036

Embassy of the Republic of
Kenya
Washington, D.C.

Consulate of the State of Kuwait
50 Rockefeller Plaza
New York, N.Y. 10020

Tourist Counsellor, Embassy of
Lebanon

9 E. 76th Street
New York, N.Y. 10021

Liechtenstein: See Swiss
    National Tourist Office

Luxembourg Consulate General
200 E. 42nd Street
New York, N.Y. 10017

Permanent Mission of Malaysia
    to the U.N.
845 Third Avenue
New York, N.Y. 10022

Malta Mission to the U.N.
155 E. 44th Street
New York, N.Y. 10017

Mexican Government Tourism
    Department
630 Fifth Avenue
New York, N.Y. 10020

306 Wilshire Boulevard
Los Angeles 5, Calif.

209 Sutter Street
San Francisco, Calif.

707 Broadway
San Diego, Calif.

210 N. Michigan Avenue
Chicago 3, Ill.

First National Bank Building
    Arcade
Miami 5, Fla.

203 St. Charles Street
New Orleans 12, La.

1905 Commerce Street
Dallas 1, Tex.

209 E. Travis Street
San Antonio 5, Tex.

809 Walter Avenue
Houston 2, Tex.

Moroccan Consulate General
757 Third Avenue
New York, N.Y. 10017

Netherlands Information Office
711 Third Avenue
New York, N.Y. 10017

601 Calfornia Street
San Francisco 8, Calif.

Holland, Mich.

New Zealand Government
        Travel Commissioner
630 Fifth Avenue
New York, N.Y. 10020

510 Sixth Street
Los Angeles, Calif. 90014

153 Kearny Street
San Francisco, Calif. 94108

Norway: See Scandinavian
    National Travel Offices

Pacific Area: For unlisted coun-
    tries, see Pacific Area
    Travel Organization un-
    der ORGANIZATIONS

Consulate General of Pakistan
12 E. 65th Street
New York, N.Y. 10021

Philippine Travel Center
535 Fifth Avenue
New York, N.Y. 10017

212 Stockton Street
San Francisco 8, Calif.

Poland: Institute for Interna-
    tional Youth Affairs (see
    ORGANIZATIONS)

Casa de Portugal
570 Fifth Avenue
New York, N.Y. 10036

Commonwealth of Puerto Rico
Travel Information
666 Fifth Avenue
New York, N.Y. 10019

Rumania: KLM Royal Dutch
Airlines (see MAJOR AIR-
LINES)

Embassy of the Republic of
Rwanda
Washington, D.C.

Saudi Arabian Information Service
150 E. 42nd Street
New York, N.Y. 10017

Scandinavian National Travel
Offices
505 Fifth Avenue
New York, N.Y. 10017

612 S. Flower Street
Los Angeles, Calif. 90017

Singapore Government Tourist
Information Office
500 Fifth Avenue
New York, N.Y. 10020

South African Tourist Information Office
610 Fifth Avenue
New York, N.Y. 10020

South African Tourist Corp.
9465 Wilshire Boulevard
Beverly Hills, Calif. 90212

South America: For unlisted
countries, see South Am-
erican Travel Organiza-
tion under ORGANIZA-
TIONS

Soviet Union: See U.S.S.R.

Spanish National Tourist Office
589 Fifth Avenue
New York, N.Y. 10017

23 W. Jackson Boulevard
Chicago 4, Ill.

Casa del Hidalgo
Hypolita and George Streets
St. Augustine, Fla.

453 Post Street
San Francisco, Calif.

Surinam Tourist Bureau
10 Rockefeller Plaza
New York, N.Y. 10020

Sweden: See Scandinavian
National Travel Offices

Swiss National Tourist Office
608 Fifth Avenue
New York, N.Y. 10020

661 Market Street
San Francisco 5, Calif.

Consulate General of Syrian
Arab Republic
527 Madison Avenue
New York, N.Y. 10022

Tourist Organization of
Thailand
20 E. 82nd Street
New York, N.Y. 10028

Trinidad and Tobago Tourist
Board
400 Madison Avenue
New York, N.Y. 10017

Tunisia Trade Office
65 E. 56th Street
New York, N.Y. 10020

Turkish Information Office
500 Fifth Avenue
New York, N.Y. 10036

United Arab Republic Tourist
Office
630 Fifth Avenue
New York, N.Y. 10020

U.S.S.R.: Information Center
for Travelers to the
Soviet Union (a non-
profit American subsidi-
ary of Government Af-
fairs Institute)
345 E. 46th Street
New York, N.Y. 10017

Venezuelan Government Tourist
Bureau
485 Madison Avenue
New York, N.Y. 10022

Yugoslav State Tourist Office
509 Madison Avenue
New York, N.Y. 10022

ORGANIZATIONS

AAA World-Wide Travel, Inc.
750 Third Avenue
New York, N.Y. 10017

American Friends of the Middle
East
222 E. 46th Street
New York, N.Y. 10017

American Society of Travel
Agents, Inc. (ASTA)

360 Lexington Avenue
New York, N.Y. 10017

American Youth Hostels, Inc.
14 W. Eighth Street
New York, N.Y. 10011

Association for the Study of
Business Economics
663 Fifth Avenue
New York, N.Y. 10022

Council on Student Travel
777 United Nations Plaza
New York, N.Y. 10017

The English-Speaking Union
16 E. 69th Street
New York, N.Y. 10021

Experiment in International
Living
Putney, Vt.

French Book Guild
101 Fifth Avenue
New York, N.Y. 10003

Government Affairs Institute
1726 Massachusetts Avenue
N.W.
Washington 6, D.C.

Hadassah
65 E. 52nd Street
New York, N.Y. 10022

Information Center for American Travelers to the So-
viet Union
345 E. 46th Street
New York, N.Y. 10017

Intermedic, Inc.
777 Third Avenue
New York, N.Y. 10017

Institute for International Youth
Affairs

211 E. 43rd Street
New York, N.Y. 10017

Junior Tourism (Britain)
52 Chester Square
London S.W. 1, England

Pacific Area Travel Association
442 Post Street
San Francisco, Calif.

Pan American Women's Association
20 W. 40th Street
New York, N.Y. 10018

Special Interest Tours
48 E. 43rd Street
New York, N.Y. 10017

South American Travel Organization
100 Biscayne Boulevard
Miami, Fla. 33131

The Tourist Hospitality Service (Britain)
13 Montagu Place
London W.1, England

United States National Student Association Educational Travel, Inc.
265 Madison Avenue
New York, N.Y. 10016

Young Women's Christian Association of the U.S.A.
600 Lexington Avenue
New York, N.Y. 10022

PASSPORT AGENCIES

Passport Office
Department of State

22nd and E Streets N.W.
Washington, D.C. 20524

Federal Office Building
300 N. Los Angeles Street
Los Angeles, Calif. 90012

Federal Office Building
450 Golden Gate Avenue
San Francisco, Calif. 94102

New Federal Office Building
51 S.W. First Avenue
Miami, Fla. 33130

Special Passport Representative
Room 304, Federal Building
Honolulu, Hawaii 96813

Federal Office Building
219 S. Dearborn Street
Chicago, Ill. 60604

U.S. Customs House
423 Canal Street
New Orleans, La. 70130

Salada Tea Building
330 Stuart Street
Boston, Mass. 02116

Rockefeller Center
630 Fifth Avenue
New York, N.Y. 10020

1410 Fifth Avenue
Seattle, Wash. 98101

INOCULATIONS INFORMATION

The Division of Foreign Quarantine
Public Health Service
Department of Health, Education, and Welfare
Washington, D.C. 20201

CUSTOMS, VISA INFORMATION,
POCKET GUIDES

Bureau of Customs
Treasury Department
Washington, D.C. 20226

Superintendent of Documents
Government Printing Office
Washington, D.C. 20402

BOOK PUBLISHERS

Appleton-Century-Crofts
440 Park Avenue South
New York, N.Y. 10016

Committee on International
Relations
National Education Associa-
tion of the U.S.
1201 Sixteenth Street N.W.
Washington, D.C. 20036

Crown Publishers, Inc.
419 Park Avenue South
New York, N.Y. 10016

Doubleday & Co., Inc.
277 Park Avenue
New York, N.Y. 10017

French & European Publications,
Inc.
610 Fifth Avenue
New York, N.Y. 10020

C. S. Hammond & Co., Inc.
Maplewood, N.J.

J. B. Lippincott Co.
E. Washington Square
Philadelphia, Pa. 19105

David McKay Co., Inc.
750 Third Avenue
New York, N.Y. 10017

New American Library, Inc.
(Meridian)
1301 Avenue of the Americas
New York, N.Y. 10019

Rand McNally & Co.
P.O. Box 7600
Chicago, Ill. 60680

Random House, Inc.
457 Madison Avenue
New York, N.Y. 10022

William Sloane Assoc.
425 Park Avenue South
New York, N.Y. 10016

Simon and Schuster, Inc.
630 Fifth Avenue
New York, N.Y. 10020

MAGAZINE PUBLISHERS

Popular Photography
Ziff-Davis Publishing Co.
One Park Avenue
New York, N.Y. 10016

Saturday Review
380 Madison Avenue
New York, N.Y. 10017

PHOTOGRAPHIC SUPPLIES

Erie Scientific Corp. (Cover
glass plates and masks)
Buffalo, N.Y.

Kimac Co. (Masks)
Old Greenwich, Conn

GEMounts (Mounts)
26705 Curie Ave.
Warren, Mich.

Porter Mfg. & Supply Co.
(Mounts)
2215 N. Chico Ave.
El Monte, Calif.

Spiratone, Inc. (Mounts)
369 Seventh Avenue
New York, N.Y. 10001

MAJOR STEAMSHIP COMPANIES

Alcoa Steamship Co., Inc.
17 Battery Place
New York, N.Y. 10004

American Export Isbrandtsen
Lines, Inc.
26 Broadway
New York, N.Y. 10004

American President Lines
29 Broadway
New York, N.Y. 10004

523 W. Sixth Street
Los Angeles, Calif. 90014

601 California Street
San Francisco, Calif. 94108

Canadian Pacific
581 Fifth Avenue
New York, N.Y. 10017

Cunard Steam-Ship Co., Ltd.
25 Broadway
New York, N.Y. 10004

Farrell Lines, Inc.
1 Whitehall Street
New York, N.Y. 10004

French Line
17 Battery Place
New York, N.Y. 10004

Furness Bermuda Line
34 Whitehall Street
New York, N.Y. 10004

Grace Line
628 Fifth Avenue
New York, N.Y. 10020

Greek Line, Inc.
32 Pearl Street
New York, N.Y. 10004

Hamburg American Line
17 Battery Place
New York, N.Y. 10004

Holland-America Line
609 Fifth Avenue
New York, N.Y. 10017

Home Lines Agency, Inc.
42 Broadway
New York, N.Y. 10004

Italian Line
1 Whitehall Street
New York, N.Y. 10004

Matson Lines
630 Fifth Avenue
New York, N.Y. 10020

523 W. Sixth Street
Los Angeles, Calif. 90014

215 Market Street
San Francisco, Calif. 94105

Moore-McCormack Lines, Inc.
2 Broadway
New York, N.Y. 10004

North German Lloyd
666 Fifth Avenue
New York, N.Y. 10019

Norwegian America Line
29 Broadway
New York, N.Y. 10004

P & O–Orient Lines
155 Post Street
San Francisco 8, Calif.

25 Broadway
New York, N.Y.

Stockyard Shipping Co.
17 Battery Place
New York, N.Y. 10004

Swedish American Line
636 Fifth Avenue
New York, N.Y. 10020

United States Lines Co.
1 Broadway
New York, N.Y. 10004

Zim-Israel Navigation Co., Ltd.
42 Broadway
New York, N.Y. 10004

MAJOR OVERSEAS AIRLINES

Aerolineas Argentinas
9 Rockefeller Plaza
New York, N.Y. 10020

Air France
683 Fifth Avenue
New York, N.Y. 10022

Air-India
410 Park Avenue
New York, N.Y. 10022

Alitalia Airlines
666 Fifth Avenue
New York, N.Y. 10019

Avianca
6 W. 49th Street
New York, N.Y. 10020

Braniff International
7 W. 49th Street
New York, N.Y. 10020

British Overseas Airways Corp.
(BOAC)
530 Fifth Avenue
New York, N.Y. 10036

Delta Airlines
5 W. 49th Street
New York, N.Y. 10020

El Al Israel Airlines
610 Fifth Avenue
New York, N.Y. 10020

Finnair
10 E. 40th Street
New York, N.Y. 10016

Iberia Air Lines of Spain
518 Fifth Avenue
New York, N.Y. 10036

Icelandic Airlines–Loftleidir
630 Fifth Avenue
New York, N.Y. 10020

Irish International Airlines
572 Fifth Avenue
New York, N.Y. 10036

Japan Air Lines
620 Fifth Avenue
New York, N.Y. 10020

KLM Royal Dutch Airlines
609 Fifth Avenue
New York, N.Y. 10017

Lan-Chile Airlines
500 Fifth Avenue
New York, N.Y. 10036

Lufthansa German Airlines
410 Park Avenue
New York, N.Y. 10013

Northwest Airlines, Inc.
537 Fifth Avenue
New York, N.Y.

Minneapolis–St. Paul International Airport
St. Paul 11, Minn.

Pakistan International Airlines
608 Fifth Avenue
New York, N.Y. 10020

Pan American Airways
Pan Am Building
New York, N.Y. 10017

Airlines Building
80 E. 42nd Street
New York, N.Y. 10017

Pan American–Grace Airways, Inc.
135 E. 42nd Street
New York, N.Y. 10017

Philippine Air Lines
609 Fifth Avenue
New York, N.Y. 10017

Qantas Airways
542 Fifth Avenue
New York, N.Y. 10036

Sabena Belgian World Airlines
720 Fifth Avenue
New York, N.Y. 10019

Scandinavian Airlines System
138–02 Queens Boulevard
Jamaica, N.Y.

Swissair
10 W. 49th Street
New York, N.Y. 10020

Trans World Airlines, Inc.
605 Third Avenue
New York, N.Y. 10016

Varig Airlines
634 Fifth Avenue
New York, N.Y. 10020

REDUCED-RATE RAILWAY AND
BUS TICKETS

British Rail International, Inc.
630 Fifth Avenue
New York, N.Y. 10020
510 W. Sixth Street
Los Angeles, Calif.

Europabus
630 Fifth Avenue
New York, N.Y. 10020

French National Railroads
610 Fifth Avenue
New York, N.Y. 10020

German Federal Railroad
11 W. 42nd Street
New York, N.Y. 10036

Italian State Railways
11 W. 42nd Street
New York, N.Y. 10036

Scandinavian Railways
630 Fifth Avenue
New York, N.Y. 10020

Swiss Federal Railways
608 Fifth Avenue
New York, N.Y. 10020

CAR HIRE AND MOTOR ROUTING

AAA World-Wide Travel, Inc.
750 Third Avenue
New York, N.Y. 10017

Auto-Europe, Inc.
25 W. 58th Street
New York, N.Y. 10019

Caltex
  380 Madison Avenue
  New York, N.Y. 10017
Car Tours in Europe, Inc.
  2 E. 46th Street
  New York, N.Y. 10017
Esso Touring Service
  15 W. 51st Street
  New York, N.Y. 10019
Europe by Car
  630 Fifth Avenue
  New York, N.Y. 10020
Hertz Corporation
  660 Madison Avenue
  New York, N.Y. 10021
Kinney System
  10 Rockefeller Plaza
  New York, N.Y. 10020
Shell Oil Co.
  50 W. 50th Street
  New York, N.Y. 10020

FOREIGN EXCHANGE DEALERS

Deak & Co., Inc.
  29 Broadway
  New York, N.Y. 10004

1478 Broadway
New York, N.Y. 10036
East Side Airlines Terminal
First Avenue at 37th Street
New York, N.Y. 10016
1406 New York Avenue,
  N.W.
Washington, D.C. 20005
349 Sutter Street
San Francisco, Calif. 94108
605 South Hill Street
Los Angeles, Calif. 90014
Honolulu International
  Airport
Honolulu, Hawaii

Perera Company, Inc.
  10 Broadway
  New York, N.Y. 10004
636 Fifth Avenue
New York, N.Y. 10020
Room 2127, also Main Lobby
International Arrivals
  Building
John F. Kennedy Interna-
  tional Airport
Jamaica, N.Y.
327 E. Flagler Street
Miami, Fla. 33131

Index

accommodations: American plan, full or modified, 30, 103; castles, 19; government-fixed prices, 19; paying guest in private home, 225; pension plan, full or demi-, 103. *See also* hotels; tourist offices (gov.); tourist-accommodation desks

Aer Lingus, 27, 118

Aerolineas Argentinas, 27

Afghanistan, 55, 75, 160, 166

Africa, 21, 222

Air France, 15, 25, 26, 47; eating on, 119; shopping guide, 166

airlines: Kinds of flights: charter, 45–46; economy, 119, in affinity groups, 46, "peak-period" fare, 45, regular fare, 44–5, "21-day excursion," 44–45; first-class, 118; "fly now—pay later," 47; non-affinity groups, 46; package plans, 22; round trip with optional stopovers, 22; thrift, 48. Reservations: confirming, 26; deposits, 25; reconfirming, 74, 76, 77; transferring to another line, 25; validation, 67. Services: information brochures, 22; reserving rooms, 27; routing flights, 26; shopping guides, 166. *See also names of individual lines*

alcohol, restrictions on, 106

Alexandria, 8, 53, 132

Alitalia, 133; eating on, 119

AAA, in Europe, 52; Paris, 127

American consulates and embassies, help from, 37, 112; temporary registration with, 199–200; visitors' bureaus, 224; marriage record, 245

American Express, 43; credit cards, 37; holding mail, 147; traveler's checks, 38

American Friends of Middle East, 224

American Youth Hostels, Inc., 52

Amsterdam, 7, 20, 27, 49, 79, 135

Angkor, 140, 205

Around the World by Passenger-Carrying Freighters, 48

Asia, 14, 15, 21, 153, 199, 205, 222

Athens, 26, 49, 119, 121, 166, 226

Australia, 13, 223

Austria, 19, 34, 161; Tyrol, 131

Auto-Europe, 128

Avianca, 113, 120

Bali, 65, 78, 79, 86, 125, 152, 185

Balitours, 125–6

Banaras, 26, 51, 87, 88, 153, 158

Bangkok, 16, 21, 77, 84, 179, 226; eating in, 102

banks, in international airports, 73, tipping advice, 73

Barcelona, 19, 34, 138

bathing facilities, 158–9

Beirut, 26, 55, 157, 218

Belgium, 19

Bermuda, 13, 62, 87, 135, 227; shopping in, 171

Bethlehem, 18

Biarritz, 33, 102

bicycles, renting, 134–5

BOAC, 14, 15, 25, 47, 118; room reservations, 27

Brasilia, 151

Britain's Tourist Hospitality Service, rooms in Great Britain, 226

British Isles, 6, 13, 14, 19, 106, 223–224, 226; eating in, 53

British Overseas Airways Corp., *see* BOAC

British Petroleum, 128

259

Bruges, eating in, 101–2
Brussels, 154, 171, 205; guests in private homes, 225
Budapest, 39, 50, 81, 166, 201; eating in, 82
Buenos Aires, 151, 166, 226; shopping in, 171

Cairo, 12, 132, 163, 202; shopping in, 169
Calcutta, 26, 118, 171, 174, 207
Caltex, information, maps, 128
Cambodia, 14, 65, 199
cameras, 182–98; photographing strangers, 194, 196. *See also* Eastman; film
cargo-liners, 116
Caribbean, the, 13, 227, 231
cars, renting or buying abroad, 127, 128; chauffeur-driven, 124
Car-Tours in Europe, 128
Casablanca, 169
Ceylon, 13, 14, 54, 65, 75, 165, 229; guided tour in, 207–17
citizenship, proof of, needed, 62–3
clothing, for air travel, 89; purchased abroad, 179; mailing home, 179
Colombo, 93, 207–8, 216
conversation pieces, 229–30
Cook's (Thomas), 43, 57; traveler's checks, 38
Copenhagen, 135, 160, 219, 231; eating in, 102; shopping in, 171
Council on Student Travel, 46, 47
courtesy: avoiding overcasualness and brashness, 150–1; considering customs of country, 152–4; dressing modestly, 159–60, in Catholic churches, 87, Eastern Orthodox churches, 87, Israel's Orthodox sectors, 87, Moslem countries, 86, Turkish mosques, 149; learning polite phrases of countries visited, 104; removing shoes, in Buddhist, Hindu, and Shinto holy places, 150, Orthodox churches in Middle East, 150, Turkish mosques, 149; sending gifts to hosts, 163; shaking hands, 152–3; taboo on left hand in Moslem countries, 153–4

credit cards, *see* American Express; Diners' Club
cruise ships, 120
Cuernavaca, 165
customs, foreign, 71; duty-free items, 71–2; holding in bond, 72
Customs Hints for Returning Residents, 180
Cutty Sark (houseboat), 171–7
Cuzco, 112, 159, 165, 195

Dalmation Coast, 31, 138, 159, 237
Danish National Tourist Office, 226
Deak, foreign exchange, 43, 44
Denmark, 135, 152, 223
Denpasar, 78, 79, 112, 125, 159
Diners' Club, credit cards, 38
disembarkation card, 69, 70
Djakarta, 43, 77, 78, 120, 152, 184
drinking, indigenous liquors, 102; regional beer or wines, 102; water, 111–12
Dubrovnik, 17, 79

Eastman Kodak, shows of native costumes, dances, 195
eating, 53; on planes, 119. *See also cities or countries; restaurants*
Ecuador, 61, 113, 133; eating in, 98
Egypt, 8, 11, 151, 202, 224, 228; eating in, 101
England, *see* British Isles
English-Speaking Union of Commonwealth, 223; of the U.S., 46, 223–224
Esso Touring Service, 128
Eurailpass, 53
Europabus, 24, 53
Europe by Car, 128, 258
"Europe on $5 a day," *see* tours
"Exciting Student Trips Abroad," 47
Experiment in International Living, 222

"Facts on Travel" series, 167
Festivals, SAS brochure, 16
festivals, folk and cultural, 15–18, 41, 65
festivals, religious, 16, 18, 126–7, 195
Fez, 169, 191; shopping in, 169–70

Fielding's Travel Guide to Europe, choosing Atlantic liners, 115
film, 185–8; duty on, 187
Finnair, 27, 118, 166
Finnish Tourist Association, 20
Florence, 7, 12, 20, 53, 131, 150, 166
Fodor's Modern Guides, 15
Foreign Independent Trip (FIT), 14, 26
France, 19, 131, 154, 199, 202, 222; eating in, 101
Freiburg im Breisgau, 129
freighters, 116
French Book Guild, 222
French Gov. Tourist Office, 24
French National Railroads, 24; Eurailpass, 53

Garuda, 78, 79, 113, 120, 152
German Federal Railroad, 53
Germany, 19, 161
Government Affairs Institute, 200, 201, 204
Government of India Tourist Office, 51
Greece, 13, 199; eating in, 122
Greek islands, 121
guides, multilingual, 122; native, 124, 125
Gulf Oil Corporation, maps, 128

Hadassah Tourist Clubs, 224
Hammond Map Company, 12; *Map Library,* 12; *Ambassador World Atlas,* 12
Handicrafts and Handlooms Exports Corporation of India, 177
Holland, 19; eating in, 53, 100
Holy Land, the, 13, 16, 199, 231
holy places, *see* courtesy
Hong Kong, 13, 14, 43, 47, 73, 78, 118, 132, 157, 178, 229; shopping in, 74, 167, 171, 177
Honolulu, 43, 47, 48, 67, 120
hotels, choosing, 21; Class A or I, Class B or II, Class C or III, 21; confirmation from, 32; luxury, 21, 52; reservations, made by airlines, 27, hall porter, 30, travel agent, 20, yourself, 31–2

How to Read a French Menu, 102
Hvar, 76, 159, 236; eating in, 99

IATA, 44, 45, 49
Iberia Airlines, 27, 118
Icelandic Airlines, 45
imports, foreign trademarks, 178; prohibited products, 179–80; state laws on, 179
India, 13, 159, 160, 187, 207; eating in, 101
Indian Airways, 26, 48, 120; food, 48
Indonesia, 13, 54, 65, 77, 100, 155; Consulate of, 151
inoculations: cholera, 61; smallpox, 61; yellow fever, 61
Institute for International Youth Affairs, 167
Interlaken, 86
Intermedic, 112
International Air Transport Asso., *see* IATA
International Certificates of Vaccination, 61, 67, 69, 111
International Youth Hostel Fed., 135
Iran, 38, 43, 139, 160, 166, 224
Iraq, 224
Ireland, 19, 150, 224
Iron Curtain countries, 64; shopping in, 167
Isfahan, eating in, 100
Israel, 64, 202, 224; eating in, 53
Istanbul, 26, 55, 56, 119
Italian Line, 85, 114
Italian State Railways, 24; Eurailpass, 53
Italian State Tourist Office, 22, 84
Italy, 76, 154, 223; eating in, 101

Japan, 13, 27, 28, 29, 87, 145, 158, 160, 199; eating in, 100, 143, 144
Japan Air Line, 27, 47, 89, 120; shopping, 166
Japan National Tourist Office, New York, 27, 28; Tokyo, 29
Japan: The Official Guide, 27
Jerusalem, 16, 64
Jordan, 16, 64, 86, 224
Junior Tourism (Britain), 226

Kabul, 55, 164, 230
Kandy, 18, 208, 212
Kashikojima, 130, 165
Kashmir, 51, 111, 157, 177; shopping in, 171–7; eating in, 175. *See also* Cutty Sark
Katmandu, 17, 18, 26, 76, 124, 206; eating in, 99
Khedive Ismail, 9
Kinney System, 128
KLM, 27, 79; charter flights, 45–6
Knossos, eating in, 98
Kyoto, 130–1

ladies' rooms, foreign names for, 156
language, learning pronunciation of one's hotel, street, 139; simple menu language, 104, 106, 139
La Paz, 124, 166, 194, 231
Lebanon, 64, 86
Lisbon, 19, 39, 112, 218
Living Language records, 137–9, 245
London, 14, 20, 132, 165, 219; eating in, 101, 107–8; shopping in, 171
Luxembourg, 45

Madrid, 19, 49, 165; shopping in, 171
Madurai, 34, 35, 203
Majorca, 34, 165
maps, city, for walking, 135; road, 128; for train use, 129. *See also* Hammond Map Company; Rand, McNally
Marrakesh, 108, 169, 191; eating in, 108–10; shopping, 170
Mexican Gov. Tourist Dept., 151
Mexico, 13, 18, 44, 61, 86, 102, 152, 205, 223, 231; Mexico City, 112
Michelin Red Travel Guides, 52
Middle East, 86, 199, 202; eating in, 101. *See also individual countries*
Milan, 20, 49, 50
Ministry of Tourism in Italy, 49
money, carrying American currency, changing, 39, 54–7; declaration form, 70; how much to take, 36; letters of credit, 39; vouchers for prepayment, 38
money-changing: *cambios* (Argentina), 54; "Change" offices (Swit-
zerland), 55. *See also* banks; Deak; Perera
Morocco, 18, 83, 109, 156, 191, 205, 224, 229; eating in, 108–10
Munich, 20, 234–6

Nagoya, 145, 157
Naples, 12, 131
National Educational Asso., 14
Nazaré, 141
Nepal, 18, 86, 124, 159, 206; eating, 99
Nepalese Department of Tourism, 17
New Cosmopolitan World Atlas, 13
New Delhi, 6, 89, 134, 175; restaurants, 13
New Horizons World Guide, 15
New Zealand, 13, 223
Nice, 12, 19, 67, 105
Northwest Orient Airlines, 27
Norway, eating in, 102
Norwegian National Tourist Office, 152
Nuwara Eliya, 208, 212

Obidos, 40, 183–4
Olson's Orient Guide, shopping for Pacific liners, 115
Opatija, 237–44; eating in, 240
Osaka, 30, 118, 130
Other Lands, Other Peoples: A Country-by-Country Fact Book, 14

packing, 93–4; cosmetics, 89–90; for customs inspection, 179
Pakistan, registering in, 75
Pakistan International Airways, 27
Panagra, 98, 133
Pan Am, 15, 25, 26, 27, 37, 97, 227; Panamac, 27; shopping guide, 166
Pan American-Grace Airways, 27
Pan American Airways, *see* Pan Am
Pan American Women's Association, 224
Paris, 12, 20, 22, 25, 30, 33, 36, 47, 132, 160, 164; eating in, 101; shopping in, 171; walking in, 135
passport, American, 62; Consular Report of Birth, 62–3; cost, original

or renewal, 64; registering with police, 75; showing at airline terminals, 67, 69, to hotel clerks, 75, at piers, 70–1; Supplementary Affidavit of Change of Name, 64. *See also* American consulates, visas

Perera, 43, 44, 54, 168

Peru, 102, 138, 155, 199

Peshawar, 142

pets, importing, 179

physical checkup, 111

Piraeus, 121, 226

Pocket Guide to the Middle East, 154

police registration, 75

Poor Man's Guide to the Orient, 15

Portugal, 19, 39, 75, 141, 161

Provence, eating in, 111

Qantas Airways, 15

Quito, 98, 113, 133

Raffaello, 85, 114–15

Ramayana, 18, 88, 126

Rand McNally, *see New Cosmopolitan World Atlas*

Rangoon, 65, 66, 118

Rawalpindi, 142, 160

Realm of the Evening Star, 229

restaurants, listed in guidebooks or hotel brochures, 103; with airline offices, local tourist bureaus, tour guides, 104; women alone in, 103–104, 107–8

Rio de Janeiro, 16, 124; shopping, 171

Rome, 12, 20, 22–3, 25, 131, 132, 231; eating in, 101, 244; shopping in, 171

Sabena Belgian World Airlines, 15, 27; charter flights, 45; shopping guide, 166

Salzburg, 17, 166

SAS, 16, 25

Saturday Review, 16, 197, 222

Saudi Arabia, 106

Scandinavia, 102, 224; eating in, 53

Scandinavian Airlines System, *see* SAS

Scotland, 14, 19, 223

Seville, 135; walking in, 228

Shannon, 20; shopping at airport, 167

Shell Oil Company, 128

shopping: avoiding taxes, Britain, Japan, 167; *carnet d'achats,* 167; duty-free at airports, 167; antiques, 179; gifts sent direct, 180; limit on duty-free imports, 180; original art, 179; guides from government tourist organizations, hotels, major airlines, 166–7; haggling, 169; price reductions for American money, 169; shipping purchases, 177. *See also cities and countries*

Sicily, 86, 138; unescorted women in, 122–3

Singapore, 179; shopping in, 171

Sodom, 106

South America, 21, 25; eating in, 98

Soviet Russia: A Guidebook for Tourists, 200

Soviet Union, 38, 87, 152, 204; satellites, 38

So You Want to Import a Pet, 179

Spain, 19, 86, 138, 205, 223

Special Interest Tours, 221

Split, 237

Srinagar, 51, 157, 171

Sweden, eating in, 102

Swissair, 27, 118

Swiss Federal Railways, 53

Switzerland, 19, 52, 54, 130, 224

Syria, 64, 224

Teheran, 166

Tel Aviv, 47

Thailand, 166

Thailand Tourist Organization, 150

Three Ways of Asian Wisdom: Hinduism, Buddhism, and Zen and Their Significance for the West, 14–15

ThriftRail Coupons, 53

tipping: Airlines, terminals only, 67; Ships: cargo-liners, 118; cruises, 117; freighters, 117–8; liners, 117; For service: doormen, 104; guides, 123; hall porters, 77; natives who pose for pictures, 124; porters, 73; taxi, 73–4; toilet attendants, 56; waiters, service charge on bill, 76; wine stewards, 105

Tobago, 16

toilet facilities, 155–7

Tokyo, 28, 47, 145, 227, 230; shopping in, 171

tourist-accommodation desks, 32, 33, 34

tourist card, needed, 61

tourist offices, foreign government, general information, 34; group sightseeing rates, 19; guided tours, 22–3; price information, 19; private car and guide, 19; shopping guides, 166–7

Tourist Trademark Information, 178

tours, "Big Splurge," 49; conducted, on bus or train, 19, 122–3; Desert Journey, 222; "Europe on $5 a day," 49, on $10 a day, 51; French Book Guild tour, 228; Rome by Night, 231–3; special, for handicapped, 222. *See also* airlines; tourist offices (gov.); Special Interest Tours

trains, first class, 132; saving ticket stubs, 132; second-class, 128, 131, tours, 122–3. *See also* Eurailpass

Trans World Airlines, *see* TWA

Travel Routes Around the World, 118

travel agents, booking reservations, 20, sightseeing, 22; charges, 21; FIT, 14; getting visas, 64; routing transportation, 20; saving time, 23; using because of language problem, 28

traveler's checks, useful denomina-

tions, 38. *See also* American Express; Cook's

Travel Guide to Europe, 15

Travellers Digest, 14

Trinidad, 16; shopping in, 171

Tunisia, 224

Turkey, 26, 228–9; eating in, 101

TWA, 15, 19–20, 25, 26, 27, 67, 118; shopping guide, 166

Tyrol, the, 33

Union of South Africa, 13

United Arab Republic, 64

U.S. Immigration form, 67

United States Line, 115

USNSA (U.S. National Student Asso.), 46, 128; International Student Identity Card, 47

Velden, 34

Venice, walking in, 135

Vienna, 34, 171

visas, procuring outside U.S., 67; where necessary, 64

Wales, 14, 17, 223

Western Europe, 8, 13, 22, 44, 137, 231

West Germany, 129

World Almanac, 202

World Travel Calendar, 16

Young Women's Christian Association, 52; in Europe, 52

youth hostels, 52

Yugoslavia, 102, 151, 236–44; eating in, 240

Zurich, 20, 27, 129